Interactive teaching in the primary school

D0418573

Interactive teaching in the primary school

Digging deeper into meanings

Janet Moyles, Linda Hargreaves,
Roger Merry, Fred Paterson and
Veronica Esarte-Sarries

with Eve English, Jane Hislam, Neil Kitson and
Morag Hunter-Carsch

Open University Press
Maidenhead · Philadelphia

Open University Press
McGraw-Hill Education
McGraw-Hill House
Shoppenhangers Road
Maidenhead
Berkshire
England
SL6 2QL

email: enquiries@openup.co.uk
world wide web: www.openup.co.uk

and

325 Chestnut Street
Philadelphia, PA 19106, USA

First published 2003

A catalogue record of this book is available from the British Library

ISBN 0 335 21213 1 (pb)   0 335 21214 X (hb)

The Library of Congress data for this book has been applied for
from the Library of Congress

Typeset by RefineCatch Limited, Bungay, Suffolk
Printed in Great Britain by Biddles Ltd, *www.biddles.co.uk*

Contents

Tables and figures

Tables

Figures

Acknowledgements

The authors and contributors are grateful to several individuals and institutions who contributed both to the SPRINT Project and to the completion of this book. First, to all the teachers, children and schools who shared the project with us and gave their time and energies in the search for a better understanding of interactive teaching. Their support and commitment were crucial. And we could not have conducted the research without the support of the Economic and Social Research Council, which funded the SPRINT Project (Grant R000238200).

We are grateful to Shirley Hord for her e-mail communications (via our colleague, Dr Siân Adams) and her interest in promoting the use of the Concerns-Based Adoption Model (CBAM) in the UK context. Also to Professor Maurice Galton, not only for writing the Foreword to the book but for supporting the use of the ORACLE teacher observation schedule. Dr Anthony Pell helped with the quantitative data from the project and we could not have managed without his clear support in deriving the new 5-point scale in the Anglicized version of CBAM. Dr Sue Beverton was initially involved in the SPRINT Project and, despite an illness that caused her to withdraw, has continued to show her interest in its development and outcomes. For this we owe her our thanks.

The two administrative assistants working on the SPRINT Project, Kathy Ashley at Leicester and Claire Rogerson at Durham, both deserve our thanks for their hard work and good humour in handling the various individuals who, as part of the project, demanded their attention. We are also grateful to Open University Press, especially Shona Mullen for encouraging the project and showing patience when initial deadlines could not be acted (or interacted) upon! Finally, Virginia Taylor has been immensely efficient and stalwart in completing the challenging task of helping to prepare the manuscript and ensure that all the various writers had an approachable contact with whom to interact.

Foreword
Maurice Galton

Over the last decade, primary teachers in England have come under intense pressure to change the way they teach. At first it was argued that they should engage in more 'direct teaching'. However, in recent years the language has changed and the term 'interative whole-class teaching' is now commonly used by those responsible for reconstructing the primary curriculum, most notably in the case of the English National Literacy and Numeracy Strategies. Among those charged with providing advice to teachers about how to operate this pedagogic strategy, however, there appears to be some uncertainty about what exactly the term itself means. For some classroom researchers, a teacher's interactions with the whole class could involve an exchange with a single pupil, provided the rest of children are expected to listen and learn from the experience and the teacher makes his or her expectations clear to the class. For David Reynolds, who chaired the Numeracy Working Party, interactive whole-class teaching was seen mainly to involve question-and-answer sessions, but whether such questions were relatively brief – designed to find out what pupils knew – more opened-ended and probing or a mixture of both remained unclear. Others, notably Tony Edwards and Neil Mercer (see Edwards and Mercer 1987), who have studied teachers' classroom discourse in great detail, wish to exclude what they term 'cued elicitations' – that is, when teachers are attempting to help pupils to learn how to think through the medium of conversation. More recently, Robin Alexander (2000) has stressed the importance of scaffolding these conversations so that, in Jerome Bruner's words, 'the degrees of freedom in carrying out the task are reduced and the pupil can concentrate on the difficult skill which he or she is in the process of acquiring' (Bruner 1996: 42). Alexander notes that in Russian classrooms, for example, an important strategy is to have an extended conversation between the teacher and a pupil during which other children are expected to listen and learn. In China, according to Martin Cortazzi (Cortazzi and Jin 1996), extended class dialogue often takes place between two pupils and one child corrects the other's errors. At present, how such strategies can easily be translated across their respective cultural barriers is, however, uncertain.

It is not surprising, therefore, to discover that these different interpretations are reflected in the explanations that teachers themselves offer if asked to say what they do when they are engaged in interactive whole-class teaching. How valuable, then, to set up a project with the support of the Economic and Social Research Council (ESRC) in which both teachers' thinking and actions were to be studied when engaged in teaching the whole class *interactively*. The fruits of this research are now published in this volume, which will be essential reading for policy-makers and those whose task it is to design and train teachers to implement successfully new and recent innovations, such as the 'literacy hour'.

Using the ORACLE (Observational Research and Classroom Evaluation) schedules was a systematic and useful way of describing teachers' actions and interactions during lessons. But an attempt to probe teachers' thinking on these issues required a different approach and the team used videotaped extracts of lessons to stimulate recall by teachers. In this they appear to have adopted a process first used in English classrooms by John Elliott (1976) and the late Lawrence Stenhouse (1980) in the Ford Teaching Project at the beginning of the 1970s. These researchers confronted a similar problem, although in the context of the time the emphasis was very different, in that great uncertainty surrounded the interpretation of such terms as 'discovery learning' and 'teaching for discovery'. In the Ford Teaching Project, the participating teachers and the collaborating researcher, together, viewed lessons in which teachers tried to use the 'discovery approach'. the teacher was invited to stop the tape and comment on any incident that was thought to have a significant impact on subsequent outcomes. The present project developed a variation of this approach in which individual teachers viewed the tape of the lesson in private before sharing their reflections with the academic research-partner.

The results of the SPRINT Project are, I believe, highly significant. The not wholly unexpected finding that there are layers of meaning attached to 'catch-all' terms such as 'interactive teaching' is a warning for those who wish to introduce a technicist approach to pedagogy, whereby teachers, like air traffic controllers, are drilled in the use of a range of procedures until they can reproduce the approved sequence automatically and reliably. What we learn from this study is that although there may be certain principles governing attempts to help children to think, to improve their self-esteem, to regulate their own learning, and so on, different contexts require the application of immense creativity from teachers if these principles are to be adapted so that they work effectively in practice. As the authors affirm in their concluding chapter, teaching is an art as well as a science.

Another lesson for would-be reforms is to be found in the analysis of the observation data in Chapter 6. Since the introduction of the National Curriculum and the implementation of the 'literacy hour', the proportion of questions asked has increased, but so has the proportion of teacher statements. There is, therefore, more talk in today's primary classroom than there was previously, but the ratio of *talking at* as opposed to *talking with* pupils is very similar. In this study, the proportion of questions increased, although there were still twice as many teacher statements. More importantly, questioning consisted of closed rather than open exchanges, particularly at Key Stage 1. The pupils initiated few of these questioning sequences so that, for the most part, whole-class interactive teaching remains a one-way teacher-dominated activity. And this despite the massive investments in in-service training that have gone into recent initiatives such as the National Literacy Strategy. In searching for ways to redress this imbalance, rather than 'blame and shame' teachers, we need to ask serious questions about the dynamics of classrooms, which seems to lock teachers and their pupils into these restricted forms of conversation.

It is clearly not an easy matter for teachers to break away from this pattern of discourse. Indeed, it has been shown that teachers are often unaware of how much guidance they give. This is because, unlike 'direct instruction', in which the teacher mostly controls the exchanges, during class discussion pupils are able to manipulate proceedings for their own ends. When asked, pupils offer a range of strategies for avoiding being picked by the teacher to give an answer. This mainly involves giving the impression that they require more thinking time. Pupils liken being asked a difficult question to 'moving on a tightrope'. They say they are worried that they might lose face with their peers. If they volunteer too many acceptable answers too quickly, they could earn the repu-tation of being a 'boff'; if they offer too few answers, they might be regarded as 'thick'. It is safer, therefore, to persuade teachers to answer their own question (Galton 1995).

This suggests that an important factor in promoting a more productive dialogue between teachers and pupils is the extent to which the relationship between parties is one of mutual trust and respect. Most teachers know that such a relationship develops through informal contacts rather than during formal periods of teaching. It could result from an incident in the playground in which a child discovers a bird's nest and the excited pupil, not normally given to participating in group or class discussion, is allowed time in the lesson after break to tell the rest of the class how they watched the mother feed its young. It can occur during a lesson, when a chance remark by a pupil causes the work to stop briefly to allow both teacher and children to enjoy a moment of spontaneous laughter. Teachers often refer to such times as 'magic moments' but, sadly, these have decreased considerably in recent years. This is because of the need to compete in the 'league tables' of high stakes, tests, increased supervision time and meetings, and the need to shorten lunch and break times in an attempt to prevent music and the arts being squeezed out of the overcrowded curriculum. In the 1970s, primary teachers worked a 42-hour week and estimated that over one hour per day was spent in various informal contacts with pupils. Today, teachers work a 55-hour week and only half an hour a day is available for similar activities. Developing interactive teaching beyond the surface level identified in this research will require a radical reappraisal of teachers' workloads.

Finally, the research has important messages for those involved in initial and in-service training. The analysis of the 'stages of concern' and interview data indicated that teachers were initially apprehensive about using interactive teaching and about coming face to face with a permanent pictorial record of their own practice. However, over time, the teachers overcame these fears and grew in confidence. This resulted in increased awareness when it came to analysing classroom events. Instead of restricting their comments to 'surface' observations, they were prepared to risk more speculative comments indicating attempts to 'theorize' at a deeper level. The success of engineering this transformation appears to be due, in part, to the sensitivity of the researchers and teacher trainers in the team who were able to encourage teachers to take ownership of their data, despite the teachers' initial feelings that the team 'already knew the answer'. Those responsible for introducing the Key Stage 3 strategy might do well to think about the dynamics underpinning teachers' thinking as described in these chapters.

The research team is, therefore, to be congratulated on bringing the enterprise to a most satisfactory conclusion. This book, which sets out the results of their labours, deserves to be widely read, not only for the many important things it has to say about changes and innovation in the classroom, but also because it is a lesson to other researchers in how to make flexible use of a variety of methodologies. The team were able to break down any ideological barriers that may have existed among themselves in the use of qualitative or quantitative approaches, and the resulting analysis is at all times both rigorous and informative. If, in the end, the authors raise more questions than they are able to answer, it can be argued in their defence that this is the hallmark of all good research. I congratulate them, most sincerely, on a satisfactory outcome to this interesting and illuminating project.

References

Alexander, R. (2000) *Culture and Pedagogy: International Comparisons in Primary Education*. Oxford: Blackwell.

Bruner, J. (1996) *The Culture of Education*. Cambridge, MA: Harvard University Press.

Cortazzi, M. and Jin, L. (1996)'Cultures of learning: language classrooms in China', in H. Coleman (ed.) *Society and the Language Classroom*. Cambridge: Cambridge University Press.

Edwards, D. and Mercer, N. (1987) *Common Knowledge: The Development of Understanding in the Classroom*. London: Routledge.

Elliott, J. (1976) *Developing Hypotheses about Classrooms from Teachers' Practical Constructs: An Account of the Work of the Ford Teaching Project*. Grand Forks, ND: North Dakota Study Group on Evaluation, University of North Dakota.

Galton, M. (1995) *Crisis in the Primary Classroom*. London: David Fulton.

Stenhouse, L. (1980) *Curriculum Research and Development in Action*. London: Heinemann.

Notes on contributors

Eve English is a lecturer on the Initial Teacher Training course at the School of Education, University of Durham. She teaches English and also supports students' school experience as a tutor. She is especially interested in the induction year for newly qualified teachers. Before joining the university, she was headteacher of an infant school. Recent journal articles include 'The teaching of reading – a decade of change in curriculum' (*Curriculum Journal*) and 'Teaching for understanding: curriculum guidance for the Foundation Stage' (*Evaluation and Research*). She was a tutor-researcher on the SPRINT Project.

Veronica Esarte-Sarries has worked on several educational projects at Leeds and Durham Universities. While intending to continue in educational research, she is also planning a project in environmental psychology. She was the Durham-based researcher on the SPRINT Project and was involved in all stages of the research process.

Linda Hargreaves is a lecturer in the University of Cambridge Faculty of Education where she teaches on the Primary PGCE and M.Ed (Research) courses. She has extensive experience of classroom research in collaboration with Maurice Galton and as director of her own projects. She first used observational methods at the University of Leicester on the original ORACLE Project in 1978–87 and, most recently, in the ORACLE '20-years-on' studies. She is co-author of *Inside the Primary Classroom – 20-years-on* and *Transfer from the Primary Classroom – 20 years on* with Maurice Galton and colleagues from Leicester. She was a co-director of the SPRINT Project.

Jane Hislam lectures in primary English at the University of Leicester, where she is course leader of the Primary PGCE English course. She has many years experience of working in Initial Teacher Training. Her main teaching and research interests relate to language and literacy development, especially oral storytelling and children's literature, and she has lectured and given workshops widely in this field. Current research includes a study of trainees' perceptions and understanding of grammar. Her publications include articles about oral story and children's literature. She was a tutor-researcher on the SPRINT Project.

Morag Hunter-Carsch lectures in primary education at the University of Leicester. She is a chartered psychologist with an interest in interactive learning and multi-lingualism and has been involved in action research and teacher education at pre-service and continuing professional development level for a number of years. Her research and publications include evaluation of literacy and study support, and teaching students with specific learning difficulties (e.g. dyslexia). She was a tutor-researcher on the SPRINT Project.

Neil Kitson lectures in primary education at the University of Leicester. In recent years he has been involved in research on the role of teacher–pupil interactivity in relation to the teaching of drama. Much of the focus of this work has been the implicit effect that this has on young children's language acquisition. He has published and broadcast widely on a variety of issues. He was a tutor-researcher on the SPRINT Project.

Roger Merry is senior lecturer in primary education at the University of Leicester with research interests in cognitive psychology, special needs education and English teaching. His research interests are in children's learning and children with special educational needs. He is author of *Successful Children: Successful Teaching* and his previous publications range from book chapters and journal articles in these areas to children's stories and activity books. He was a co-director of the SPRINT Project.

Janet Moyles is professor of education and research at Anglia Polytechnic University and an early childhood education specialist, especially in the areas of play, teaching and learning. Her books include *Just Playing?*, *Organizing for Learning*, *The Excellence of Play* (ed.) and, more recently, *Beginning Teaching: Beginning Learning* and *StEPs: A Framework for Playful Teaching*, the latter of which has arisen from a recent research project. She has directed several funded research projects on effective pedagogy and has also written a variety of articles on different aspects of early years and primary education. She was principal director of the SPRINT Project.

Fred Paterson is currently a research officer at the National College for School Leadership. He previously conducted research at both the Universities of Nottingham and Leicester. In his present position, Fred continues to develop links with primary schools throughout the country. His current work focuses on innovations in professional development for school leaders and in particular the use of video. Fred was previously a primary practitioner and advisory teacher. He remains fully engaged in his own learning, blissful ignorance and ecstatic enlightenment! Fred was the Leicester-based research assistant for the SPRINT Project.

Glossary

Many of the terms used in the book are specific to certain contexts within the national scene in England and within the SPRINT Project. For this reason, we hope this Glossary will support readers in identifying clearly the meaning behind our use of certain acronyms and terms.

Comparison teachers Teachers who acted as a comparison for the focus teachers

Concerns-based adoption model (CBAM) The tool used to assess the levels of teachers' concerns and use of interactive teaching at the beginning and end of the project

Continuing professional development (CPD) Courses and other training provided by various bodies for teachers to further develop their knowledge and skills

DfES Department for Education and Skills (formerly DfEE: Department for Education and Employment)

ESRC Economic and Social Research Council: the funding body for the project

Focus teachers Teachers who undertook reflective dialogues with their tutor research-partners

Initiation → response → feedback (IRF) The process of interaction between teacher and pupils in which initiation by the teacher is followed by the pupil response, which, in turn, initiates brief feedback from the teacher

INSET In-service education of teachers, now generally called Continuing Professional Development (CPD)

ITE Initial teacher education

ITT Initial teacher training

Key Stage 1 (KS1) The 5- to 7-year-old phase of the National Curriculum structure

Key Stage 2 (KS2) The 7- to 11-year-old phase of the National Curriculum structure

Literacy hour The time period within each school day that focuses on the activities prescribed by the National Literacy Strategy

'Lunchbox' The box of activities provided by the National Literacy Strategy for teachers as ideas for teaching and learning

NLNS National Literacy and Numeracy Strategies

NLS National Literacy Strategy

NLS: 'show me', 'get up and go', 'time out' The activities described in the NLS literature that are intended to support teachers in prescribing particular activities to be undertaken with children

NNS National Numeracy Strategy

NUD*IST Non-Numerical Unstructured Data Indexing Searching and Theorizing: a software package used to support the analysis and interpretation of transcriptions of interviews and reflective dialogues

OfSTED Office for Standards in Education: the government body responsible for the inspection of standards within English schools

ORACLE Observational Research and Classroom Evaluation: the SPRINT Project used the ORACLE structured teacher observation schedule to compare pre- and post-Literacy Strategy teaching

Reflective dialogue The process through which the intervention within the project was undertaken, which consisted of a discussion (based on a theoretical framework) between a teacher and higher education tutor as research-partners

SPRINT Study of Primary Interactive Teaching: the name of the project

Typology The list of features of interactive teaching derived from the observations, interviews and reflective dialogues with primary teachers

VSRD Video-stimulated reflective dialogue: the research tool that enabled researchers and teachers to explore teachers' interactive pedagogy through in-depth discussion of video clips of the teachers' practices

Introduction
Just what IS interactive teaching?

Janet Moyles and the SPRINT team

In the past few years, the government and its educational advisers have become progressively more involved in telling teachers not only *what* to teach within the curriculum but *how* to teach it, using a range of methods perceived to be appropriate (for example, see Alexander *et al.* 1992). Depending on the age, experience and partialities of teachers, some have welcomed these incursions into their professional practice while others have been more sceptical. The National Literacy and Numeracy Strategies (DfEE 1998, 1999c) are arguably the most prescriptive of these incursions and they have received mixed responses from teachers. The National Literacy Strategy (NLS) provided a wealth of documentation and information about *how* to teach literacy and *what* to teach; it also categorized pupils' skill development but was 'thin' on *why* specific skills and knowledge ought to be taught. This applies equally to any rationale for teaching using particular techniques or strategies. In addition, the NLS framework document describes 'The most successful teaching' as, *inter alia*, 'interactive – pupils' contributions are encouraged, expected and extended' (DfEE 1998: 8). It is clear that the content of the curriculum is often confused with the pedagogy.

Beard's (1999) retrospective review of research relevant to the National Literacy Strategy (see also Reynolds and Farrell 1996; Reynolds 1998) related interactive teaching to a three-phase framework of questioning in which teachers use: (i) questions of increasing difficulty to solve an initial problem to assess skills; (ii) rapid recall questions to assess pupils' knowledge; and (iii) slower paced higher-order questions within whole-class discussion to promote pupils' thinking.

The NLS training materials have not, however, provided any pedagogical rationale or, dare we say it, theory, or even empirical research evidence to underpin any of these recommendations. The simultaneous requirement for teaching to be 'well-paced' with a 'sense of urgency' would seem to limit the possibilities for 'extended' pupil contributions or interaction as teachers might conceive of it. Issues related to the metacognitive development of pupils and teachers appear to be regularly disregarded.

Despite these confusions, primary teachers were expected to teach 'inter-actively' and were left to decide for themselves what this might mean and how it might be interpreted in practice. Unsurprisingly, then, when asked what 'interactive teaching' meant to them, some Key Stage 1 (KS1) and Key Stage 2 (KS2) teachers responded as follows:

> I don't really feel clued-up.

> I'm not really sure what it is at all.

> I guess it's just in terms of the teacher presenting something, and then the child feeding something back, and then you start the cycle again.

> I would guess that interactive teaching is quality teaching, quality relationships and trust.

> It is not really a discussion that we have had in the staff room. People tend not to like to talk about wider issues; they are more concerned with what happened that morning.

A few clearly felt somewhat more knowledgeable:

> I do feel fairly knowledgeable about interactive teaching, and fairly confident about it as well.

> [I feel] comfortable in my knowledge of [interactive teaching] in terms of its use in my classroom.

However, a deeper explanation or interpretation was not forthcoming. We suspect, too, that some teachers did not like to admit they didn't know because they felt that somehow they *ought* to know. Little wonder that Alexander (2000) expresses his strong reservations about:

> exercises in process–product correlation, such as the one which during the 1990s caused the UK government and Office for Standards in Education (OfSTED) to elevate 'interactive whole class teaching' to the status of pedagogical panacea and seek to impose it on every primary teacher in the land.
>
> (Alexander 2000: 321)

Teachers' weak awareness of interactive pedagogy is perhaps under-standable when we consider that the earliest NLS literature provided little tangible advice for teachers seeking a clear definition or examples of interactive teaching. More recent classroom-focused literature and video materials do offer examples of teaching technologies designed to model interactive teaching practices (DfEE 1999b), but they still provide few clues about the pedagogical principles or educational philosophies that underpin interactive teaching. Rather belatedly, the National Literacy Centre responded to requests for information about the research base for the NLS with the publication of the *National Literacy Strategy: Review of Research and Other Related Evidence* (Beard 1999). Clear information about the principles underlying interactive teaching, however, has not been forthcoming.

How, then, can teachers decide how to teach interactively without significant knowledge of what it is and what it might involve in practice? This was the first basic question a group of tutors on initial and continuing teacher education courses raised in discussions on course content and implementation during the early period of the advent of the National Literacy Strategy. This initial discussion led the group (originally six tutors) to explore among themselves how they were going to support students in teaching interactively. It did not take long for the group to realize that the concept of 'interaction' was complex when related to classroom practice. For example, did it mean the interaction between teacher and whole class, teacher and group or teacher and individual? Or did it mean all of these?

We began the process of exploring interactive teaching by considering among ourselves a range of circumstances in which interaction might take place. We observed videos of classroom practice and tried to identify what was – and was not – 'interactive' by our own uninformed and undeveloped criteria. Sometimes the teacher appeared to encourage interaction between children – did this equally constitute interactive teaching in the broadest sense? What about story time, when teachers told or read the story and children listened – was this interactive? Did interaction only encompass those strategies that prompted pupils to think for themselves or to use higher-order thinking skills? What types of questioning were implicit within teachers' use of interactive teaching strategies? Was interactive teaching likely to be the same in different parts of the country or across the two different key stages? With so many questions requiring investigation, the ideas in time developed and were formulated into a bid for research funding: by then we had decided that the issues were important enough to warrant a full-scale research study.

Undertaking the research into interactive teaching

With funding secured from the Economic and Social Research Council (ESRC), we were able to embark upon a five-term study of primary teachers' understanding and use of interactive teaching, particularly within the National Literacy Strategy, although there was some opportunity to make a comparison with other areas of the curriculum. So it was that the SPRINT Project – Study of Primary Interactive Teaching – eventually transpired. The project ran for two years until autumn 2001. It involved several tutors and researchers in two geographical areas – Leicester and County Durham. These two areas were chosen on the basis of convenience: originally the project had been planned to take place in Leicester, but one of the co-directors moved to Durham and thus the two-centre research became feasible and desirable.

The SPRINT team consisted of three co-directors (two in Leicester and one in Co. Durham), four tutor-researchers (three in Leicester and one in Co. Durham) and two part-time researchers, one each in the two locations. The research involved 30 teachers (20 in Leicestershire and 10 in Durham) who were either self-selected or approached through their headteachers. All took part based on their willingness and enthusiasm to be involved in working with the SPRINT team. The 27 female and three male teachers had a range of experiences from newly qualified to 20 years. Sixteen worked in Key Stage 1 and 14 in Key Stage 2. Fifteen were classified as 'comparison' teachers: these teachers would be involved initially and towards the end of the project through questionnaire completion, video observation and individual inter-views, to determine how far their practice changed *without* any specific inter-vention through working with the research team. The remaining 15 teachers were designated as 'focus' teachers, who would work as research-partners with individuals within the research team. As the research design was essentially a pre- and post-test intervention study, the focus teachers were similarly interviewed and completed questionnaires, but their video observation was accompanied by a new method we termed 'video-stimulated reflective dialogue', essentially an opportunity to reflect with a knowledgeable research-partner on one's own teaching (see Chapter 8 for further details). The practical fieldwork with teachers lasted three terms during the first year of the project and the analysis and interpretation of data was undertaken during the follow-ing three terms. Focus teachers were videoed on three occasions and also engaged in three video-stimulated reflective dialogues.

The data gathered have continued to generate rich and significant infor-mation on teachers' thinking and their development of pedagogic skills. The data collection methods involved gathering both quantitative and qualitative data. This has proved to be a powerful means of digging deeper into teachers' knowledge, perceptions, views, beliefs and understanding of a range of pedagogical practices, including various types and forms of interaction. The differences in approach of different teachers has been informative and has also led to many more questions being addressed than those previously outlined.

In writing this book we hope that primary teachers who read it will be able to see themselves within its pages and identify with the practitioners who were an integral part of the research. Most teachers have, for example, recognized the dilemma of listening to children while at the same time feeling the urgency of 'moving them on' so that targets can be reached and time-scales (particularly with the literacy hour) adhered to. While some of the language is based in research terminology (this is necessary to show the integrity and rigour of the research process), there are also significant numbers of 'stories' about teachers with which teacher readers will no doubt empathize.

The research was grounded in what is usually termed a 'socio-constructivist' paradigm applied to teachers' pedagogical development. In effect, the research examined the thesis that, through review and reflection on practice with a sophisticated partner and in the light of video evidence, teachers might articulate their conceptualizations of interactive teaching and refine their practice of it. The project adopted the framework of the Concerns-Based Adoption Model (CBAM) (see, for example, Hall *et al.* 1979), which details a progressive series of 'statements of concern' about an innovation (in this case, interactive teaching) interlinked with a sequence of 'levels of use' of the innovation. Further explanation will be provided in later chapters.

Reflecting on and about practice (Schön 1983, 1987; Day 1999a, b) has challenged both teachers and researchers to reconsider their teaching practices in some depth and has involved 'systematic inquiry into . . . practice . . . to deepen one's understanding of it' (Lucas 1991: 84). At the outset of the research, researcher–practitioner collaboration was thought likely to be particularly effective because of the complementary exchange of skills and knowledge (Day 1999a). Schulz (1987: 482) agrees, suggesting that it is during moments of 'co-reflection' that we explore and extrapolate pedagogical understanding and that it is often through reflection that we retrospectively construct the meaning of our work. Day (1999a: 153) further suggests that those leading change must ensure participants have 'intellectual, practical and affective support': this was an embedded part of the process of the reflective dialogues, intended to extend and deepen understanding. This is something available to all teachers, particularly through peer-evaluation of actual teaching or through the use of video as in this project.

A specific feature of the project was teachers working in partnership with experienced tutor-researchers. Some chapters in this book are written by these tutor-researchers, who present their own and the teachers' perspectives. We asked the teachers to both deconstruct their practices and also to engage in the process of reconstruction of the meanings of their practices as part of the research. We will argue later that these are important aspects of teachers' professional understanding and development. The process of deconstruction seeks to provide understanding and to make meaning from teachers' actions. According to LaBoskey (1993) and Zeichner (1994), professional reflection requires a clearly defined focus and criteria for making judgements if understanding is to be achieved. Having an explicit focus on interactive teaching, its meaning and use gave just this kind of clear springboard for discussion, analysis and interpretation. Significantly, Bullough and Gitlin (1991) identified the need for practitioners to talk about practice to enhance understanding of it, not just at a polite conversational level but within deeper, focused discourse, underpinned by mutual respect and characterized by a willingness to tolerate differences in opinion and values. Teacher readers might consider for a moment the opportunities they have for actually thinking and talking about practice in depth: all too often 'action' is associated with the rush to feel that at least some targets have been met by the end of each day and week. Time to reflect seems like a luxury and so it was to the teachers within the SPRINT Project.

The research: qualitative and quantitative methods

The SPRINT research aimed to explore classroom practice based on teachers' frames of reference. This provided the research team with several challenges, including how they might:

- facilitate teacher development without promoting particular theoretical or conceptual models of interactive teaching;
- respond when teachers asked for information or theoretical perspectives on interactive teaching;
- ensure teachers benefited from the skills and experience of their higher education research-partners, all of whom were experienced education tutors, mentors, advisers or researchers.

In addition, the SPRINT Project had several clear objectives, which informed both data collection and its analysis and interpretation, including:

- construct a typology of interactive teaching derived from practising teachers' definitions;
- examine teachers' concerns about 'interactive teaching' in the absence, at that time, of relevant training;
- observe primary teachers' implementation of interactive teaching within the various components of the 'literacy hour' and compare these with pre-NLS classroom interaction;
- compare primary teachers' use of interactive teaching in the literacy hour with that undertaken by them in other subject areas within the curriculum;
- evaluate the process of video-stimulated reflective dialogue as a means to enhance teachers' reflection on, and development of, their interactive teaching practice.

The investigation of teachers' underlying understandings and values generated several research questions, namely:

- How do primary teachers define interactive teaching and what aspects of their own practice do they see as being particularly interactive?
- How and why do they actually use interactive teaching?
- Would they refine their definitions and enhance their use of inter-active teaching through a process of self-observation, reflection and discussion?
- What are their concerns about, and values related to, interactive teaching?
- Would self-observation, reflection and discussion change these concerns?
- Has interactive teaching in the literacy hour, as defined by teachers, made a noticeable difference to their patterns of teacher–pupil interaction?

To address these various issues and questions, the research team decided to:

- follow a reflective practice model of development (Schön 1987; Zeichner and Liston 1987; Hatton and Smith 1995; Smyth 1995; van Manen 1995), with the aim of developing generic professional skills that focused on interactive teaching and the teachers' current awareness, knowledge and practice;
- evolve a methodological framework that would offer some coherence of experience across the teachers involved in the developmental aspects of the project, but still allow individual autonomy within the process;
- provide an empirical focus for 'reflective dialogues' by using video of teachers' own practice. This focus could be revisited and audited as part of the research process, as well as linking individual teacher practice at the start and end of the project and to historical teaching practice via the ORACLE research.

Several intervention measures were included within the project methodology with the purpose of establishing (a) teachers' current knowledge and use of interactive teaching and (b) whether it was possible to develop pedagogical practices. These pre- and post-intervention measures included:

- determining teachers' definitions and conceptualizations of inter-active teaching by means of semi-structured interviews;
- establishing teachers' concerns about interactive teaching as measured by a 35-item questionnaire from the Concerns-Based

Adoption Model (CBAM) research of Hord (1987) and Hall *et al.* (1979);

- making systematic observations, using an adapted version of the Observational Research and Classroom Learning Evaluation (ORACLE) teacher record (Galton *et al.* 1980, 1999), of interactive teaching in the literacy hour.

The intervention itself was carried out with the focus teachers using video-stimulated reflective dialogue (VSRD). The professional development aspirations of the SPRINT Project meant that interviews alone would not have been sufficient. How far the effects of the intervention were felt became evident in the interview transcripts, the questionnaire responses and the observations made three times during the project of both literacy hour teaching and other areas of the curriculum.

Analysis of the qualitative data (from interviews and reflective dialogues) took a grounded approach using *in vivo* terminology facilitated by NUD*IST software (see Glossary). The CBAM questionnaire data were subjected to factor analysis, while mean ratings and observation frequencies were compared between groups by statistical methods. Greater explanation of the outcomes of these methods are given in the appropriate chapters. The methodology included teacher workshops in both geographical locations that provided checks on the authenticity, validity and ethics of the processes of the research. All together, four workshops were held and they served a useful purpose in ensuring that we fed back to teachers the ongoing findings of the project for verification and comment. At the first teacher workshops, convened half-way through the data collection process, the research team presented the *focus* teachers with elements from the then current transcriptions of data and sought their views and confirmation that what was reported was valid. At this juncture, teachers' discussions about their statements informed the evolving typology through grouping the statements into trial categories and commenting on their suitability. At the second teacher workshops, towards the end of the final term of the data collection, both focus and comparison teachers were invited to share the emerging findings from the research and to challenge and authenticate our interpretation of the results at that time.

In addition to the workshops, at each VSRD session the individual focus teachers were provided with the main points from their previous session and were asked to comment on our analysis and interpretations. They also decided upon a maximum of three action points for issues and practices they might pursue between reflective dialogue sessions; these were reviewed and examined collaboratively at the start of each reflective dialogue. Thus the teachers – the focus teachers in particular – were intentionally and overtly an integral and embedded part of the research process throughout the project.

Ethics of the research

Entering into classrooms and videoing teachers and children during their interactions can clearly be sensitive. We were aware at the start of the project that offering full information about the project to heads and teachers who had indicated a willingness to take part was crucial in securing informed consent and negotiating access to classroom events (see, for example, Foster 1996: ch. 2; Anderson and Arsenault 1998). In accordance with good practice, we developed a contract with teachers and schools that had to be signed by all parties, and which stated the role to be played by each contributor throughout the project and beyond. Although the project did not focus directly on individual children, they were inevitably part of the classroom observation processes. Headteachers agreed in writing to seek parents' written permission for their children to be videoed and these constituted part of the written contract between researchers and researched.

Issues of confidentiality and anonymity were respected and continue to be respected. For that reason, all the names of participating teachers have been changed to pseudonyms for the purposes of formalized writing and, where we felt that teachers might identify themselves or be identifiable even without naming, we have taken steps to counteract this while keeping the data intact.

What did we find out?

Substantial and significant qualitative and quantitative evidence was gathered, analysed and interpreted concerning interactive teaching across Key Stages 1 and 2 in two regions of England. As will become clear in the pages of this book – and not to give too much away! – our evidence suggests that teachers' conceptions of interactive teaching are more sophisticated than that offered in the NLS documentation and indicates various surface and deep interpretations. In the book, we offer our typology and describe its content and how it was interpreted through case studies of some of the teachers. Teachers' concerns about interactive teaching showed some parallels with Hall and co-workers' (1979) CBAM model, but we were also able to see intercultural differences and to develop an 'English' structure that can be tested in further studies of teachers' responses to innovation in England. Alongside this, it became clear that teachers' knowledge and understanding of the pedagogical principles involved in interactive teaching need to be developed further to foster pupils' higher-order thinking, especially in Key Stage 1. Major differences were found between the key stages in terms of cognitive task demand. We also found that video-simulated reflective dialogues proved to be an effective means of developing professional thinking. Finally, teacher talk in interactive sections of the literacy hour is considerably different from pre-NLS teacher–pupil interactions.

What can the book do for readers?

Although the book grew out of a research project, the authors are intent upon it being a readable and accessible account of the processes of the research, as we feel strongly that there is much to be learned about the ways teachers construe and practise interactive teaching within all aspects of the curriculum. The subtitle of this book comes from the response of one teacher who thought that interactive teaching was mainly about the need to 'dig deeper into meanings', to consider how pupils are thinking and to encourage pupils to reflect and explain their thinking processes in depth. This is what we want to encourage teachers to do through this book. As we have found, there are many ways of interacting with pupils. Teachers who want to 'dig deeper' into children's understandings will need to consider whether they are encouraging more sustained interactions through the way, for example, that they ask questions and how they assess and extend children's knowledge. The younger the children, the more time they need to offer a considered response: if teachers do not allow this time, then children will learn only in a superficial way, without meaning. Ensuring that what children do has meaning and relevance for them and relates to their lives out of school as well as in, and paying attention to extending children's thinking skills, rather than only imparting information, are also key areas for teachers to consider. This also means putting children's learning before their own teaching intentions. Reflecting regularly on practices and the effects upon children and one's own role, is also likely to make teaching more effective and enjoyable.

How the book is organized

This book reports on and extends the SPRINT research project. The project, as we have seen, was rooted in primary school practices. It has engaged with the practice of interactive teaching within the literacy hour across Key Stages 1 and 2, working with a group of 30 teachers to investigate their perceptions and uses of this style of teaching, as one of the English government's key strategies. The project was somewhat unique in that it set out, using its own interactive VSRD process, to support primary teachers in making sense of their own teaching within the National Literacy Strategy. Springing as it did originally from the government's educational advisers' notions of the benefits of 'whole-class teaching' in primary practice, it was interesting to the researchers that teachers, in general, were unsure about what interactive teaching actually was intended to be and what its components looked like, as readers will discover throughout the various chapters that follow. Perhaps teacher readers feel like this. By offering stories and case study information about teachers' views and perceptions, as well as examples of their actual practice, we hope that readers will share the experience of data handling and get close to the teachers with whom we worked. Some teacher readers may find in Chapter 2, for example, their own concerns reflected in the views of SPRINT teachers. In Chapters 3, 4, 7 and 9 we can see something of the teacher's struggle to understand what interactive teaching might be and how to put it into practice. Other chapters give more detailed information about the research methodology and processes through which our findings emerged.

In Chapter 1, we explore interactive teaching from the perspective of what it means to teachers and children. The chapter begins by setting out briefly the context of the research, looking at the origins of a dramatic increase in interest in interactive teaching, particularly through the National Literacy Strategy. It then goes on to outline the main features that formed the basis for the research itself, including previous observational studies in classrooms and other research into children's learning and the impact of teaching.

Teachers showed inevitable apprehension about interactive teaching and what they were intended to be doing within the literacy hour and in other facets of their teaching. They were especially concerned about the likely effects upon the children. In Chapter 2, we provide information about teachers' affective and cognitive positions on interactive teaching at the beginning of the project. Both concerns were investigated, since they were likely to be interdependent and to affect teachers' motivation to engage with the project, and demonstrate and refine their practice of interactive teaching. The chapter begins with the main issues, such as the limited information about interactive teaching for teachers despite its declared importance in recent educational policy. The chapter goes on to report the teachers' concerns and how these developed during the fieldwork when they were actively focusing on the use of interactive teaching. Based on questionnaire data, this section is pitched at the group level and considers the similarities and differences between the focus and comparison teachers.

The SPRINT Project teachers were concerned about their lack of information and theoretical knowledge of interactive teaching. Some teachers wanted a definition and others wanted a description of strategies and techniques that would exemplify interactive practice. In Chapter 3, we show that, compared with their theoretical knowledge, these teachers had rather more confidence in their personal, experiential knowledge. This work is based on qualitative interview data and looks in detail at how the teachers described their own knowledge of interactive teaching and its sources. It distinguishes between the teachers' formal and informal knowledge of interactive teaching and takes into account their attitudes to the literacy hour, since this was the main arena for the research and, potentially, a major source of their knowledge about interactive teaching. We see also that the SPRINT teachers equated inter-active teaching with 'good' and 'usual' practice, and we show that interactive teaching was not considered by them to be an innovation or new development in teaching practice. Given the contention of Reynolds and Farrell (1996) that interactive pedagogy is a harbinger of improved literacy standards not currently associated with UK practice, the fact that these teachers saw interactive teaching as 'nothing new' suggests that continuing professional development messages about innovative teaching practices had either not been received or had not been promoted. We argue that this was based on at least two factors: (i) a lack of clarity about the features of interactive teaching within the teacher-focused literature and (ii) the lack of attention paid to interactive teaching in contemporaneous professional development opportunities. By the end of the SPRINT Project, however, less concern was voiced about lack of information and knowledge and there was a greater awareness and more thought being given to interactive practice. There remained, though, a desire for a definition, theory and description of strategies and techniques. Perhaps due to the increased reflection encouraged by the project, there was also some evidence to suggest that interactive teaching was beginning to be viewed as an innovation or, at least, that it was something more than 'usual' practice.

As we also set out to consider how teachers conceptualize interactive teaching, Chapter 4 explores the initial and changing views of teachers over the period of the project. It outlines how we gathered baseline information and plotted developments in teachers' growing construction of the concept. Although there is an absence of detailed information on interactive teaching in the official National Literacy and Numeracy Strategies literature, teachers constructed multidimensional definitions of the construct. We present a typology of the main features identified, followed by a more detailed descrip-tion of each feature drawing upon the interview data of both groups of teachers, across the age phases and within each level of experience. This led to the notion that there are both 'surface' and 'deep' features of interactive teaching, the latter of which are addressed in detail in Chapter 5. The variables of experience and geographical location did not appear to alter views of inter-active teaching substantively, but different key stages appear to be associated to some extent with the incidence of one particular feature. Length of experi-ence appears sometimes to be associated with more negative initial attitudes to the National Learning Strategy. Changes in teachers' views over the course of the project on both general and individual terms are analysed and a summary of the main points is presented.

The chapters up to this point discuss how SPRINT teachers described their understanding of interactive teaching in interviews and, in the case of 'focus' teachers, reflective dialogues with members of the research team.

Chapter 5 follows on from Chapter 4, which sets out the five 'surface features' of interactive teaching that emerged from these interviews and dialogues. Chapter 5 examines the 'deeper' features, which tended to be constructed in less extensive ways and to be articulated with less sophistication than the surface features. It also explores how teachers' constructs of these features changed over the life of the SPRINT Project.

Having established the forms of teachers' knowledge and the ways in which they conceptualized interactive teaching, Chapter 6 explores the various ways in which primary teachers used interactive teaching in the classroom. This chapter teases out in some detail, using the ORACLE teacher schedule, the changes that have occurred in practice since the mid-1970s up until the advent of the National Literacy Strategy and during its first full year – the period of the SPRINT Project. It reveals both dramatic changes in teachers' interaction patterns since the 1970s, as well as some surprising stability. The SPRINT teachers' examples of interactive teaching were characterized by remarkably high levels of questioning, yet teacher talk overall was still dominated by teachers giving information and telling children what to do. Although consistent differences between the focus and comparison teachers did not emerge, the critical differences we found in the literacy hour and other curriculum teaching at Key Stages 1 and 2 have serious implications for both pedagogy and educational policy.

Although it was possible to develop the typology of interactive teaching outlined in Chapters 4 and 5, what was extremely interesting was to build case studies of different teachers to show how they compared in practice with one another when it came to interactive teaching. Thus Chapter 7 explores how some of the teachers' perspectives shifted between these dimensions, and we hypothesize a developmental progression in interactive teaching pedagogy. By comparing and contrasting case examples, we explore some of the influences on SPRINT teachers' constructions and use of interactive teaching, and explore the complex influences of experience, attitudes, knowledge, thinking and practice.

The video-stimulated reflective dialogue (VSRD) method is the focus of Chapter 8. This method is both a professional development strategy and a research tool. A key element of the process during the SPRINT Project was that the practitioner was in control – of what was videoed, where attention was focused and the direction and pace of events. Although many of the teachers reported some discomfort, anxiety and difficulty with the process, *all* those involved considered it essentially worthwhile. All nine higher education tutor research-partners who supported these VSRDs also reported growing allegiance to the method. This chapter reports on how teachers and tutors viewed the reflective dialogue process and what was gained from the experience.

Needless to say, some teachers felt there were significant conflicts between the National Literacy Strategy and what they felt was most appropriate for the children and their learning – for example, in relation to the pace at which lessons were intended to proceed. In Chapter 9, these conflicts and tensions are explored with the focus on individuals' concerns and experiences. Drawing on teachers' interviews and VSRDs, we see how four teachers reacted to the inherent contradictions in the NLS framework document, and how they variously wrestled with, and solved, the problems and confusions this evoked. While the chapter develops the theme of the VSRD process, its inevitable conclusion is that policy-makers must begin to recognize and value practitioners' expertise if the profession is to retain and attract people who wish to 'dig deeper into meanings' and extend children's cognitive skills.

Finally, in a chapter we have called 'Interactive teaching: digging even deeper into meanings' (Chapter 10), we summarize the achievements of the project in relation both to its findings and the innovations in methods, particularly the use of video-stimulated reflective dialogue. The chapter presents a framework for understanding and developing interactive teaching, based on the findings of the project and in the context of the research background explained at the outset. It then draws parallels between the methodology of the project and interactive teaching itself. Finally, the chapter sets out some questions and challenges to encourage teachers and other readers to further their understanding and development of interactive teaching and consider future research into such practice.

But first, Chapter 1 frames the research in the context of the theoretical and psychological perspectives of interactive teaching and lays the foundations for the following chapters.

1 Scuppering discussion?

Interaction in theory and practice

Roger Merry and Janet Moyles

Introduction

Let us begin with registration.

Teacher:	John?
John:	Here Miss.
Teacher:	Suhila?
Suhila:	Yes Miss.
Teacher:	Claire? . . . Has anybody seen Claire?
Rest of class:	No Miss.
Teacher:	OK. Jason?
Jason:	Miss.

There is undoubtedly some sort of interaction going on here. The teacher is asking questions to which the pupils respond in different ways, and further teacher questions depend on the response or not of the children. One question is directed at the whole class, all the children respond and the teacher's next question is affected by this response. We might argue that this isn't 'proper' teaching, but what if the children are in a new reception class and the teacher is trying to get them to learn to sit quietly and respond to their names? Is this an example of interactive teaching?

Another teacher is describing everyday life for Neanderthal people. She asks the children to close their eyes and imagine what it must have been like to live in a cave in the depths of winter. As the children listen, she paints a vivid picture of a dozen emaciated people huddled together against the cold at the back of a low, damp cave, with no fire, no food, the wind howling outside and drifts of snow piling up in the entrance to the cave. The children listen, eyes closed, enthralled. They can almost hear the wolves howling. The teacher then asks them to draw the scene they have imagined and later, when she looks at their pictures, realizes that several have drawn their Neanderthal people wearing modern clothes. She decides to change her plans for the next lesson to accommodate this misconception. The teacher has asked no questions and there has been no discussion, yet the children's thinking has apparently been affected by the teacher and vice versa. So is this an example of interactive teaching?

This chapter introduces the background to the SPRINT Project. It begins by setting out briefly the context of the research, looking at the origins of a dramatic increase in interest in interactive teaching, particularly through the National Literacy Strategy. It then goes on to outline the main features that formed the basis for the research itself, including previous observational studies in classrooms and other research into children's learning. Finally, brief summaries of the methodology and findings are presented as background for the more detailed discussions in the later chapters.

So what IS interactive teaching?

The concept of interaction is clearly not a new one and educational researchers have long been interested in the interactions that take place in classrooms. The original ORACLE research, which forms part of the basis for the SPRINT Project, was published in an influential book by Galton *et al.* (1980). ORACLE used systematic observation to study interactions in primary classrooms, and produced typologies of both pupils' and teachers' behaviours.

To give a sense of context and background, it is interesting to look for a moment at some other publications about classroom interaction, which appeared at the same time the ORACLE research was being carried out. Stubbs (1976), for example, showed how socio-linguistic principles could be applied to the study of classroom talk, especially in the context of disadvantaged groups of children, and encouraged teachers to become more aware of their own language and to carry out investigations of their own. Another example from the same year is the work of Barnes (1976), who also wrote about the importance of communication in the class-room. He noted, for instance, that teacher questions dominated and that pupils rarely initiated exchanges or asked questions of their own. Barnes recognized the conflict for teachers between the need to promote learning and the need to maintain control, but saw the way forward as being through genuine pupil discussion in groups, enabling them to create meanings for themselves:

> The question-and-answer method of control must in the long run devalue – in the pupils' eyes as much as the teacher's – the pupils' capacity for taking a responsible part in learning. Implicitly it

devalues both the knowledge they have and their capacity to use speech to apply this knowledge to a new task.

(Barnes 1976: 181)

Although there has been much research over many years into classroom interaction, the notion of 'interactive teaching' itself has received interest only relatively recently. A major impetus was in 1996 when, in the context of growing concern that many 'Pacific Rim' countries were apparently producing higher levels of classroom achievement than the UK, Reynolds and Farrell (1996) proposed that one of the most important reasons for their success was the widespread use of whole-class interactive teaching. This conclusion has been criticized by Galton *et al.* (1999) among others, who note the many other variables that could affect test scores when international comparisons are made. These range from major differences in underlying social values and attitudes towards learning, to more specific ones such as primary teachers being given time for preparation and even the samples selected for testing in each country. In stark contrast to the conclusions of Reynolds and Farrell, Maehr and Maehr (1996), for example, argued that the real way to improvement lies in alleviating much deeper social problems and supporting families in need whose children are disadvantaged whatever teaching methods are used. Conversely, Alexander (1996) pointed out that some Pacific Rim countries do use whole-class interactive methods, yet their test results are no better than those of the UK.

In spite of the dangers of selecting just one teaching technique as the major cause of international academic success, Reynolds and Farrell's proposal was enthusiastically taken up by the National Literacy Strategy. Interactive teaching is listed as one of the major features of the strategy (DfEE 1998) and teachers are explicitly required to use it in the 'literacy hour'. But what exactly does it mean?

Reynolds and Farrell (1996) present a brief analysis in which the emphasis is almost entirely on teacher questions (see Introduction). They include a whole chapter on interactive teaching in their book, although the chapter deals almost exclusively with questions posed by the teacher. Advice is given on mixing different types of questions and on what to do, for example, if a pupil answers a question incorrectly. Although there is also a brief section on discussion, with advice about how to keep it focused on the teacher's objectives, interactive teaching is identified almost exclusively with teacher questions.

There is, however, considerable evidence that teacher questions have *always* dominated classrooms (e.g. Galton *et al.* 1999), and it is instructive to return to Barnes for a moment here. Barnes describes a teacher who:

is the centre of everybody's attention: she asks many questions, and demands answers of right. 'What other ways are there of measuring it?' she asks, and goes on urgently, 'Come on, more hands up. Have you all gone to sleep?' In spite of this urgency she seems to know the answers already, for she dismisses several suggestions until one comes up which she greets with, 'That's it. Good answer, John'. Her young pupils ask hardly any questions, except for permission to fetch ink from the cupboard.

(Barnes 1976: 11)

The dominance of teacher questions to the whole class, the clear objectives she appears to have in mind and the overall sense of urgency are all apparent. Barnes is clearly concerned about the limitations of such an approach, but it is only the reference to fetching ink from the cupboard which reveals that this is not an extract from a model literacy hour – or, more likely, a numeracy period – a quarter of a century later!

If whole-class interactive teaching really is an innovation for British teachers that will result in significant improvements in pupil achievement, then it must surely involve more than continuing the age-old process of asking children question after question and, essentially, not interacting with their responses to promote further learning. So what else might it be? Another obvious source to turn to for help would be the vast amount of material produced by the National Literacy Strategy (NLS). The strategy has certainly offered teachers a range of lively ideas, whose aim is to engage children in active ways rather than sitting passively listening to the teacher. Thus the NLS flier 'Engaging all pupils' (DfEE 1999b) suggests some techniques that involve children, for example, in 'get up and go' activities, where they come out to the front of the class, or 'show me' activities, where they all hold up small boards or fans to show the teacher their responses to questions directed at the whole class. Similarly, other materials produced to support teachers in teaching the literacy hour are full of practical examples of what is apparently interactive teaching. Medwell *et al.* (2001: 83–6), for instance, use the heading 'interactive approaches to reading' to set out several techniques for trainee teachers, including advice on how to reproduce texts so that all the class can see them.

What still appears to be missing is any explicit discussion of the under-lying rationale behind this central concept of interactive teaching. The emphasis on requirements and techniques in the literacy hour, while certainly telling teachers what to do, has been at the expense of such discussion and is not universally welcomed. Thus Harrod (2002), for instance, bemoans the 'skills based approach to the teaching of reading and the excessive regimenta-tion and fragmentation of the Literacy Hour' (p. 53).

Similarly, where there are hints of explanation, they are not always useful. Another NLS document (DfEE 1998), for instance, simply states that inter-active teaching is where pupils' responses are 'expected, encouraged and extended' (p. 8), but this is more problematic than helpful. For example, it is difficult to imagine any sort of lesson in which some sort of pupil response is neither expected nor encouraged, and the cameo of registration at the beginning of the chapter would certainly meet these criteria. So is the key term 'extended'? However, if teaching is not interactive unless pupils' responses are extended, then only the third of Reynolds and Farrell's (1996) three stages (slower paced, higher-order questions) definitely qualifies as interactive, and the second (rapid question and answer) is deliberately designed not to. At the very least, there is an apparent discrepancy between the NLS definition of interactive teaching and the one offered by Reynolds and Farrell, who proposed it in the first place. Even Beard's (1999) review of research and related evidence seen as underpinning the National Literacy Strategy, produced when the strategy was already well established, has relatively little to say about what interactive teaching might mean in terms of children's learning, and instead emphasizes the contribution of the school effectiveness and improvement literature (Mroz *et al.* 2000).

A word of caution is necessary, however. The educational research literature is full of books and articles bemoaning the lack of agreement about how to define major educational concepts, including 'education' itself. Although this may be lucrative for educational philosophers but problematic for more pragmatic researchers, a lack of clear consensus about exactly what is meant by a term need not necessarily matter and it sometimes appears that, the more important something is, the harder it may be to define (Merry 1998). We would all define 'happiness' in different ways, but this lack of agreement does not mean we should all stop pursuing it until a clear and agreed definition can be found by researchers. However, there is a major difference between the pursuit of happiness and interactive teaching. The difference is that, while we are all free to pursue happiness in our own idiosyncratic ways, all primary teachers are now formally required to use 'interactive whole-class teaching' for large parts of the day, and may be severely criticized if outside assessors such as Of STED (Office for Standards in Education) inspectors judge that they are not doing so.

This lack of clarity is, therefore, not just a theoretical inconvenience. Apart from teachers' understandable anxieties about arousing the wrath of the inspectors, a clear underlying rationale for interactive teaching is vital for at least three important overlapping reasons:

1   As professionals, teachers need to understand what the concept means, rather than just slavishly to imitate the specific activities described in the NLS materials. Anybody can get children to wave fans in the air, but as an activity it is pointless unless we understand why we are asking them to do it, when it is appropriate and what sorts of information it can and cannot lead to.

2   Teachers need this understanding to be able to reflect upon and to evaluate their own planning and teaching. Without it they will be reduced to the dreadful question that was frequently asked by SPRINT teachers: 'In the literacy hour, are we allowed to . . .?' If we agree that we do not wish to encourage dependency among children, it is hardly appropriate to appear to require it from teachers.

3   Similarly, teachers need to be able to create activities of their own that are not only true to the spirit of interactive teaching, but also relate to their particular circumstances and the needs of their particular children.

The National Literacy Strategy, which not only tells teachers what they must do but also how they must do it, is arguably one of the most radical changes in the history of primary education in this country. Yet one of its central concepts – a vital and apparently radical new strategy that teachers must adopt and which of its own accord is intended to bring significant improvements in children's achievements – has not been explained in any depth to those who are required to use it.

Interactive teaching and the SPRINT Project

The two cameos at the beginning of this chapter imply that interactive teaching involves both observable or 'surface' features and deeper, non-observable ones. This list also includes both 'surface' questions about observable classroom practice and 'deep' questions about teachers' perceptions and understandings, so that, to try to provide answers, two quite different approaches had to be used in the project. The first was quantitative research using structured classroom observation; the second was generally more qualitative research based on ideas about teaching and learning mainly derived from cognitive psychology. These complementary approaches are discussed in the following two sections.

Observational research: the background

There is a long history of classroom research using structured observation in the series of ORACLE and related studies at the University of Leicester, and a large amount of information was available from both the earliest work in the 1970s through to data collected just before the advent of the literacy hour. From the start of the SPRINT Project, the intention was that comparisons would be made between this collection of data and observations of teaching during the literacy hour. There were four main areas of interest.

First, if interactive teaching is mainly about teachers asking questions, we would expect to find teachers doing less 'telling' and asking more questions than in previous ORACLE studies. The data would offer a simple but very reliable way of making such comparisons, using exactly the same categories as before. Second, the ORACLE observation categories also distinguish between different sorts of teacher question and pupil response, so that it was also important not only to count the number of questions, but also to analyse them more closely. In particular, we wanted to look out for higher-order questions, extensions of pupil responses and more sustained teacher–pupil interactions generally, in line with the points discussed earlier. Third, in spite of the lack of an underlying rationale for interactive teaching, the National Literacy Strategy has certainly offered a range of practical techniques for teachers to use, and we wished to determine if teachers were actually using these specific techniques, not only during the literacy hour but also outside it, in other curriculum areas. If the literacy hour had resulted in observable changes in patterns of teaching, have these had any wider effects. Finally, if these techniques involve qualitative as well as quantitative changes in teaching, the original ORACLE categories might not be able to record them properly. We were aware of this possibility from the start and were interested to see how observers, already trained and experienced in the use of the categories, would cope with recording new techniques such as the use of fans and whiteboards, where each pupil makes a verbal but unspoken individual response to the teacher's question.

A further area of interest emerged during the project, through other research into the literacy hour published after the start of the SPRINT study, using discourse analysis to look for changes in patterns of teaching. Mroz *et al.* (2000) suggested that a shift to higher-order questions was not taking place in the literacy hour. They found that interactions were still dominated by the classic 'initiation→ response → feedback' (IRF) pattern reported so frequently in much previous research, in which the teacher initiates a question, a pupil responds and the teacher gives feedback. As the SPRINT research proceeded, we were also interested to see if our data generally agreed with those of Mroz and her associates.

A decision was taken early in the project to use video for the systematic observation, rather than recording the observations 'live'. This was partly to allow observers to compare their categorizations and to gain a measure of reliability and partly to allow for more detailed and, if necessary, repeated analysis of the same lessons, in line with the fourth aim above about the ability of the ORACLE categories to cope with apparently new teaching techniques. There was another reason for using video, however, which arose from our central intention to combine quantitative and qualitative approaches in the project. As we discuss later, we were able to use the same video clips both for ORACLE analysis and as the basis for in-depth unstructured interviews with the teachers.

Structured observational research formed a very important part of the SPRINT Project, not only as a systematic method of collecting new quantitative data about the literacy hour, but also as a continuation of the ORACLE studies, acting as part of the background to the research into what interactive teaching might mean in terms of observable changes in classroom practice. However, from all that has been said, it will be clear that, from the start, we considered interactive teaching to go beyond strictly observable classroom techniques to an interest in teachers' perceptions, concepts and attitudes. The research background to these 'deeper' aspects of the project was much less specific than the observational studies, and our thinking was clearly affected by a wide range of studies of children's learning rather than classroom events, generally derived from the work of cognitive psychologists. The next section reviews very briefly some of these aspects of the background to the SPRINT Project, as possible ways of developing a rationale for interactive teaching.

Research into children's learning: the background

In the past, the impact of cognitive psychology on classrooms has been mainly indirect at best, largely because of the different agendas of teachers and psychologists (Merry 1998). Those working in the experimental or 'laboratory' tradition have often simply concluded that teachers 'should be aware' of whatever the psychologists had discovered, without always recognizing the differences between laboratory and classroom learning. However, there has been a shift in cognitive psychology away from a Piagetian emphasis on 'private' individual learning towards a much greater awareness of the social contexts of learning and of the ideas of writers like Vygotsky and Bruner. This shift has important implications for practitioners and their classroom interactions with children, and terms like 'scaffolding' are passing into the everyday language of teachers.

This shift is even more apparent when examining research in the general area of children's learning, which, although trying to go beyond observable behaviour, has been carried out in classrooms and has often resulted in actual materials or programmes. Some of the better known of these studies formed part of the background to the SPRINT Project and are briefly summarized below.

Higher-order thinking. If interactive teaching is intended to develop higher-order thinking skills as well as those which can be taught at a fast pace and in a teacher-directed way, as Reynolds and Farrell (1996) propose, then Resnick (1987) offered a potentially useful list of 'higher-order thinking skills' that is widely accepted and is still often referred to by other Western educationalists. She says that such thinking tends to:

- be non-algorithmic (that is, the path to the solution is not completely clear in advance and the learner cannot simply follow a series of known steps);
- be complex, involving, for example, different points of view;
- have several possible solutions, each with advantages and disadvantages to be weighed up;
- involve nuances of judgement and interpretation;
- depend on multiple criteria for making decisions;
- involve uncertainty because not all the necessary information is available in advance;
- depend on self-regulation rather than on instructions from someone else;
- involve imposing meaning and structure;
- involve considerable mental effort.

As with other research into children's learning discussed in this section, it is important not to see this as some sort of 'theoretical' or idealized list, which is irrelevant to the demands being made on busy teachers. Attempts to develop thinking skills such as these could easily be linked to literacy hour activities. For instance, many of the items on Resnick's list relate clearly but not exclusively to NLS text-level objectives, and some might be developed during guided reading and writing sessions or even in unsupervised groupwork. Thus, for example, a persuasive non-fiction text being studied in year 4, term 3 could be ideal for understanding 'different points of view' (Resnick's second item), while a sequencing activity could certainly involve 'imposing meaning and structure'. A list like Resnick's could, therefore, supplement NLS materials and give teachers a rationale and way of understanding the techniques they might choose to use in practice.

Cognitive acceleration. Adey and Shayer (1994) discuss teacher intervention, which could be seen as the teacher's role in interactive teaching. They emphasize the value of features such as concrete preparation, cognitive conflict, meta-cognition and the 'construction zone' in which the teacher supports the child in the joint construction of new knowledge or skills. In line with several other researchers (e.g. McGuinness 1999), Adey and Shayer consider that such skills are best taught in the context of curriculum subjects rather than in separate 'thinking skills' lessons, and they apply their ideas to science through the CASE (Cognitive Acceleration through Science Education) programme. The underlying rationale, however, applies just as well to other subject areas and might be particularly useful in discussions in English lessons.

Reciprocal teaching (Brown and Palincsar 1989; Rosenshine and Meister 1994). This is based on an approach in which the teacher initially acts as a model, after which pupils take it in turns to lead the group through four stages of discussion – a question posed by the leader, group clarification and discussion, a summary of the discussion by the leader, and a group decision about the next step. Here, the teacher's role is clearly being taken on by the pupils in a supportive and structured way in the hope of developing their independence and meta-cognitive awareness. Again, the approach is not simply a list of activities, but has a clear rationale derived from studying children's learning, in this case being closely related to a Vygotskyan theoretical perspective.

Innovative thinking (Hart 2000). This begins with the sorts of unexpected pupil responses seen as problematic in the literacy hour. Hart proposes that, far from indicating that something has gone wrong and that the teacher's objectives have not been met, these unexpected responses can be very revealing and can form the basis for important learning, provided the teacher uses various 'questioning moves' to try to understand them. These are very different from the rapid-fire questions that tend to dominate the literacy hour, and include teachers questioning their own assumptions and recognizing the importance of the children's and their own feelings. This contrasts strongly with the NLS view, which emphasizes the teacher's objectives rather than the pupils' learning:

> Of course, things don't always work out the way you intend. Discussion can be scuppered in many ways. Sometimes a child provides an unexpected – even bizarre answer and throws you off key . . . Worst of all, perhaps, are the occasions when a pupil comes up with a fully-fledged answer that pre-empts all your carefully laid plans.
>
> (DfEE 1999a: 4)

Here, the unexpected fact that one child suggests a really good answer, which can form the basis for further discussion (even perhaps led by the pupil), is seen not as an opportunity but as a nuisance.

Accelerated learning. Smith (1998) combines research from neuroscience and cognitive psychology to produce not only a series of practical ideas, but also a rationale for them through an understanding of learning processes that seem to be lacking in the National Literacy Strategy. Particular emphasis is given to preparing the learner before the content is 'delivered' through techniques such as 'brain gym' and providing the 'big picture'. During the presentation of new material, teachers are not just given useful techniques to keep the learners busy, but are helped to understand the invisible processes involved in learning, including individual differences in modality and learning style preferences. Again, accelerated learning, like the NLS materials, includes many lively ideas, but here they are offered in the context of reflection and a rationale based on research findings.

Interactive and reactive teaching. Cooper and MacIntyre (1996) propose that effective learning usually results from a blend of 'interactive' and 'reactive' teaching. The former has an emphasis on the teacher's pre-determined objectives and pupils' responses are taken on board only to the extent that they do not conflict with these objectives. If the responses do conflict, the teacher tries to modify them. This definition of 'interactive' is totally compatible with the emphasis on rapid teacher questions commonly found in the literacy hour. However, as later chapters will show, it is rather different from the definitions preferred by many teachers, who tend to see it more in terms of what Cooper and MacIntyre call 'reactive' teaching. Here, the emphasis is much more on the pupils' contribution, negotiation and the joint construction of meaning, in line with several of the approaches being outlined here.

Teaching for thinking (Sternberg and Spear-Swerling 1996) is in many ways similar. The first step, 'familiarization', involves the teacher in trying to make their own and the children's thinking explicit, particularly through dialogue, so that they can work together on this shared cognition, with a gradual shift of responsibility from teacher to learner. Sternberg and Spear-Swerling recognize that this view of learning may not appear compatible with tight objectives and a rapid pace, but they note that it is relevant to 'real-life' learning outside school, which tends, for example, to involve several possible solutions, nuances of judgement, different points of view and multiple criteria.

Many of the above approaches share common themes, particularly the emphasis on the child's learning as opposed to the teacher's objectives, and the notion of knowledge being constructed jointly rather than content being delivered. It might be argued that such an emphasis is unrealistic, given the demands of the National Curriculum and the literacy and numeracy hours. Conversely, it might also be argued that, if some aspects of these initiatives are not compatible with the ways in which children learn, then it is the value of the initiatives that is questionable. Ideally, of course, we should not be looking for conflicts between officially required practices and ideas developed from research into children's learning. The two should complement each other. Overall, it does appear that research might help us to understand the underlying rationale behind interactive teaching, especially those unobservable aspects that seem to be concerned with developing reflection and higher-order thinking.

Such research is not purely 'theoretical' with only vague implications for the teacher. Just before the start of the SPRINT Project, Merry (1998) drew on this body of research literature to provide some examples of the kinds of interactive activities that teachers might use to try to develop their children's learning. Merry (1998: 118) conjectured that they should:

- listen to the children to find out about their current understanding, or use other ways of making it explicit, such as mind maps;
- ask questions to check on this understanding and to point out mismatches;
- direct the children's attention to particular aspects of the materials or activity – the 'significant features';
- remind children about relevant events or findings from the past;
- encourage them to make hypotheses or predictions;
- amplify what they say and involve them in dialogue;
- model various courses of action, using expert protocols and similar devices;
- suggest strategies to help the children to learn and to build mental models;
- draw attention to the results of their activity, as feedback;
- encourage them to suggest different possible ways to proceed;
- allow them space and time to try things out without any teacher intervention!

So far, this chapter has discussed the background to the SPRINT Project in terms of the research questions we set out to answer and the research context of previous work in classroom observation and the psychology of children's learning. The rest of the book will set out the methodology and findings of the project in detail, but the chapters clearly have to be presented in sequence, unfolding one area at a time. Several early chapters, for example, refer to the video-stimulated reflective dialogues (VSRDs) that formed an important part of the research, but these are not explained in any detail until Chapter 8. The final section of this opening chapter will, therefore, briefly introduce the range of methods and main content areas of the project to give readers an overall understanding of what is to come – in line with Smith's (1998) notion of 'the big picture'. In doing so, it will also set out what we feel are the main research contributions of the whole project, under four headings: (i) qualitative methodology, (ii) quantitative methodology, (iii) qualitative findings and (iv) quantitative findings.

SPRINT's research contribution

Qualitative methodology

The major contribution to qualitative methodology was the development of VSRDs, with a clear shift in the roles of researcher and research-partner to encourage genuine reflection based as far as possible on the teacher's own perceptions and understandings, in keeping with one of the major aims of the research. These dialogues were carried out with only half the teachers – the 'Focus teachers' – mainly to see if such interventions had any effect on their thinking. The key features of VSRD involve an attempt both to probe and develop each focus teacher's individual understanding, while still collecting data systematically. These features included:

- *Video analysis.* Unlike most previous research, ownership of the video was both literally and metaphorically given to the teacher. The lesson to be recorded was chosen by the teacher as one which they expected to involve a lot of interactive teaching. After each classroom recording, the video was given to the teacher to view privately and to select what they considered to be a few minutes of particularly interactive teaching, using their own definition.
- *Video as a stimulus for prompted recall.* The video offered not simply raw data to be analysed by the researcher, but a shared experience that gave some structure to the dialogue and acted as a focus for both research-partners. The researcher's role was not to pose pre-set questions, but primarily to listen, to encourage the teacher to explore their ideas and to develop them through a balance of support and challenge.
- *Questions.* Teachers and researchers shared a list of possible headings and questions, but the questions were selected by the teachers as far as possible, to allow them to illuminate their own ideas.
- *Targets.* At the end of each dialogue, both participants agreed on two or three targets to be considered for the next phase. Again, this joint agreement provided a focus in terms of the teacher's own individual concepts and priorities, but also involved some challenge.

Overall, both researchers and teachers commented that they found the VSRDs more stimulating and more illuminating than previous interviews in which they had been involved. All agreed that the approach would be beneficial for both teachers' and researchers' professional development.

Quantitative methodology

As noted already, a major strength of the project was its ability to build on almost 25 years of previous research and data in the ORACLE tradition of systematic classroom observation. The video episodes chosen by the focus teachers for the reflective dialogues were also analysed using slightly revised ORACLE categories. Direct comparisons were possible between teaching before the advent of the National Literacy Strategy and in the literacy hour. The original categories had to be adapted slightly to take account of new techniques brought in by the National Literacy Strategy. The adapted categories will be of value to other researchers studying teaching in British primary schools now the literacy hour has been introduced.

Another widely used instrument, the Concerns-Based Adoption Model (CBAM; Hord 1987), originally developed in the USA in the 1970s, was used in the initial and final interviews with all teachers to probe their concerns about interactive teaching. However, it was found to be not entirely appropriate for probing these particular teachers' attitudes, and our analysis suggested a slightly different structure that might make it more suitable for future British use. Teachers' responses also questioned the notion of 'innovation' as applied to interactive teaching.

Qualitative findings

Analysis of interviews and reflective dialogues revealed a lack of teacher consensus about interactive teaching, in spite of its importance in the National Literacy Strategy. All the teachers had received some training for teaching the literacy hour, but they did not regard this training as having helped them to understand what interactive teaching might mean. Perhaps because of this, they often associated it with existing good practice rather than NLS-inspired innovation. However, several key features of teachers' thinking did emerge. These could be seen as being on a continuum, ranging from an emphasis on 'surface' features such as teaching techniques, to the development of pupils' higher-order thinking, as emphasized in the NLS view of interactive teaching. This continuum suggests a way forward for teachers' professional development, if the aims of the strategy to enhance pupils' thinking are to be realized.

Quantitative findings

Even taking into account the slightly revised observation categories, some striking differences emerged between the initial ORACLE results of 1976–77, data collected before the National Literacy Strategy in 1996 and the SPRINT literacy hour data. For example, although there was more interaction overall, some categories of teacher talk, such as 'task supervision', had declined considerably with the advent of the literacy hour. Analysis of the data (discussed in depth in Chapter 6) suggests some differences in patterns of interaction between Key Stages 1 and 2, and in the extent to which teachers encouraged more extended pupil responses, in line with the discussion earlier in this chapter.

The other main source of quantitative data was the CBAM Stages of Concern Questionnaire. Responses showed that the 'focus' teachers in general moved towards more sophisticated and strategic adoption of interactive teaching with significantly reduced concern about its everyday practicalities than the 'comparison' teachers. The focus teachers also moved to a more holistic and integrated profile of factors, indicating their professional commitment to interactive teaching and its dissemination, than the comparison teachers.

Summary

This chapter has introduced the background to the SPRINT Project and has outlined the main features that formed the basis for the research, including previous observational studies in classrooms and research into children's learning. It has set out the contribution of the research, in terms of both methodology and findings, to act as a context for the analysis chapters.

One major theme running through the chapter, from the introductory cameos onwards, has been the distinction between 'surface' and 'deep' strategies and interactions. It is a distinction that has been made by some previous researchers (e.g. Biggs 1994) and spontaneously recognized by at least some of our teachers. It is also a distinction that could be usefully applied not only to interactive teaching as the content area of the project, but also to the methodologies we employed. Classroom research in the ORACLE tradition understandably focuses on observable behaviour – the 'surface' features of what is going on – with all the advantages of being as objective and quantitative as possible, allowing various comparisons between individuals and between groups. Conversely, of course, it does not claim to identify the 'deeper' meanings, attitudes and perceptions that shape the behaviour, and for this we had to turn to our interviews and particularly to the VSRD transcriptions. Here, far richer, more qualitative data complemented the observations, and the two were brought together through the focus of the videos, which provided both data to be analysed into categories and a starting point for deeper reflection.

However, the parallel does not stop there. During the research it became apparent that the reflective dialogue process itself embodies several features that the results of the project suggest are central to interactive teaching. In a shift away from more traditional didactic approaches, interactive teaching would appear ideally to go beyond observable 'surface' features and classroom techniques, however beneficial they might be in encouraging practical involvement. 'Deep' interactive teaching appears to be a reciprocal process, genuinely taking on board the pupils' thinking as well as the teachers' objectives, and trying to encourage the children to reflect on and develop their own ideas. Similarly, the reflective dialogues were an attempt to move away from the more traditional relationship between researcher and interviewee, to set up genuine dialogue in which both participants shared and tried to develop their own understandings as research-partners. The result, a powerful balance between support and challenge for children, teachers and researchers, gives the SPRINT Project a coherence that underlies the following chapters.

2 Interactive teaching

A cause for concern?

*Linda Hargreaves, Anthony Pell and
Janet Moyles*

Introduction

This chapter and the next deal with two basic issues associated with teachers' understanding and use of interactive teaching. These are their concerns about, and knowledge of, interactive teaching. At the beginning of the project, it was important to try to determine the nature and direction of the teachers' concerns about interactive teaching as well as their attitudes to the literacy hour itself, since these were likely to affect their subsequent motivation to examine their practice of interactive teaching in depth. Our investigation of the teachers' concerns used the Concerns-Based Adoption Model (CBAM) of Hall *et al.* (1979). This was constructed from studies of teachers in the USA in the process of adopting educational innovations (see also Hord 1987). The CBAM identifies knowledge about an innovation as the first of a series of concerns that include practical implementation, effects on children and dissemination to colleagues. When, as we saw in the Introduction, several teachers whispered, 'Actually, I haven't heard of it', we felt justified in treating interactive teaching as an innovation. At the same time, we wished to determine whether the nature of primary teachers' concerns in England in 2000 differed from that of the teachers in Texas in the 1970s on whose responses the CBAM was based.

In this chapter, after describing the CBAM in a little more detail, we consider the overall patterns in the teachers' concerns and how these developed when they were actively involved in refining and evaluating their use of interactive teaching. A major part of the chapter is devoted to the methods we used in the study, and we are aware that some sections may be of more direct interest to researchers than to practising teachers. On the other hand, we think it important to indicate how our findings have been derived and how they differ from the original CBAM, so that all readers can evaluate our conclusions.

Teachers' concerns about interactive teaching

As noted in Chapter 1, although the National Literacy Strategy (DfEE 1998) informed teachers that successful teaching was, among other things, 'interactive', thus implying that primary teachers should adopt an interactive teaching style, the first edition of the framework document offered no advice on how this might be achieved, and clearly failed to acknowledge the difficulties associated with the adoption of new or different teaching styles. As Hargreaves and Fullan (1998) point out, there is a general failure to realize that 'teaching is hard emotional labour' (p. 60). They note that, 'Emotions are virtually absent from the literature and advocacy of educational change in areas like . . . teachers' competencies' (p. 59). Since the SPRINT Project was inviting teachers to demonstrate and develop their practice of interactive teaching, we thought it reasonable to investigate the nature of their concerns about it. To this end, we decided to use the Concerns-Based Adoption Model (Hall *et al.* 1979), as recommended by Hord (1987) as a means to evaluate teachers' adoption of innovation.

The Concerns-Based Adoption Model

Hall and co-workers' (1979) Concerns-Based Adoption Model (CBAM) explores the affective, cognitive and behavioural aspects of teachers' responses to any innovation. First, teachers' concerns about interactive teaching were measured by means of a questionnaire to determine their 'stages of concern' about interactive teaching. Second, questions derived from the CBAM 'levels of use' (LoU) were included in the interviews conducted at the beginning and end of the project. These interviews also included cognitive aspects and asked the teachers to talk about their knowledge and conceptualization of interactive teaching. Third, observation of practice, a central part of the SPRINT methodology, provided the information about performance or behaviour in implementing interactive teaching. Together, these three components provided methodologically triangulated information about the process of change. In this chapter, we concentrate on the affective and cognitive aspects and how these changed during the project.

The CBAM originated from Fuller's (1969) work, which identified three main phases of trainee teachers' concerns about teaching. These became known as concerns with 'self' (personal adequacy to teach), 'task' (the content of teaching) and 'impact' (the effect on pupils) (Hall *et al.* 1979). Beginning with a pool of over 500 items that related to Fuller's model, Hall *et al.* (1973) took two and a half years to develop the present 35-item

Stages of Concern Questionnaire (SoCQ). The 35 items are divided into seven subscales, each representing a stage of concern from 0 to 6. The items constituting each stage were derived from factor analysis of teachers' questionnaire responses, and were congruent with the theoretical constructs based on Fuller's work. Abbreviated definitions of the seven stages are shown in Table 2.1.

To adapt the SoCQ for SPRINT, 'interactive teaching' was inserted in place of 'the innovation', and a few American words such as 'faculty' were replaced by appropriate terminology for an English primary context. The teachers were asked to complete the questionnaire at the beginning and end of the fieldwork period when they were actively involved in the project. Each teacher rated the 35 items on a 7 point Likert scale ranging from 1 = 'not true of me now' to 7 = 'very true', with 0 = 'irrelevant'. In the analysis, zero was used as the lowest point on the 8-point scale following the procedure used by Hall and colleagues. According to CBAM, progress in the adoption of an innovation means a reduction in concerns about the basic practicalities of organizing and managing the classroom (Hall's 'management' stage) and greater concern about the 'consequences' for the children and 'collaboration' with other teachers. Ultimately, experienced users of the innovation might 'refocus' their concerns on something that would work better. If the SPRINT Project was being effective through its use of video and reflective dialogue with the focus teachers, then these teachers were expected to move further through the stages of concern than the comparison teachers.

Table 2.1 The seven Stages of Concern (Hall *et al.* 1979)

Stage		Description
0	Awareness	Little concern about, or involvement with, the innovation is indicated
1	Informational	A general awareness of the innovation and interest in learning more detail is indicated
2	Personal	Uncertainty about the demands of the innovation, adequacy to meet those demands and role with the innovation
3	Management	Attention is focused on the processes and tasks of using the innovation and the best use of information and resources
4	Consequence	Attention focuses on the impact of the innovation on students in his or her immediate sphere of influence
5	Collaboration	Focus on coordination and cooperation with others regarding use of the innovation
6	Refocusing	Focus on exploration of more universal benefits, including the possibility of major changes or replacement with a more powerful alternative

Video-stimulated reflective dialogue (VSRD)

The process of video-stimulated reflective dialogue was the main vehicle for pedagogical development in the SPRINT Project. The 15 'focus' teachers were videoed on four separate occasions engaged in what they defined as 'interactive teaching'. Three of the four videos were used as the basis for VSRD, which is described in full in Chapter 8. These were the initial and final literacy hour videos and a video taken when the teacher was teaching another curriculum area about half-way through the fieldwork phase. After the video had been recorded, the teacher took it away for independent viewing and selected a 20-minute section to illustrate interactive teaching for subsequent systematic coding. The section of video formed the focus for a reflective dialogue with a member of the research team a few days after the lesson had taken place. A framework for reflection and a set of reflective questions were used to provide a 'theoretical' basis and to focus attention during the discussion. The teachers stopped the video at points of significance and chose reflective questions to discuss. Action points were agreed and reviewed at subsequent meetings. A crucial aspect of the VSRD was that it gave teachers ownership of the reflection process and, by asking them to select the portion of video that best demonstrated interactive teaching for analysis, encouraged them to look critically at their practice.

The SPRINT Scales of Concern

It is plausible, without questioning the rigour used in the development of the Stages of Concern Questionnaire, that a sample of primary teachers in England in 2000 might have had a different constellation of concerns than Texan teachers and trainees in the 1970s. The SoCQ data were, therefore, analysed twice. The first approach was to apply a statistical method called 'factor analysis', which is used to identify several underlying factors in a test or inventory that has many items, and which was used by Hall and his colleagues originally. The second analysis involved applying Hall's original scales to see how the results compared.

SPRINT's factor analysis showed that our teachers' concerns did have a slightly different structure from that found by Hall. Five new scales, as opposed to Hall's original seven, made more sense of the SPRINT teachers' questionnaire responses. Three items (12, 13 and 35) did not fit into the new SPRINT scales, but none of these differentiated significantly between the groups of teachers. The five SPRINT scales achieved higher reliabilities than the analysis based on Hall's stages of concern. In further analyses, therefore, we used the SPRINT scales to maximize both the validity and reliability of our results.

Table 2.2 Characteristics of the five SPRINT Scales of Concern

Scale	Variance extracted (%)	Typical item (and its correlation with scale total less this item)	Score per item (mean ± s)	N
1 Lack of information	8	17. I would like to know how my teaching is supposed to change (0.55)	3.63 ± 1.19	26
2 Conflicting demands	10	8. I am concerned about conflicts between my interests and responsibilities (0.75)	3.28 ± 1.54	26
3 Professional adoption	30	14. I would like to discuss the possibility of using interactive teaching more effectively (0.87)	5.52 ± 1.17	27
4 Collegial development	16	18. I would like to familiarize other teachers and other schools with the way I am working during interactive teaching (0.68)	4.19 ± 1.37	27
5 Critical concern	7	22. I would like to modify our use of interactive teaching in this school based on the experience of our pupils (0.59)	4.08 ± 1.14	26

Note: 'Professional adoption' and 'Collegial development' correlate significantly at $r = 0.46$ ($N = 26$, $P = 0.02$). s = standard deviation.

The resultant SPRINT Scales of Concern, with example items, are shown in Table 2.2 and are shown in full in Appendix A.

The five SPRINT concerns

The first SPRINT scale, 'lack of information', correlated closely with both Hall's 'informational' and 'personal' stages. It included items such as 'I have a very limited knowledge of interactive teaching' and 'I would like to know how my teaching is supposed to change'. Since so many teachers had told us that they were not sure what interactive teaching was, it seemed reasonable to expect quite high scores on this scale at the beginning of the project.

The second scale, 'conflicting demands', correlated almost perfectly with Hall's 'management' stage. This scale was about the basic practicalities of implementing interactive teaching and included concerns about not having enough time to organize the sessions or to coordinate tasks, children and other people. According to Hord (1987), moving beyond basic implementation appears to be a critical step towards adopting the innovation.

The third SPRINT scale, 'professional adoption', was the strongest and most wide-ranging one, which took in concerns about achieving more effective use of interactive teaching, coordination with other teachers and using feedback from children. It was an important factor for our teachers and was associated significantly with several CBAM stages, including the first two. Its closest links, however, were with the more advanced CBAM scales. This applied in particular to Hall's 'consequences' stage on second administration. The original 'consequences' stage focused on the effects of the innovation on the children. In the SPRINT analysis, however, concerns about the effects on the children did not appear separately but were distributed across all three more advanced scales, and perhaps indicated a general concern that underlay the others. Thus 'professional adoption' included two items concerning children's responses, such as 'I would like to use feedback from children to change the way I undertake interactive teaching'. Similarly, while three of the five items that made up the fourth SPRINT scale, 'collegial development', included items such as 'I would like to help other staff in their use of interactive teaching', two were concerned with the effect on the children.

Finally, SPRINT's fifth scale, 'critical concern', consisted of items which suggest that the teachers had begun to re-evaluate interactive teaching and to adapt it or modify it to suit their own practice. Item 22, for example, reads: 'I would like to modify our use of interactive teaching in this school based on the experience of our pupils'. (This item had been amended from Hall's original to include the words ' in this school', making it more specific.)

Progress through the scales of concern

Hall *et al.* determined an order of progress through their seven stages that was derived from Fuller's original theory. They validated this by examining the concerns of people at various stages in innovation adoption, and use the resultant sequence as an aid to professional development to guide teachers through change (e.g. Hall and Hord 1987; Hord *et al.* 1987). We did not attempt the lengthy process of trying to establish an order of progression empirically, but used another statistical device. By plotting the highest inter-correlations (i.e. the items that were most similar to each other) against each other, we found a sequence that corresponded neatly with the original CBAM progression. It is important to remember, however, in the words of Hord *et al.* (1987), that 'the progression is not absolute and certainly does not happen to each person in a like manner' (p. 32).

Relationships between the CBAM stages of concern and the SPRINT scales

Although the total number of factors differed, the SPRINT scales and CBAM's stages of concern overlapped considerably. The items that made up the SPRINT 'conflicting demands' scale, for example were almost identical with CBAM's 'management' stage. Only one of Hall's scales, entitled 'consequences', was disrupted. Rather than appearing as a separate factor, these concerns about the effects on the children were spread across the three scales of 'professional adoption', 'collegial development' and 'critical concern'. Major change and innovation have been familiar events for teachers in England for well over a decade. We might hypothesize, therefore, that concern about the effects on the children has become a constant and wide-ranging anxiety that might accompany and inform other concerns, rather than forming a separate strand.

The similarities between the CBAM and SPRINT scales beyond the 'management/conflicting demands' level probably also reflect the idea that teachers do not show a profile of a single 'peak' at one stage, but high scores on two or three consecutive stages, as they become more experienced users of the innovation (Hall *et al.* 1979: 35; Hord 1987: 107). Hall and co-workers' profile of an experienced user, for example, shows high ratings on the 'consequence', 'collaboration' and 'refocusing' stages. Thus the overlap among the SPRINT scales was not surprising and reflects the original model, while the modified structure might account for the effects of England's decade of rapid multiple educational reform. It is reasonable to suggest that this has produced teachers who are not only concerned with the impact of these changes on the children, but who are also more critical of change. As we shall see in Chapter 3, while generally positive about interactive teaching, several SPRINT teachers were indeed critical of the National Literacy Strategy.

To summarize, even though we used a slightly different method of factor analysis, the SPRINT scales were closely correlated enough with the original CBAM stages of concern to suggest that they were representing similar constructs. However, the SPRINT solution does suggest that teachers in England at the turn of the twenty-first century may have responded in a slightly different way psychologically than teachers in the USA 30 years ago.

Having shown the similarities and differences between these two structures, we turn now to the SPRINT teachers' concerns and to the differences between the 'focus' and 'comparison' teachers.

The SPRINT teachers' concerns

If the process of video-stimulated reflective dialogue was effective in assisting the SPRINT teachers to refine their use and understanding of interactive teaching, then we would expect the focus teachers to move to greater concerns at the 'impact' level, namely 'professional adoption', 'collegial development' and 'critical concern', on the second administration of the SoCQ. Somewhat disappointingly, this simple hypothesis was not supported. There were no significant differences between the focus and comparison teachers' concerns overall on either the first or final questionnaire. This can be explained in part by the relative brevity of the focus teachers' active participation in the project and the small amount of time spent on VSRDs. Hord (1987) pointed out that the time needed for teachers to adopt and subsequently adapt any innovation is usually underestimated. She suggested, for example, that it could take two years to move from the 'awareness' to the 'management' stage in CBAM. Unfortunately, the SPRINT Project's original intention to spend a full year with the teachers was thwarted by the difficulty of identifying schools that felt able to take on the project when faced with the introduction of the National Numeracy Strategy, or an imminent OfSTED inspection. The latter is ironic at a time when evidence-based practice is being promoted, but in our own experience at least, it has constrained several innovative schools from participating in research projects.

Within the focus group, however, there were significant changes in the predicted directions, as shown in Figure 2.1 and Tables 2.3 and 2.4. Moreover, as we shall see later, when we compared focus teachers with their comparison teacher-partners, there were greater pre- and post-intervention changes among the focus teachers.

Both focus and comparison teachers became less concerned about their knowledge of interactive teaching. However, the focus teachers' concerns

Table 2.3   Changes in focus teachers' concerns

		Mean score per item (mean ± s)		
Attitude scale	Teachers (n)	First round	Final round	Difference
Lack of information	14	3.73 ± 1.25	2.96 ± 1.27*	−0.77
Conflicting demands	15	3.63 ± 1.83	2.85 ± 1.35*	−0.78
Professional adoption	15	5.36 ± 1.45	5.42 ± 0.98	+0.06
Collegial development	15	4.28 ± 1.32	4.68 ± 1.04	+0.40
Critical concern	15	4.20 ± 1.18	4.36 ± 1.06	+0.16

*$P < 0.05$, paired t-test. s = standard deviation.

Table 2.4   Changes in comparison teachers' concerns

		Mean score per item (mean ± s)		
Attitude scale	Teachers (n)	First round	Final round	Difference
Lack of information	12/12	3.58 ± 1.21*	3.00 ± 1.30*	−0.58
Conflicting demands	11/12	2.81 ± 0.90	2.80 ± 0.84	−0.01
Professional adoption	13/12	5.69 ± 0.78	5.41 ± 0.95	−0.28
Collegial development	12/12	4.08 ± 1.47	4.82 ± 1.07	+0.74
Critical concern	11/11	3.92 ± 1.12	4.15 ± 1.41	+0.23

*$P = 0.052$, paired t-test. s = standard deviation.

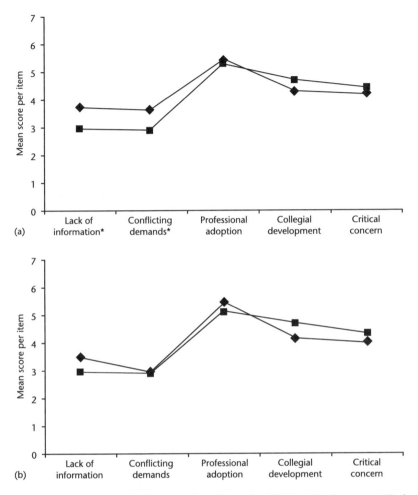

Figure 2.1   (a) Focus (◆) and (b) comparison (■) teachers' first and final concerns. *Reduction in level of concern significant at $P < 0.05$ (t-test, $n = 15$).

about their lack of knowledge fell significantly, whereas the decline for comparison teachers was small enough to be simply due to chance factors. (Chapter 3 is devoted to the change in the teachers' knowledge of interactive teaching and so we will not discuss it further here.) The critical development, however, was that the focus teachers returned significantly lower ratings on the 'conflicting demands' scale in the second questionnaire. This marks the shift from Fuller's 'personal' to 'task' concerns, and passes a critical threshold in innovation adoption. To put it crudely, teachers became less worried about how the innovation would affect them personally and began to think about how to put it into practice. This is clearly an important step because, prior to this, as Hord put it:

> One of the most common problems afflicting school improvement efforts has been the consistent failure to recognise the existence and significance of this stage . . . [in which] . . . teachers are typically frantic and frustrated; their connection with the innovation may be tenuous, and their use of it superficial, since most of their time and energy are taken up with basic material and logistical preparations.
>
> (Hord 1987: 102)

Hord went on to point out, however, that, crucial as this shift is, once achieved, further refinement of implementation is not inevitable. Instead, having sorted out the day-to-day management issues, some teachers simply 'coast' rather than develop their use of the innovation for their pupils' benefit (Hord *et al.* 1987). This was a very important development for the SPRINT Project because it was seeking first to access teachers' existing understanding of 'interactive teaching' and subsequently to support their refinement of it.

Differential progress between the focus and comparison groups on the three 'higher' stages, however, was not significant, but concerns about 'collegial development' increased markedly in both groups. Not surprisingly, perhaps, this was the most marked increase in concern for the comparison group, and represents an effect reflecting a desire on their part to be more involved in the project. The fact that both the focus and comparison groups showed the greatest increase in concerns abuot 'collegial development' might indicate a general shift in teachers' expectations of collaboration. It is arguable that the emphasis on whole-school curriculum planning and assessment trials to ensure progression, during the 1990s, and the NLNS cascade strategies, have created an expectation of collegiality, shared professional development and cooperation in schools. Both groups, therefore, were keen to collaborate on interactive teaching.

We suggested above that the relatively short time devoted to the intervention with the focus teachers might explain the lack of major differences between the focus and comparison groups. A second reason could have been the extent of teachers' existing knowledge of interactive teaching; in other words, whether interactive teaching was perceived as a real innovation (this is discussed in depth in Chapter 3). As we shall see, while few teachers claimed to be knowledgeable about interactive teaching, it was quite common for them to refer to it as part of standard practice, or, indeed, as part of their practice before the introduction of the National Curriculum or the National Literacy Strategy. Hord *et al.* (1987) pointed out that this is not uncommon: 'Another way teachers express personal concerns about a change is to characterize the innovation as nothing new, but something they have always done or used to do' (p. 31). It may have been that the innovation for the SPRINT teachers was the term 'interactive teaching', rather than the practice itself. However, as recent observational studies of primary teaching have shown (e.g. Alexander 1995, 2000; Galton *et al.* 1999) and as we shall see in Chapter 6, there was little that could be described as interactive teaching before the National Curriculum and this has declined, if anything, since its introduction.

A third explanation for the similarity between the focus and comparison teachers' concerns may lie in the nature of the comparison group. Many of these teachers were more experienced, or more senior, than their focus counterparts. When the teachers were first introduced to the project, heads had encouraged teachers who were keen to develop their practice to become focus teachers and asked experienced and perhaps more confident staff to take the role of comparison teachers. Laura, for example, was deputy head of her school and a recognized teacher leader in her local authority. She held a brief within her school to foster independent learning and saw interactive teaching as a medium for its development. Her focus counterpart, however, was a mature entrant to the profession, had only three years experience and was much less confident. In the light of these characteristics of many of the comparison teachers, the changes within the focus group are a strong positive outcome.

Stages of concern and levels of use: qualitative evidence

As well as the stages of concern, the CBAM includes 'levels of use' of an innovation. The levels of use are explored by means of interviews. The first level is 'non-use', which is followed by six stages, punctuated by critical decision points, leading to 'renewal' (see Table 2.5). Level IV marks a critical threshold between a teacher simply 'bolting on' the innovation to their usual practice and moving on to refine their use of the innovation to increase its value for the children. In the SPRINT Project, the interviews tapped teachers' initial and final levels of use, while the video-stimulated reflective dialogues (VSRDs) provided the opportunity for the focus teachers to discuss how they could refine their use of interactive teaching. Methodologically, the qualitative levels of use data can be used to check and enlarge on the questionnaire findings.

For example, the significant reduction in the focus teachers' concerns on the 'conflicting demands' scale (similar to Hall's 'Management' stage) was consistent with the evidence from the VSRDs in which they identified and confronted the dilemmas of implementation, as well as elaborated and clarified their understanding of interactive teaching (see Chapter 7). Thus, items about time pressures on the questionnaire were backed up by teachers' comments in the interviews when asked if there might be any constraints on their use of interactive teaching.

Table 2.5   Concerns-Based Adoption Model: Levels of Use (Hord 1987)

Level of use	Title	Brief definition
Level 0	Non-Use	Not using nor intending to use the innovation
Level I	Orientation	Taking steps to find out about the innovation
Level II	Preparation	Preparing for first use
Level III	Mechanical Use	Initial attempts to master use of the innovation
Level IVA	Routine	Stabilized use of innovation with little change
	non-user/user interface	
Level IVB	Refinement	Variation in use to increase effect on children
Level V	Integration	Working with others to increase benefits to children
Level VI	Renewal	Re-evaluating use and seeking modifications

Time was a concern for most of the teachers, an issue taken up in detail in Chapter 9. Kathleen and others were concerned about the time needed to cover the learning objectives laid down in the NLS framework document (DfEE 1998), which might not be met if children were given more opportunity to tell their own stories. Another practical constraint was the noise likely to ensue from increased verbal interaction which might disturb others, particularly in open-plan settings, or where classes were separated by 'concertina doors' (as Kelly put it) or shared a mobile classroom unit. Some of the teachers who said they worked in particularly quiet schools were especially worried about this as a constraint. Karen, for example, worked in a partly open-plan area and also mentioned the potential problem of noisy interactions. She had solved this problem, however, by 'taking steps to inform others' when she was expecting to have a 'noisy' lesson. Karen had also dealt with the problem of time by being 'flexible' and feeling able to manage time constraints. Thus these were not particular concerns for Karen, who was a deputy head and leading teacher; her concerns profiles showed minimal change between the first and final rounds. Practical constraints were concerns, however, for some of the less experienced focus teachers or those who felt constrained by school policy. These comments, then, could be interpreted as reflecting conflict between the teachers' 'interests' – to use interactive teaching – and their 'responsibilities' – for example, to conform to school policies and ethos or to meet the literacy or numeracy targets in the time allowed.

The reflective dialogues enabled teachers to pursue such conflicts in greater depth, and included issues from the 'professional adoption' scale. This referred to more wide-ranging and analytic aspects of the use of interactive teaching, detailed in Chapters 4 and 5, such as the desire to use it more effectively (item 14). Teachers were often aware of individual differences, for example. As Xena recognized, '[interactive teaching] is sometimes harder for the middle group'; and, for Karen, the need to ensure that less assertive children could benefit as much as those who volunteer to talk. The content of the interviews and VSRDs corroborated the concerns highlighted by the questionnaire, while placing the focus teachers beyond the critical user/non-user threshold at Levels II ('preparation') and III ('mechanical use') and, in most cases, clearly in IVb ('refinement') (Hord 1987: 111). Further examples from the interviews and VSRDs are given in later chapters (see Table 2.5).

A strength of the CBAM is that it can be used to consider change in individuals as well as groups, and the fact that it is based on the individual's understanding of the innovation is particularly pertinent to the objectives of the SPRINT Project. We turn now to consider briefly some individual profiles and the differences between pairs of focus and comparison teachers.

The focus teachers and their comparison partners: changes in concerns

It could be argued that it is fruitless to search for overall change in a group of teachers when stages of concern profiles are highly individualized and influenced by contexts and personal responses. According to Hord *et al.* (1987: 43):

> Concerns do not exist in a vacuum. Concerns are influenced by participants' feelings about an innovation, by their perception of their ability to use it, by the setting in which the change occurs, by the number of other changes they are involved in and, most of all, by the kind of support and assistance they receive as they attempt to implement change.

In the SPRINT Project, each focus teacher was paired with a comparison teacher in his or her own school. Since each pair of teachers was in a different school, each with a different ethos, level of collegiality and physical environment, this suggests that variation between the pairs in a relatively small sample was likely to outweigh general trends. On the other hand, variation *within* the pairs, and within these different settings, might show whether each focus teacher's concerns had developed more than those of their comparison counterpart, as a result of even a brief opportunity to demonstrate, observe and discuss interactive teaching.

We therefore compared each focus teacher with their comparison teacher-partner on each of the five scales, and used a standard measure (statistically half a standard deviation) as the criterion for deciding whether or not a change had occurred. We found that the focus teachers met this criterion on more scales than the comparison teachers. In two cases where there were no comparison data, the focus teachers met the criterion on four of the five scales. For only one pair did the comparison teacher appear to have changed on more scales (3) than the focus teacher (2), but the data for the focus teacher were not quite complete in this case. In other words, these results provide encouraging support for the value of the VSRD process and the hypothesis that, given more time, even greater developments might have ensued.

Figures 2.2–2.4 show a range of profiles for teacher pairs. Hord (1987) showed how the stages of change profiles change as teachers become experienced users of an innovation. Typically, as new users they have more concerns during Hall and co-workers' 'awareness', 'informational' and 'personal' stages. As their concerns about 'self' reduce in intensity, so the 'task' or 'management' concerns become more prominent. Finally, as practical management of the innovation becomes routine, so the 'impact' concerns become more intense, as teachers think about the effects on children and wish to share use of the innovation with colleagues.

One teacher, Queenie, showed relatively little change in any of her concerns over the course of the project. In response to the questions about her levels of use of interactive teaching, Queenie, an experienced teacher, regarded interactive teaching as 'good infant practice' and said she already used it '80 per cent of the time'. By the end of the project, Queenie felt that she had not changed her practice of interactive teaching, and demonstrated its use in role-play in a history session. Her profile in Figure 2.2a reveals her confidence in her knowledge and practice of interactive teaching. However, these are well below the focus teachers' final mean scores. Although 'professional adoption' remained her greatest concern, this eased during the project, while her concern to share interactive teaching with other staff increased. Overall, however, Queenie was one of the focus teachers whose concerns profile changed least. In shape it most resembles the single peak profile typical of someone with intense concerns in the CBAM 'management' stage (Hord et al. 1987: 36). Although not strictly comparable, in the SPRINT model this would be equivalent to concerns about 'professional adoption'. Queenie's second profile, however, shows a slight progression from 'professional adoption' to SPRINT's collegial concerns (or Hord and co-workers' 'collaboration'). Leonie, a comparison teacher and one of Queenie's younger colleagues, also displayed very low levels of concern compared with the other SPRINT teachers, and her concerns changed less than Queenie's during the project (Figure 2.2b).

Katrina's profile shows a considerable change during the project, with significant reductions in concern in most areas. As we shall see in the next chapter, Katrina felt comfortable with her knowledge of interactive teaching, but showed a considerable reduction in concern about the practical management ('conflicting demands') of interactive teaching, as well as in the 'impact' concerns about 'professional adoption' and 'collegial development'. By the final administration, her greatest concern was 'collegial development'. Her

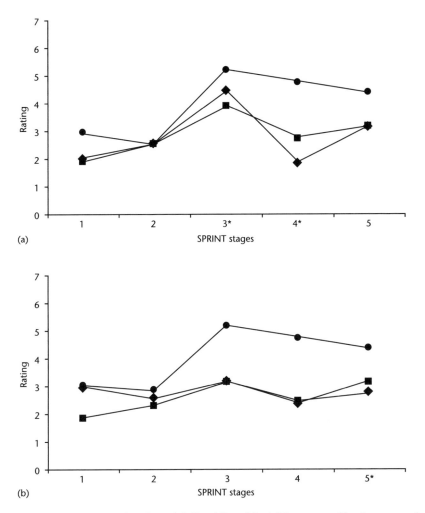

Figure 2.2 (a) Focus teacher Queenie's first (♦) and final (■) concerns (● = focus group's final concerns). (b) Comparison teacher Leonie's first (♦) and final (■) concerns (● = comparison group's final concerns). SPRINT scales: 1, lack of information; 2, conflicting demands; 3, professional adoption; 4, collegial development; 5, critical concerns. *Denotes a change of more than 0.5 of a standard deviation based on first administration of the questionnaire.

profile moves from affinity with Hord and co-workers' 'inexperienced user' towards a more experienced profile concerned with 'management' of the innovation. Her comparison teacher, Iris, has a profile showing fewer changes. She becomes more concerned to find out about interactive teaching, yet stays at the level of a relatively experienced user who is still focusing on the consequence of the innovation. Both Katrina and her colleague

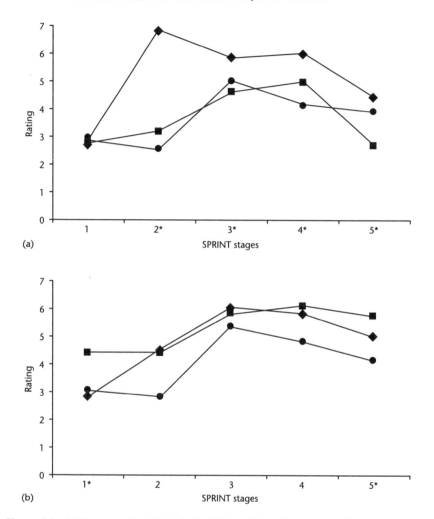

Figure 2.3 (a) Focus teacher Katrina's first (◆) and final (■) concerns (● = focus group's final concerns). (b) Comparison teacher Iris' first (◆) and final (■) concerns (● = comparison group's final concerns). SPRINT scales: 1, lack of information; 2, conflicting demands; 3, professional adoption; 4, collegial development; 5, critical concerns. *Denotes a change of more than 0.5 of a standard deviation based on first administration of the questionnaire.

became less concerned about alternatives to interactive teaching as the project progressed.

Finally, Kim's profile suggested someone who was extremely critical of interactive teaching initially (see Chapter 3). By the second round, however, her concerns showed a change of mind about 'professional adoption' and 'collegial development'. None of Hord's profiles resemble this dramatic

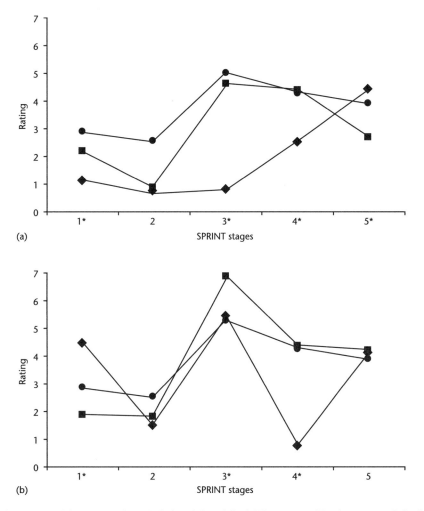

Figure 2.4 (a) Focus teacher Kim's first (◆) and final (■) concerns (● = focus group's final concerns). (b) Comparison teacher Irene's first (◆) and final (■) concerns (● = comparison group's final concerns). SPRINT scales: 1, lack of information; 2, conflicting demands; 3, professional adoption; 4, collegial development; 5, critical concerns. *Denotes a change of more than 0.5 of a standard deviation based on first administration of the questionnaire.

change. Her partner, Irene, in common with many other comparison teachers, becomes concerned about 'collegial development', perhaps as a result of talking to Kim, and felt she was now more knowledgeable about interactive teaching.

[Note that we used an oblique factor solution, which allows for correlation between the factors, whereas Hall *et al.* (1979) used a 'varimax' orthogonal factor solution, which imposed a condition of independence on the factors. When Hall *et al.* carried out their factor analysis, it was more usual to use orthogonal solution.]

The evidence presented here shows that the focus teachers as a group became less concerned about the lower-order stages of CBAM – their knowledge of interactive teaching and the day-to-day demands it made on their teaching. In addition, five of the 15 focus teachers, but none of the comparison teachers, significantly changed their concerns on four of the scales (statistically by over half of a standard deviation). A further three focus teachers changed by that amount on three scales and the remainder on two. Five comparison teachers changed their concerns on three scales, but three did not change their concerns at all. Considered this way, we would suggest that the project had a positive impact on the focus teachers' concerns about interactive teaching. The video-stimulated reflective dialogues provided an effective tool for professional development, and a longer period of time with even just one more VSRD would have furthered this development.

Summary

SPRINT's statistical analysis of the Stages of Change Questionnaire found that five scales correlated sufficiently with the original CBAM stages of concern to indicate comparability. We suggest that the main differences may indicate a teaching profession that has become more critical of change and is more generally concerned about the effects of change on children, compared with teachers in Texas in the 1970s. In view of the pace and scale of change that teachers have had to adopt – or adapt to – in England since the late 1980s, a different configuration of concerns than the Texan pattern is not surprising. In particular, the SPRINT teachers' concern about the effects of innovation on the children appears to have become more generalized and associated with other more specific concerns, although it must be remembered that the differences may be due, in part, to the method used to isolate the structures. Our sample was small, and a larger-scale study of teachers' innovation adoption concerns in England is needed to examine this suggestion of a new 'English' concerns structure.

This chapter began with the idea that concern about our knowledge of an innovation is the first step in beginning to adopt it. As we have seen, this is the substance of the first level of concern, which Hall *et al.* (1979) labelled 'informational' and SPRINT identified as a concern about 'lack of information'. The next chapter turns to look in more detail at the whole question of teachers' knowledge of interactive teaching.

3 It's what I've always done!
Teachers' knowledge of interactive teaching

Fred Paterson and Janet Moyles

Introduction

This chapter explores SPRINT teachers' knowledge of interactive teaching during the project. This was a time of unprecedented attention to literacy teaching and learning and to government's moves to change teaching strategies. In Chapter 1, Merry and Moyles have argued that even though it was considered a 'key determinant of educational achievement' by Reynolds and Farrell (1996), within the National Literacy Strategy (NLS) literature 'interactive teaching' was not clearly defined in ways that enabled teachers to understand why and how they might consider teaching in this way. Galton *et al.* (1999) make a similar point when they suggest that, 'Currently the distinctions between terms such as "direct teaching" and "interactive or whole class teaching" are not well defined' (p. 189).

The earliest NLS literature provided little tangible advice for teachers seeking a clear definition or examples of interactive teaching. Although the National Literacy Strategy promoted interactive teaching as an effective pedagogical response to low standards of literacy, within the classroom-focused literature available to teachers, interactive teaching was inadequately defined and lacked a clear basis in pedagogical principles. More recent classroom-focused literature and video material has offered examples of teaching technologies designed to model interactive teaching practices (DfEE 1999c), but has still provided few clues to the pedagogical principles or educational philosophies that underpin interactive teaching. Somewhat belatedly, the National Literacy Centre responded to requests from many quarters for information about the research base for the NLS with the publication of *National Literacy Strategy: Review of Research and Other Related Evidence* (Beard 1999). Although the promotion of higher levels of pupil thinking was a key aspiration of the National Literacy Strategy, little attention was paid to the research literature addressing the development of these skills, and clear information about the principles underlying interactive teaching remained unforthcoming. In their largely positive evaluation of the implementation of the National Literacy and Numeracy Strategies, Earl *et al.* (2000: 11) agree, stating: 'although traditional goals associated with literacy and numeracy are well defined, there is less attention in [NLS/NNS] to goals related to higher order thinking and deep understanding'.

In Chapters 1 and 2, we discussed the research of Mroz *et al.* (2000), who suggested that even 'effective' teachers are not always successful in addressing the NLS aspiration to promote higher-order pupil thinking. This chapter describes how many of the SPRINT practitioners had an understandably minimal awareness of its pedagogy, did not consider it to be an 'innovation' in practice and, at the same time, lacked confidence in their 'theoretical' knowledge of interactive teaching. Given all the above it is, perhaps, unsurprising that the SPRINT teachers equated interactive teaching with 'good', 'quality' or 'usual' practice, rather than differentiating interactive methods from 'common' practice or 'what I've always done'. We argue that this was a reflection of the lack of (a) clarity in the NLS literature and (b) attention to 'interactive teaching' in professional development opportunities provided for teachers. We also show that the SPRINT Project went some way to relieve teachers' informational concerns, albeit that their desires for some form of definition and indicators of appropriate strategies were still apparent by the end of the project.

Data from the 30 SPRINT teachers were collected via interviews, question-naires and systematic observation of classroom practice (initial and final inter-view schedules are shown in Appendices B and C, respectively). To identify ongoing teacher conceptualizations of interactive teaching and their attitudes towards its implementation, all the project teachers undertook an initial and final interview. The analysis presented below is based largely on the inter-views with the teachers, supplemented by analysis of data from the videos, questionnaires and reflective dialogues. The influences upon teachers' knowledge of interactive teaching reflect a complex arena, and the findings presented here do not necessarily describe generalizable themes. Rather, the analysis and case examples are used to portray potentially interesting and use-ful perspectives on the factors that influence teachers' knowledge of practice.

'Tell me more'

At the start of the SPRINT Project, the Concerns-Based Adoption Model (CBAM; Hord 1987) analysis showed the two most significant teacher concerns about interactive teaching focused on their requirements for information ('tell me more') and the professional adoption of interactive practices. By the end of the project, concerns about their lack of awareness and knowledge were significantly reduced. The basic data offered by the CBAM analysis, however, hide a much more complex and intriguing picture about SPRINT teachers' thinking.

Concerns about knowledge and information were reduced during the project but still only four of the SPRINT teachers said, categorically, that they felt more knowledgeable by the end of the project. Interestingly, though, all four were focus teachers. Half the SPRINT teachers suggested that they were more conscious of interactive teaching or talked about giving 'interactive practice more thought' since their involvement in the project. Other teachers said that they felt there had been little change in their knowledge. These teachers fell into two categories: those that did not feel 'at all knowledgeable' and those that had been confident in their own knowledge from the start of the project. Given the point made above about the focus teachers, that this group were all comparison teachers potentially adds credence and significance to the influence of video-stimulated reflective dialogue.

Apparent contradictions in teachers' knowledge

As is often the case with qualitative data, teachers' confusions about inter-active teaching became obvious by the number of occasions on which they appeared to contradict earlier statements. What one teacher meant by 'feeling knowledgeable' was not necessarily the same for another and cross-relating emerging concepts was vital to our understanding. When asked if they felt knowledgeable, some teachers' were based on their perceived theoretical understanding, whereas others responses were based on their 'lay understanding' and expertise. For example, one teacher said, 'I don't feel at all knowledgeable' about interactive teaching, while adding, 'I do know what I find effective in the classroom'. Another expressed 'a lay understanding' but confessed that 'I still haven't got it clear in my mind'. Yet others talked about theoretical influences of various kinds, including continuing development courses, but expressed little confidence in their own knowledge. As we argue later, this latter must be of concern to all those who value teaching as a profession. These statements may reflect a diminishing of professionals' self-confidence as a result of over-prescriptive policies such as that embodied in the National Literacy Strategy.

In analysing teacher knowledge, we feel that it is useful to distinguish between personal and public forms of knowledge as outlined by Eraut (1994):

- *personal knowledge* is that which is developed through personal engagement with the issues;
- *public knowledge* refers to knowledge that is considered to have certain claims to theoretical validity and generalizability and is widely available.

For our teachers, these two appeared to be merged in their thinking, potentially another indicator that teachers in general feel they have little control over what they are required to do and what they must simply do as bid by their political masters. As a profession – if teaching truly is a profession – teachers should be querying and challenging practices, which, in their professional knowledge and judgement, are not appropriate for teaching and learning.

At the start of the SPRINT Project, 12 of the 30 SPRINT teachers expressed some satisfaction with their own personal knowledge of interactive teaching, and ten of the teachers referred to public or theoretical forms of knowledge about interactive teaching. Some teachers were comfortable with their personal knowledge, but not at all confident with their theoretical knowledge. Other teachers referred to theoretical knowledge, but did not 'feel knowledgeable' about interactive teaching. These contradictions are the reason for minor discrepancies readers may notice in the figures reported in this chapter. For example, one teacher said, 'I have my own views, but I wouldn't like to say I was that knowledgeable really'. Although this teacher was satisfied with her own views about interactive teaching built on several years practice and personal experience, she did not feel 'knowledgeable' or, as we have suggested, feel she had relevant or necessary public knowledge. This suggests that, for some teachers, 'being knowledgeable' was determined only by public or theoretical knowledge, while others used their own personal experience as a gauge of their knowledge.

Teacher attitudes

To make sense of what teachers said about their personal knowledge, it is useful to consider as a starting point their attitudes to interactive teaching and its context within the National Literacy and Numeracy Strategies. The initial interviews showed that, from the start of the SPRINT Project, *all* 30 teachers held positive attitudes towards interactive teaching. This uniformity of positive attitude was not, however, repeated for the literacy hour. Eleven of the SPRINT teachers expressed negative or ambivalent attitudes towards the NLS, with nine of these being longer serving teachers. All 12 of the teachers with fewer years service expressed positive attitudes to interactive teaching, and most of these teachers were also positive about the NLS.

The analysis of data from longer-serving, arguably more experienced, teachers provided a wider variety of perspectives than for the shorter-serving teachers. By comparing the various combinations of public and personal knowledge with positive and negative attitudes towards the literacy hour, we see the rich variety of influences on the more experienced teachers. A variety of attitudes were expressed. Eleven of the 18 longer-serving teachers expressed positive attitudes towards the literacy hour and related interactive teaching to 'good practice', 'quality teaching', common or 'usual' practice. Seven of these 18 teachers, however, expressed negative attitudes. These teachers tended to dislike the limitations provided by the structure of the literacy hour and felt constrained and 'hemmed in' by its structure, which they deemed to be 'quite prescribed'. One teacher felt that the literacy hour promoted a 'delivery model' of teaching, while another felt that it promoted 'chalk and talk' and that her teaching had become 'more formal' since its introduction. A strong advocate of collaborative and child-centred practices was unsure whether the National Literacy Strategy promoted 'good practice' at all. Nevertheless, all the teachers with more than five years teaching experience considered interactive teaching variously to be 'the way we should be teaching', 'absolutely key' and 'very important'.

Teacher knowledge

When asked during interview whether they felt knowledgeable about interactive teaching, the SPRINT teachers offered a range of responses from the unequivocally negative – 'Actually, what is interactive teaching?' and 'I don't feel knowledgeable at all' – to the more positive – 'fairly knowledgeable' and 'comfortable in my own knowledge'. One teacher was more equivocal: '[I'm] not theoretically at all knowledgeable, but I've got quite a lot of experience using it in the classroom'. And another said, 'I don't think I am knowledgeable, I don't know the theory, I only know what I find effective in the classroom, which I think may be interactive teaching, but I don't know the theory behind it'. Here again, we see a glimpse of the uncertainties between public and personal knowledge expressed by this teacher.

Yet another teacher explained that her knowledge had 'evolved naturally' over time through her experience of teaching different year groups, abilities and mixes of pupils in different schools. These comments show how some teachers valued theoretical or public forms of knowledge over their own personal experiential knowledge. We return to this point below.

At the start of the project, 19 of the 30 teachers expressed little or no confidence in their knowledge of interactive teaching. Given its importance within the National Literacy Strategy, it is also disappointing to find that two-thirds of the SPRINT teachers felt they lacked theoretical knowledge about interactive teaching methods. More of the teachers were confident about their personal experiential knowledge (although still less than half of the cohort) and, as mentioned above, these teachers equated interactive teaching with their everyday practice rather than differentiating interactive methods from general practice or strategies they had always pursued in their teaching. A few teachers referred specifically to the issues of pace and pupil thinking skills, which form the crux of the NLS construction of interactive teaching. One can infer from this that, for many of these teachers, interactive teaching was not seen as an 'innovation' in practice, a point we illuminated below.

Chapter 2 showed how the SPRINT teachers' informational concerns decreased significantly in the analysis of the post-programme CBAM questionnaires. However, it was perhaps surprising that, by the end of the project, only four teachers stated clearly that they felt more knowledgeable. That all four were focus teachers suggests that the reflective dialogue process had a positive impact, but only one of these teachers based her opinion on a 'theoretical grounding' provided through discussions with her research-partner. It is interesting to note that six of the 30 provided some indication that they had increased theoretical or public knowledge, which suggests that heightened awareness had occurred as a result of the SPRINT Project. One-third of the teachers also implied some increase in confidence in personal knowledge and half indicated that they were more conscious of interactive teaching, or talked about giving 'interactive practice more thought' through their involvement in the project.

Although he was not more knowledgeable than before, Louis, an experienced KS2 comparison teacher, became more aware of the literature on interactive teaching. He felt that his awareness of interactive practice had been raised through the SPRINT Project and that he had developed his own thinking 'rather than more [public] knowledge'. He commented:

> I had more of an 'eye-out' for what's been going on in the field study for interactive teaching, just through my awareness being heightened, I think. Quite naturally when you see the word, whether it be in an article in the *TES* [*Times Educational Supplement*] or in any kind of literature that comes into school – 'Oh, what's that about?' and perhaps you're a bit more focused on it and that would seem to be the emphasis of what has been said. I'm not referring to a specific article, I'm just . . . little snippets from different places.

Increased awareness was not necessarily a precursor to action. Although Shelley felt that she had become more aware since her contact with the project, she said: 'I don't think anything in practice has happened, but mentally I'm thinking it through'.

Other teachers suggested there had been no change in their knowledge. These teachers fell into two categories: either they were confident in their own knowledge from the start or had never felt at all knowledgeable. All these teachers were comparison teachers. Irene, an experienced and confident teacher with more than 16 years experience, felt her knowledge was unchanged. She was positive about interactive teaching, but saw it as 'nothing new'. Laura, a KS1 teacher with just a couple of years experience, said:

> I have my own views, but I wouldn't like to say I was that knowledge-able at all really. I do what I do and my only real discussion about it has been with staff in school. Other than that I have no real . . . [unfinished] I have no knowledge of any research . . . Knowledge wise, I just sort of hope that I am quite secure in my knowledge of what I feel.

Another less experienced KS1 teacher, Teresa, was less confident or secure in her views and reflected, 'I think people have an idea of what interactive teaching is but I don't think anybody knows if their idea or concept is correct'.

Linda, a KS2 teacher with 3–5 years experience[1], was confident about her own personal knowledge and practice. When asked how knowledgeable she felt, she said: 'Talking about my classroom, fairly knowledgeable. I know about various different teaching processes, styles whatever, but I wouldn't say I am that knowledgeable. I know from experience'. Here we see a teacher who appears to emphasize personal, practical knowledge over public forms of knowledge. Linda was unaware of sources of information about interactive teaching, and her response suggests that her personal knowledge hadn't changed since the start of the SPRINT Project. Although a competent and articulate teacher, Linda appeared reluctant to consider addressing theoretical knowledge. It would have been interesting to challenge teachers such as Linda as to their reasons for such an emphasis on personal knowledge, and more opportunity for reflective dialogues may well have supported more of our teachers in addressing both dimensions and relating them to each other.

In contrast, as implied by Teresa above, about a third of the teachers had either implicit or explicit aspirations for some form of definition of interactive practice. Among this group, Dawn asserted:

> I have got so many questions. I don't feel that there are definitive answers to any of them. There are lots of opinions. I feel like I would really like lots of different techniques that I could perhaps see on a sheet of paper that I could try and use and develop.

This comment highlights teachers' anxieties about interactive practice. In the absence of 'definitive' answers about the principles that underpin inter-active teaching, less experienced teachers, in particular, looked for strategies to operationalize the concept. Perhaps more opportunity for these teachers to access public knowledge in the way we argued in Chapter 1 would support their professional development and ensure that government policy was put into practice more effectively.

The comments by Teresa and Dawn above also suggest an increasing awareness that interactive teaching is something more than 'what we've always done'. They were, however, less experienced teachers. Was there any sign that more experienced teachers had begun to see interactive teaching as something new? Or were there other reasons for the differences between experienced and less experienced teachers? We return to this in the final section of this chapter.

In the following sections, we start to explore some of the conditions for and influences on teachers' knowledge.

The impact of NLS professional development opportunities

All 30 of the SPRINT teachers had received some form of professional development focusing on aspects of the literacy hour. These included:

- multi-day in-service provision for pilot schools;
- three-day coordinator training;
- national training days – half-day sessions on specific aspects of the literacy hour, such as 'sentence level work' or 'extension work for more able pupils', offered by consultants and advisory staff;
- in-school provision in 'directed time' and 'lunchbox' activities (NLS training packages delivered by school staff) in 'un-directed time'.

However, only five of the 30 teachers recognized professional development for NLS that had specifically paid attention to interactive teaching. One example was Belinda, a year 2 teacher and literacy coordinator for her school, with more than 16 years experience. She had received training as part of the NLS pilot project, literacy coordinator training and a two-day literacy hour course, and considered that 'teaching styles have changed for the better' since the introduction of the literacy hour. Understandably, Belinda felt fairly knowledgeable about interactive teaching, although she remained keen to find out more about additional strategies for interactive teaching. Belinda was less positive about the NLS video materials, however, commenting, 'I'm not sure of the value of those really, everybody seems so well behaved'.

Extensive literacy hour training, however, was *not* necessarily a determinant of teacher knowledge about interactive teaching. Tracy, the deputy head of an inner-city primary with 5–10 years experience of Key Stage 2, had attended a three-day literacy training course and in-school INSET. She suggested that she was 'not theoretically at all knowledgeable' about interactive teaching. When asked about interactive teaching, she whispered, 'I don't know, I've never actually thought about it'. She stated later, however, 'I think I use it quite a lot and I've got quite a lot of experience of using it in the classroom'. Alongside the implication that NLS training had not delivered messages about the importance of interactive teaching methods, this comment implies a personal knowledge of interactive teaching, albeit one that may not previously have been labelled as such. Indeed, this was exactly how she appeared to view interactive teaching – as a label. Once again, this appears to signify how vital it has been – and, potentially, still is – for a professional debate on interactive teaching in the context not only of the National Literacy and Numeracy Strategies, but in terms of classroom teaching as a whole.

Louis, a deputy head with 6–10 years experience in teaching both Key Stage 1 and 2, felt the National Literacy Strategy provided an 'excellent structure with plenty of flexibility'. He confessed, however, to feeling 'a bit limited' by the literacy hour aspect. Louis' school was part of both the NLS and NNS pilot projects, and staff had received what he described as 'intensive training'. Louis was, however, 'not familiar with a definition of interactive teaching', and recalled that, when initially considering his involvement with the SPRINT Project, he thought 'I wonder what they mean by interactive teaching?' He commented, 'I have not seen personally any guidance on what interactive teaching is all about and this is what you should be doing'. He felt that 'the true definition of interactive teaching is good-quality teaching, full stop. Lots of good teachers have always been doing . . . what we now call interactive teaching – it has just been perhaps labelled in a different way now'.

Indeed, Louis, like many teachers, associated interactive teaching with straightforward 'good practice'. Given the aspiration of Reynolds and Farrell (1996) that the National Literacy Strategy and its interactive pedagogy will revive literacy standards by promoting successful teaching methods not currently associated with UK practice, the fact that these teachers saw interactive teaching as 'nothing new' at the start of the SPRINT Project suggests that continuing professional development messages about innovative teaching practices had either not been received or not been promoted in the first place.

Louis felt that his understanding of interactive teaching was based on his own personal experiences as a teacher, rather than courses or professional reading – indeed, more public forms of knowledge. However, he did mention that a course on 'accelerated learning' addressed the principles of interactive teaching. He added:

> I think I know what *I* mean by interactive teaching, but is that the same model which is being put forward by the people that have come up with the term interactive teaching? . . . and so I don't know whether I am truly teaching interactively . . . I am sure that there are many more strategies I could adopt.

Like Belinda, Louis expressed a desire for further 'know-how', although, like several other SPRINT teachers, he was comfortable with his own personal knowledge, but recognized that he was unaware of public knowledge – definitions or theories – of 'interactive teaching'. Even though, in many cases, the same teachers were comfortable with their own personal knowledge, the above example emphasizes the argument that professional development for the literacy hour had not, in general, satisfied these teachers' needs or demands for public forms of knowledge about interactive teaching.

All 12 of the less experienced SPRINT teachers (1–5 years teaching experience) had received some form of NLS training, which included NLS videos, in-school directed time sessions, consultant-led sessions and national training days. All were positive about interactive teaching. Nine of these 12 shorter-serving teachers expressed informational concerns about interactive teaching, such as: 'It's not something I have really thought about . . . what is it [interactive teaching]?' (2 years teaching) and 'I don't really know if I know exactly what it [the NLS] means by interactive . . . To be honest . . . I don't really feel very clued up' (1st year teaching).

Three of the least experienced teachers (in their first or second year) noted that their initial training had not prepared them for the interactive pedagogy required by the National Literacy Strategy. However, another three of the less experienced teachers did feel knowledgeable about interactive teaching. Ursula, for example, commented, 'I've had a lot of in-service training and been kept right up to date'. This begs the question whether initial teacher training experiences had prepared the newest teachers for the pedagogy of the NLS? As noted, the confidence of these least experienced teachers appeared to be based on professional development opportunities taken as qualified teachers.

National Numeracy Strategy training

Six of the 11 teachers who expressed negative attitudes to the literacy hour at the start of the project felt that the numeracy hour was more interactive. Nine of the SPRINT teachers referred to an enhanced understanding of interactive teaching from attending NLS training. Of all the SPRINT teachers, Kylie was probably the most negative about the National Literacy Strategy. Her case provides some useful insights. She was a great advocate of the 'Collaborative Learning Project' (www.collaborativelearning.org) and stated firmly: 'I am 100% committed to collaborative learning and then the [Literacy] Strategy came along, and I've been subverting it in whatever way I could . . . trying to pick out of it what I thought was positive'.

Kylie described how her perspective on interactive teaching conflicted with the model offered by the National Literacy Strategy. She considered that the NLS advocates a delivery model of teaching, which assumes that pupils are 'empty vessels'. She also felt that it promoted a version of interactive teaching based on the teacher 'at the front of the whole class/group', in which strategies such as 'flash cards, taking turns, doing things, sticking things in the [Big] book, or writing on the board' are simply framed as whole-class activities. She considered the National Numeracy Strategy (NNS), on the other hand, to be much more concerned with 'getting pupils to think'.

This is an interesting comment, given the stated intention of the National Literacy Strategy of developing higher-order thinking in pupils. Kylie's views suggest that the NNS has actually been more successful in disseminating messages about developing pupils' higher-order thinking skills. However, Kylie had received only a half-day in-school training for the literacy hour. It may be that interactive pedagogy had not reached the level of 'craft knowledge' (Grimmet and MacKinnon 1992) in her school. That is, those colleagues who had attended more NLS training than Kylie had not received, accepted, internalized or acted upon notions of interactive teaching. These pedagogical intentions were not, therefore, spread, cascaded or disseminated in the way that techniques such as the use of fans and whiteboards have done.

Other professional development influences

Public forms of knowledge about interactive teaching were often linked in the teachers' thinking with professional development from sources other than NLS training or literature. Iris, the deputy head in a primary school with 16–20 years in teaching, had received only school-based NLS training. She was, however, confident in her knowledge, which included public forms of knowledge of interactive teaching. Iris was pursuing an MA in teaching and learning and she commented that, 'because of the MA I am mindful that I may have given [interactive teaching] more thought than colleagues in school'.

Another two teachers linked their experiences of MA courses with interactive teaching; and five others made links with various other forms of continuing professional development. These included continuing professional development that attended to accelerated learning, special needs provision, behaviour management, emotional literacy, communicative language teaching, teaching for independence and collaborative learning. It is implicit in many of these teachers' discourses that their interactive teaching was based on principles promoted or reinforced through the above-mentioned professional development. We can see, therefore, how theories, such as those mentioned here and others discussed by Merry in Chapter 1, might fill the gap in public forms of knowledge about interactive teaching.

Interactive teaching as an innovation

While the CBAM model asked teachers about innovation, and many SPRINT teachers expressed a lack of clear understanding of what interactive teaching means in practice, the following examples serve to highlight how interactive teaching was not really seen as being innovative during the early part of the SPRINT Project. Rather, teachers related it to the best of what they had always done, hence the title of this chapter.

Olive, a year 5 teacher with 5–10 years experience, was 'fairly knowledge-able' about interactive teaching 'based on what I've always done'. She added that interactive teaching '[is] the only way I know *of* teaching'. She added that it was 'part of my style of teaching' and that the National Literacy Strategy had confirmed her own practice. She felt that the literacy hour had 'freshened everybody's approaches' and that it promoted interactive teaching, but she did not refer to any theoretical knowledge, definitions or other bodies of public knowledge linked to interactive teaching. Another teacher, Natalie, whose school had been part of the NLS pilot project, felt that contact with colleagues had been more influential than any courses she had attended.

Barry had 10–15 years teaching experience in both Key Stages 1 and 2 and had received only school-based NLS training. Currently teaching a year 5/6 class, he was positive about both the National Literacy and Numeracy Strategies and felt that both lend themselves to interactive teaching. He said that the literacy hour had 'influenced my teaching style' and that 'I find things easier when I have got a definite structure'. The literacy hour had enabled him to reflect on his teaching style and 'to think about what I am doing and how I am doing it'. Barry related interactive teaching to 'quality teaching', although he reported that, 'I suppose that I am positive about it, but I am not sure what I am positive about!' When asked 'What is interactive teaching?', he replied, 'Yeah, it's a phrase I wish I knew. I don't really know'. The following comment suggests that he was at an early stage of orientating himself to interactive teaching: 'if it is something which is going to help me develop as a teacher, to make me more efficient, to improve my quality of teaching, then most certainly I shall embrace it'.

Barry's construction of interactive teaching does not pay attention to pace or thinking skills, and the video of his most interactive teaching (see Chapter 6) revealed a classic initiation → response → feedback (IRF) format (Wells 1993), albeit that many pupils offered extended responses. Even though Barry was positive about the structure provided by the National Literacy Strategy and felt he had learned from its introduction, there is little to indicate that interactive pedagogy offered anything new. He was certainly not able to articu-late any of the associated underlying principles.

Towards the end of the SPRINT Project, there was more evidence to suggest that some of the teachers were beginning to see innovative possibilities for interactive practice. Belinda had been teaching for more than 21 years, but felt that she only used practices that were the 'tip of the iceberg' and was keen to know 'what other processes were available'. Although tentative, there appears to have been a slight shift of perspective from viewing interactive teaching as 'usual' practice to an acknowledgement that there are various processes, techniques, strategies or methods associated with interactive pedagogy. This was amplified as many of the focus teachers shifted their attention from whole class to groups and back again while exploring the nature of interactive teaching with their research-partners. In her final interview Dawn said, 'Before I was really only thinking whole class for interactive teaching, but what it has really bought home to me now that it is not whole class, it is the whole class, groups, and individuals as well'. Teresa added, 'It's a very vague area. People have heard of interactive teaching but has anyone specified what it is? Have teachers had that information, because I haven't?'

Summary

Although the sample in this study was small, analysis of the data raises the concern that there is a deficit in pedagogical knowledge of interactive teaching practices among primary practitioners. Given the emphasis on NLS training over recent years, the fact that only five of 30 teachers in this sample linked knowledge about interactive teaching with NLS training suggests that the deficit reflects a gap in the provision of continuing professional development. This in itself is probably a reflection of how the government perceived the introduction of the National Literacy Strategy and of interactive teaching; that is, as something to be applied to teachers and teaching rather than strategies and their underlying rationale to be shared with the profession. The lack of discussion and training appears to have affected the least experienced teachers most, as three-quarters of shorter-serving teachers were not confident in either personal or public knowledge about interactive teaching. This has huge implications for their service within and to the profession over the coming years. We argue elsewhere in this book that reflection on and about practice and subsequent articulation of that reflection is vital for teachers' development and pedagogical know-how.

We have shown that, at the start of the SPRINT Project, two-thirds of the SPRINT teachers lacked theoretical knowledge about interactive teaching methods. Less than half the teachers felt they had personal experiential knowledge, and these equated interactive teaching with 'good', 'quality' or 'usual' practice, rather than differentiating interactive methods from 'common' practice or 'what I've always done'. Only a very few teachers referred specifically to the issues of pace and pupil thinking skills, which form the crux of the NLS construction of interactive teaching. Following their involvement in the SPRINT Project, there was a small reduction in the teachers' concerns for knowledge and information from the CBAM analysis and some qualitative evidence that a few teachers felt more knowledgeable. It was apparent that interactive teaching had been heightened in teachers' awareness and con-sciousness, but we feel that this still hides the real issue, that of ensuring that the profession understands from both a practical and theoretical position the basis and extent of newly introduced strategies.

Although not all of the SPRINT teachers were positive about the National Literacy Strategy or the literacy hour, all of them held positive attitudes towards interactive teaching. This is encouraging news for those providers of NLS training who wish to promote practice that addresses higher-order thinking skills. Although there was confusion even among those teachers who felt knowledgeable about interactive teaching, there was also a desire for further public forms of knowledge about interactive practice, especially knowledge addressing procedural interests. Based on the teachers' positive views of the National Numeracy Strategy and associated training, providers of literacy training might look no further than the NNS training for inspiration.

There is, of course, a much wider literature on interactive teaching, as discussed by Merry in Chapter 1, and attention to this might also be a profitable basis for enhancing this aspect of NLS training. Also, it should be borne in mind that this research refers to a very specific period in the history of the National Literacy Strategy, occurring as it did early in its existence. Anecdotal information suggests that the NLS literature and training materials have undergone changes intended to further support teachers. The findings of this study suggest that the strength of future developments will be determined by the clarity and utility of pedagogical knowledge – as well as strategies and procedures – of the training and associated materials promoted through the National Literacy Strategy.

Note

[1] Teachers in the project were asked to express the length of their teaching experience within year bands, i.e. 1–2 years, 3–5 years, 6–10 years, 11–15 years, 16–20 years, 21 years and upwards. Hence, the length of service descriptions used in this and other chapters is expressed in these terms.

4　Scratching the surface

A typology of interactive teaching I

Veronica Esarte-Sarries and Fred Paterson

Introduction

The SPRINT teachers described their understanding of interactive teaching in interviews and reflective dialogues with their research-partners. This and the following chapter introduce the nine features of interactive teaching, collated into a 'typology of interactive teaching', which have emerged from analysis of these dialogues. This chapter deals with surface features of interactive teaching that reflect clearly visible aspects of pedagogy. Chapter 5 describes deep features of interactive practice and refers to cognitive, affective and social processes that may be stimulated by visible practices, but which produce learning outcomes that may be much less susceptible to observation or immediate assessment. The surface features mentioned by the SPRINT teachers mirror many of the practices advocated in the National Literacy Strategy (NLS) literature for teachers.

As we have indicated in the previous chapters, the SPRINT Project was conducted in the second year of the National Literacy Strategy, a time of unprecedented attention to, and professional development for, literacy teaching in England. Even so, in Chapter 3 we showed that less than one-fifth of the SPRINT teachers felt their NLS training experiences had addressed interactive teaching, and two-thirds did not feel theoretically knowledgeable about interactive teaching.

With little detailed information about this important pedagogical principle, one might anticipate that the SPRINT teachers would construct interactive teaching with reference to their own prior experience, tacit understanding and intrinsic pedagogical principles. This, indeed, often appeared to be the case. The NLS framework informs teachers that *successful* teaching is, among other things, interactive, so it is not surprising that when we asked the teachers what they understood by 'interactive teaching', they equated it with 'good', 'quality' or 'usual' practice.

When encouraged to talk about it, however, the SPRINT teachers constructed multidimensional definitions of interactive teaching. In fact, the summation of these views presents a somewhat broader construction of interactive teaching than that presented by the National Literacy Strategy, as well as responding to wider theoretical interests. In this and the following chapter, we explore how the SPRINT teachers constructed their own versions of interactive teaching. The nine features of interactive practice that emerged from the analysis of teacher comments are shown in Table 4.1. None of the teachers referred to every one of these features and some talked about only a few. The typology does, however, represent themes talked about frequently in the teachers' dialogues with the research team.

Distinguishing between surface and deep features of interactive pedagogy

The distinction between surface and deep features was rooted in comments made by Dawn, one of the least experienced teachers, and subsequently echoed by several others. She explored the idea that there were two levels of interactive practice: using what the teacher described as 'gimmicks', such as whiteboards and fans, reflected a surface interaction, whereas encouraging pupils to discuss the ways in which they 'juggle concepts in the head' reflected deeper interactive practice. Indeed, the features emerging from the analysis of SPRINT teachers' comments at this point in the study showed that interactive practice was sometimes constructed in terms of visible pedagogy – that in which the strategies are observable by others – and sometimes in terms of cognitive, affective and social processes.

Previous chapters have shown how the NLS framework responded to Reynolds and Farrell's (1996) assertion that whole-class interactive teaching promotes student achievement. According to Reynolds and Farrell (1996), Reynolds (1998) and Beard (1999), interactive teaching involves: attention to problems and solutions; graded questions; rapid questions and answers to assess knowledge; and slower paced questions and answers that promote high levels of pupil thinking. The NLS literature aimed at teachers neither describes these methods clearly, nor explains the principles that underpin them. The emphasis in the teacher literature has, it seems, been put on **pace** and the efficient delivery of curriculum objectives (see Chapter 9). In Chapter 1, Merry argued that Reynolds and colleagues had over-emphasized the school effectiveness and improvement literature at the expense of a wide range of empirical work on children's learning. Thus, it might be argued that although attention to problems, solutions and higher-order pupil thinking constitutes attention to deep features of interactive teaching, the emphasis within the NLS teacher literature emphasizes the use of surface features in pursuance of pace and curriculum efficiency. As we will see in Chapter 6, this was reflected in a

Table 4.1 Typology of the features of interactive teaching

Surface features	
1 Engaging pupils	Constructs relating to maintaining pupil interest in the curriculum and providing fun and enjoyable experiences
2 Pupil practical and active involvement	Constructs emphasizing 'hands-on' learning and activity requiring 'movement' and practical engagement
3 Broad pupil participation	Constructs referring to strategies that involve the whole class in activity or those that allow the teacher to assess pupil knowledge through whole-class presentation of knowledge, e.g. the use of white boards or letter fans
4 Collaborative activity	Constructs relating to pupil–pupil collaboration as the basis for learning, e.g. NLS 'Time Out'
5 Conveying knowledge	Constructs referring to conveying new knowledge; particularly non-didactic methods
Deep features	
6 Assessing and extending knowledge	Constructs that refer to issues concerned with assessing and extending pupil knowledge
7 Reciprocity and meaning-making	Constructs that relate to 'two-way' communication where both teacher–pupil and pupil–teacher interaction is encouraged. Constructs that emphasize the construction of meaning through dialogue rather than didactic approaches
8 Attention to thinking and learning skills	References to attention to, and development of, pupil thinking skills, and comments that imply learning frames or attention to pupils' learning processes
9 Attention to pupils' social and emotional needs/skills	References to teaching addressing the emotional needs and social interests of the pupils

significant increase in the proportions of rapid-fire, closed and factual recall questions since the introduction of the National Literacy Strategy, commensurate with an emphasis on pace and curriculum objectives. In addition, in Chapters 5 and 6, we suggest that while they referred to both the surface and deep features, SPRINT teachers constructed surface features in more sophisticated ways than deep features.

In addition, unlike the early NLS documentation, which emphasized whole-class teacher–pupil interaction, the SPRINT teachers' constructions of interactive teaching reflect a wider focus. While individual teachers' foci shifted during the course of the project, discourse revealed that they constructed interactive teaching with reference to groups and individuals as well as to whole-class teaching. Teachers also linked interactive teaching to pupil–pupil interaction in various settings.

Surface features of interactive practice

The data gathered from interviews and reflective dialogues were analysed using a constant comparative analytic process (Straus and Corbin 1990). The research explored how the variables of key stage, school location and teacher experience interacted with the emergent 'features', but no significant correlations were apparent. The surface features (items 1–5 in Table 4.1) are discussed below in relation to their purposes as viewed by the SPRINT teachers; the main pedagogical tactics employed in their application, the conditions influencing application and identified consequences are included.

Engaging pupils

Of the 30 teachers, a majority referred to engaging pupils as part of their construction of interactive teaching. They stressed the importance of maintaining pupil interest in the curriculum and providing fun and enjoyable experiences. Teachers in both key stages and at all levels of experience saw this as an important component of interactive teaching. Engagement was one of the strategies later advocated by the National Literacy Strategy. A typical example was Olive, a less experienced KS1 teacher, who said:

> I spend quite a lot of time trying to make it interesting for them . . . because you want to know that you've *GOT* them all the time you're talking to them. You are aware that you're doing a lot of talking and that you need to have their attention for a long space of time, so you try and make it more exciting, if you like, to keep their attention.

Some teachers referred also to the need to 'know' their pupils and thus adapt or tailor their activities. For example, Hannah (a KS2 teacher) stated: 'Interactive teaching is a way of teaching that engages all pupils. It's the teacher thinking ahead, thinking where the children are at, knowing their personalities and how they would best engage those children in the activity'.

Another teacher indicated that the general atmosphere created could be beneficial to all, pupils and teachers alike. Queenie, an experienced KS1 teacher, suggested: 'One of the reasons why I like to do it . . . it all adds to the sense of fun . . . nothing nicer than children laughing in an infant school and enjoying what they are doing'.

Most teachers reflected upon a number of practices that might encourage pupil engagement and links may be seen with other features of the typology.

Engagement and questioning

The teachers' constructs of interactive teaching seemed to be largely in direct opposition, either explicitly or implicitly, to any constructs they held of didactic teaching, but many teachers elaborated upon the role of *questioning* in whole-class and group teaching. Obviously questioning is an integral part of teaching, but the types of questioning used and their extent were deemed crucial by some teachers for engaging the attention of pupils. The strategy was summarized by some as 'expecting a response from the pupils'. This view was possibly influenced by NLS material. Other teachers described more extensively the importance of deciding when to use closed or open questions, in whole-class, group or individual teaching. The issues of the type of question used and its suitability to the pace of the lesson, as well as the frustrations expressed by some teachers who wished for more time to extend pupil discussion, are considered in Chapter 9.

Some of the focus teachers, who were able to explore this issue in more depth in their reflective dialogues, made substantial changes in their handling of the timing of questions over the course of the project (for example, Dawn). The difficulties of ensuring as much engagement of pupils as possible, coupled with the greater demands of the curriculum, has led to more use of other strategies. From the comments of some experienced teachers, it is clear that, over the course of the SPRINT Project, they perceived an increase in their use of strategies recommended by the National Literacy and Numeracy Strategies, such as the use of collaborative and practical activities.

One of the most experienced teachers, Louis, explained how he saw the difference between questioning tactics in the past and the current more inter-active approach, in which he clearly links the National Literacy Strategy to the use of collaborative activity:

> there used to be a time . . . where a question is posed to the class and a child is chosen to supply the answer, and if not you move on to the next child. Now there are always going to be children – I count myself in amongst them – where I will sit and think, 'Well, hang on, my odds of being chosen are pretty remote so why bother stimulating the old grey matter, I may as well sit here and let someone else do the work'. So it is a different approach, where for example . . . like I did in literacy this morning, where everyone is expected to supply the answer by holding up a card or indeed by turning round to a partner and discussing what the answer should be or making it clear that rather than them volunteering you are actually going to be perhaps selecting someone and that gets everyone in the class thinking.

In the same school, Paula was influenced by Louis, who was her mentor, and used similar tactics to his. To involve every child in her class, when she used closed but collective questions she would only give the pupils 'a count of three' to respond either verbally in chorus, with hands or fans. This was contrasted with her use of the strategy 'time-out', which, though brief, gave the pupils a chance to rehearse responses that produced 'more talking' than individual questions and answers. Paula, like Louis, felt that with individual questions and answers some children might never be asked a question. Thus she found that while a closed question usually elicits brief responses, if the pupils are given the opportunity to talk with a peer, the interaction facilitates more open dialogue.

Information from the National Literacy and Numeracy Strategies includes practical advice on questioning. It may be argued, however, that in its brief-ness the advice stays in the realm of the tactical rather than helping teachers to explore the pedagogical basis of the questioning tactics advocated. Some of the SPRINT teachers over the course of the project (for example, Xena, KS2) reflected extensively on their use of questioning and demonstrated this in their videos, thus indicating a greater commitment to deep interactive practice. Table 4.2 summarizes the main issues relating to this feature.

Consideration of the optimal methods of engaging pupils was addressed throughout the SPRINT Project, but it was still an important element of teachers' constructs of interactive teaching. Whatever strategies teachers used, it was seen as crucial for interactive teaching that the pupils *were* engaged.

Practical and active involvement

Reference to the use of practical and active involvement was made by most teachers, at all levels of experience, in each key stage and in both locations. There was a suggestion from one KS2 teacher that the activity methods of KS1 teachers were having an influence on, and being adapted by, their KS2 colleagues. Many of the examples given came from consideration of the National Literacy and Numeracy Strategies, but a few teachers made reference also to the possibilities of activity methods in other areas of the curriculum. Most of the examples cited below come from a consideration of literacy and numeracy sessions. The extent to which teachers referred to interactive teaching in other subjects varied greatly. Science was frequently suggested to be a suitable candidate for interactive methods, but others, such as art, appeared to relate more to teachers' confidence in these subjects than to any official guidance.

Most teachers were initially satisfied with their use of practical and active involvement in literacy and numeracy, but a significant and vocal minority expressed reservations. The teachers who were mainly satisfied, though sometimes acknowledging organizational difficulties, are detailed first.

Table 4.2 Engaging pupils

Purposes and issues	Main tactics	Conditioning factors	Consequences
Maintaining pupil interest in topic	Providing fun and enjoyable experiences for pupils	Time in school day	
	Non-verbal communication	Pupil curriculum fatigue	
Managing the attention of the class	Teacher questioning tactics	Ability of pupils Size of class	Rapid questions reduce pupil thinking opportunities
Check prior knowledge		NLS and NNS literature	

By using games in the literacy hour, Karen, an experienced KS1 teacher, talked of 'involving the whole body, making it tactile, making it loud'. She used many of the games advocated by the National Literacy Strategy, such as 'Circle Swap Shop.' Lisa, a less experienced KS1 teacher, was adept at using both NLS suggestions and inventing new ones of her own: 'We do an awful lot of games, playing with words, things like that . . . It might be that children are actually taking on the teacher role sometimes, they come up and write and things and highlight things in a sentence, or highlight things in a list'.

In numeracy, Tracy (KS2) indicated how she used activity methods:

> I knew I'd presumed wrongly because they could work out the area of something with a formula but they had no clue what they were actually finding out because they had no concept of what 'area' actually meant . . . We went outside in the playground. We worked in groups, they measured various things . . . we came back with the answer. What did they get?' 'Why?' And more understood it that way.

Many teachers have found that they have been expected to keep children doing 'carpet work' for much longer than was the case before the introduction of the National Literacy Strategy, and using various physical activities is one way of coping with these demands.

At the beginning of the SPRINT Project some teachers were satisfied with using practical and active involvement as advocated by the National Literacy and Numeracy Strategies, but changed their views during the project (see section below on change). Others indicated from the beginning that they were somewhat critical of using such strategies extensively, including Iris, who concluded that the use of items such as phonic wheels or fans was not interactive teaching at all, 'because it is coming from you leading again. They're not always helping . . . it's how can you get them to generate it'.

The problem of the sustained attention of others was voiced by several teachers, including Beth, an experienced KS1 teacher: 'if the situation is that only one child can actually be performing the task at the front to demonstrate, it is very motivating for the children to have the opportunity to do that, but I do know that in the time it takes to get it done then some children will drift'.

Another teacher of long experience, Kelly (KS1), felt very keenly the pressure to provide the recommended practical activities but was an enthusiastic advocate of interactive teaching:

> Well, I think the challenge of the classroom is – the home environment is the ideal place for interactive learning in my opinion – on a one-to-one or one to small group relationship. Practical activities and experiences in a real-life context . . . In the classroom you've got thirty or more children . . . You also have got a curriculum and scheme of work . . . in the classroom context. I think the role of interactive teaching is constrained by the scheme.

Table 4.3 shows the main features we identified as part of 'practical and active involvement'.

Criticisms of too much reliance on activity methods came not only from the most experienced teachers. At least two of the less experienced teachers had serious concerns about the depth of their interactions with their pupils. As detailed above, in the introductory section, some teachers, such as Dawn, came to regard practical activities as surface practices – in her terms, 'little i' as opposed to 'Big I'. Only a few teachers reflected upon the 'deeper' goals of interactive teaching. It could be argued that, where this reflection was evident, it was prompted more by personal or professional values than by guidance from the NLNS literature.

Broad pupil participation

Both the National Literacy and Numeracy Strategies recommend the use of broad participation of pupils through whole-class methods. Activities advocated are the use of whiteboards, letter and digit fans and hold-up cards by pupils. The essential point of broad participation seems to be that the whole class should be engaged at the same time and that assessment is effected by the use of the whiteboards and so on. Eighteen of the 30 teachers referred directly to the use of broad participation as a main construct, but even more were seen to use forms of it in their practice. There were no apparent links between key stage, geographical location and length of experience in referring to this construct.

Table 4.3 Practical and active involvement

Purposes and issues	Main tactics	Conditioning factors	Consequences
Engagement	NLS and NNS suggested tactics, such as 'get up and go'	Teachers' pedagogic values and theories	Motivation
Retention of knowledge and skills	'Show me' – fans, wheels, whiteboards and 'Get up and Go'	Younger pupils sometimes lack motor skills required for manipulation of objects	Extends concentration
Collaboration	Drama/role-play	Time taken to move pupils around – particularly with younger pupils	Aids retention and linguistic skills also enhanced Cuts down on writing
	Games	'Observers' may get bored Behaviour management skills	Breaks up long periods required for 'carpet time'
Omission of links to 'deeper' aspects of interactive teaching		Class size and ability range	Opportunity to develop higher-order thinking and meaning-making not taken
Can still be too 'teacher-led'		Teacher confidence	

Attitudes towards the use of this feature, as with other features, were subject to some modification throughout the course of the project. Initially, teachers at all levels of experience were found to enthuse about the use of broad participation. Beth, an experienced KS1 teacher, expressed her attitude thus:

> I think I'm pleased it's [whole-class teaching] come back because I feel more focused and I think it's more time-efficient as well, whereas you might have been telling two or three groups the same thing but at different times, now you can tell . . . you can do your initial teaching as a whole class.

Ewan, at the other end of the experience scale (KS2), was equally enthusiastic: 'Because of the way the numeracy hour works, because of the focus on whole class teaching, you know it's almost as if you can see – I think a lot of teachers have said that almost at a glance you can see whether the class has got it or not'.

While teacher views of interactive teaching were very similar in the two geographical locations, school and classroom contexts inevitably differed markedly, and could thus affect the practice of some interactive methods. Whereas some teachers considered that the success of such methods might be modified by pupils' limited social and linguistic skills, others such as Belinda showed how she used broad participation to enhance skills:

> It demands a response from every child and I think that some children are frightened to participate and it gives them the security that everyone is doing it . . . some of the children are, I think, even at this early age, so used to not achieving that they come to school expecting to do very little and that gives them a boost – that they can participate.

By the end of the SPRINT Project, Beth had, like several other teachers, started using collaborative activity more, rather than broad participation, finding it frequently more effective (this issue is addressed further in the next section). The rationale for using collaborative activity was not just managerial, as for some teachers it obviated the need to provide whiteboards, cards and so on. As is detailed in the next section, pupil collaboration appeared to have more cognitive benefits than broad pupil participation.

For some teachers, the negative aspects of the use of broad participation included the need for fine motor skills to handle all the equipment used; others felt that the NLNS methods emphasized teacher-centred learning, with the focus on objectives, at the expense of pupil-centred learning. Although some teachers saw the use of broad participation as an efficient way of delivering the curriculum, several teachers suggested that there was still a need for differentiation of questions used within the whole class. For example, Keeley (KS2) stated:

> It really depends on what you mean by interactive, but if you are wanting children to react to you and to become involved at a whole class level, the objectives that you are focusing on vary from child to child, you know, the specifics of it, whereas within a group you know what you want them to know.

The question of whether to differentiate questions when using whole-class methods highlights the point that, although the National Literacy

Strategy advocates greater use of whole-class methods, how they are being used may differ in important respects from those used in other countries. In the SPRINT groups, teachers were clearly committed to trying to ensure that the needs of individual pupils were met. Given large class numbers, this resulted in the grouping of children both in group work and, in effect, in whole-class sessions. Teachers then felt it necessary to differentiate their questions according to their placing of pupils in high-, middle- or low-ability groups. Pupils had been thus designated in some schools at KS1. In other countries, referred to in debates about the National Literacy Strategy (e.g. the Pacific Rim countries), and in other research (e.g. Alexander 2000), it is clear that teachers are not expected to differentiate the questions in the manner practised in English classrooms. Some SPRINT teachers did consider that being part of a large class could benefit less able pupils as they might be supported by the teacher and more able peers when experiencing work at a level unachievable without support. However, there appeared generally to be an underlying assumption that, even when using whole-class methods, it was both desirable and feasible to operate a kind of covert group or individualized system. While neither group nor whole-class methods are being advocated here, it is argued that there needs to be a wider debate about the underlying assumptions of all methods advocated, and a greater examination of the conflicts and tensions with which English teachers have to cope, because of their laudable commitment to individual needs. Broad participation is outlined in Table 4.4.

While broad participation was seen in practice at the end of SPRINT, and formed the introductory part of many literacy and numeracy sessions, as advocated by the NLNS literature, it appeared for some teachers that a subtle but possibly far-reaching change in emphasis had taken place. If teachers had made the shift to using greater pupil collaboration rather than broad participation, it might be argued that they saw this as having distinct cognitive benefits. It appeared that more children were being required to explain their reasoning to each other rather than just hold up equipment or call out their answers.

Collaborative activity

Pupil collaboration was seen to have an increasingly important role in both teachers' use and understanding of interactive teaching. For some teachers, they had always used it in their practice. Others came to see its benefits in managerial, motivational and cognitive terms. Although some teachers were unsure initially whether pupil collaboration formed part of their understanding of interactive teaching, 28 of them indicated that, by the end of the project, it did indeed do so. For some of the KS1 teachers at the beginning of the year, there were understandable problems in using pupil collaboration.

Table 4.4 Broad pupil participation

Purposes and issues	Main tactics	Conditioning factors	Consequences
Engage pupils	Whiteboards, fans, 'time-out' Pupils aware that they need to respond, either to teacher or peer Eye contact, pupil centred interaction	Pupils feel secure that others around them will be offering multiple responses Class size/age Assessing engagement problematic	Pupils are motivated by active involvement with boards and fans, etc. Peer interaction promotes autonomous learning: pupils don't need to wait to interact with the teacher Methods require careful attention, which can be exhausting Variety of needs of younger pupils difficult to meet in larger groups
Assessing prior and topic-specific knowledge	Using letter and digit 'fans' Whiteboards Holding up notebooks	Ability of pupils to handle and use fans Need to train younger pupils to use fans Effective with smaller class size	Less able given opportunity to work at higher level More able pupils can support less able Individual assessment still important
Teacher efficiency	Fans, whiteboards, big books and 'follow me' cards	Whole-class teaching back in style Tendency to be teacher- or objectives-led	Discourages pupil meaning-making and thinking
Collaborative activity	'Time-out'	Pupils having/using appropriate listening skills	Reinforces the need for pupils to listen Increases engagement as all pupils are expected to be involved Requires 'less paraphernalia' than fans, etc.
Differentiation	Giving individuals attention within whole-class interaction	Objectives being addressed for subgroups of pupils	More able may be bored by work addressing needs of less able pupils

For instance, Lesley, an experienced KS1 teacher, said: 'It's very difficult at first to get children to work together and so you have to train them by introducing them to ways of working with each other through talking, through writing together and sharing ideas'. Conversely, Lisa, a less experienced KS1 teacher, while noting how young children might lack some linguistic and social skills, saw pupil collaboration as beneficial, because 'maybe one child says something that connects with another child that maybe the teacher just hasn't said. If you can encourage the discussion and collaboration between them, I think that's all part of it as well'. This point was echoed by Dawn, also KS1 and a less experienced teacher: 'Sometimes a child's explanation of why something works makes more sense to another child than the adult's does'.

Key Stage 2 teachers did not experience the same difficulties in instigating pupil collaboration as their KS1 counterparts. Xena used pupil collaboration extensively in literacy and numeracy, and got pupils to question each other about the strategies they had used. She was one of the teachers who reasoned that, following the model of literacy lessons recommended, teacher interaction with pupils instigated peer interaction, which then entailed teacher and whole-class, group or individual interaction, in a kind of chain model.

One reason for the increase in pupil collaboration was the promotion by the National Literacy Strategy of the limited use of 'time-out'. Kathleen, a less experienced KS1 teacher, referred to her own experience to justify her increased use of peer interaction: 'There is a lot more peer teaching going on . . . which I was always keen on, because I know that's how I learned . . . reading something or speaking to someone about it helps clarify it in your own mind'.

Kathleen also found that if children were given the opportunity to discuss ideas first with their peers, they were more attentive when required to listen to the responses of selected others. Similarly, several teachers felt that some pupils might gain the respect of their peers when taking part in discussion if they were less skilled in other areas. Only one teacher (Keeley, KS2) expressed doubts about the use of collaborative practices:

> I would just like to perhaps hear more evidence that they are grasping things through working with their peers, that they grasp that in a better way than they would if it was more didactic . . . I would just like to know if it's more successful – more fun – but whether it is more successful I don't know.

Keeley concluded that pair work was more successful than group work, as she felt pupils then had 'more ownership'.

Although most teachers did not refer to any theoretical underpinning of the use of pupil collaboration, some, particularly in the Leicester sample, found that having followed courses other than those for the National Literacy Strategy (such as the RSA Diploma in English across the curriculum, or for secondary school French teaching) helped them to refine their views on the benefits of pupil collaboration.

Many teachers mentioned an increase in the use of pupil collaboration over the year of the project. The reasons for this were various, including more official literature recommending the use of strategies such as 'time-out', the increased maturity of the pupils – particularly in the case of KS1 children – and, arguably, the further reflection upon methods promoted by taking part in SPRINT. Two teachers, the first experienced and the second less experienced, summarized the change.

First, Louis, who considered he had 'a fairly good record of interactivity already', added: 'I have become *more* focused on interaction between the children as opposed to just good-quality interaction between myself and the children'. For Ewan, a less experienced KS2 teacher, it was interaction between himself and another teacher at the first SPRINT workshop that had encouraged him to change his views on the use of peer interaction. Through discussion with a more experienced teacher from another school, he became a firm convert to pupil collaboration, as represented by 'time-out' and this became a part of his repertoire of interactive techniques. It should be noted, however, that the official recommendation of the use of 'time-out' is for only 30 seconds, a very brief time in which to develop ideas. Teachers have also been warned by NLS trainers about using it too much, which does not suggest that it is seen as being of enormous learning benefit. The quotation above from Kathleen, about 'speaking to someone about it helps clarify it in your own mind', appears to encapsulate the underlying views of many teachers that pupil collaboration really could produce cognitive benefits. While the official NLS guidance might advocate limited use of collaboration, some teachers were sufficiently confident to develop collaborative work according to their own professional judgements. By changing from broad participation to pupil collaboration, teachers not only found that they were solving some time management problems, but were enhancing pupils' cognitive development (see Table 4.5 for an explanation of pupil collaboration).

Conveying new knowledge

Very few of the SPRINT teachers linked conveying new knowledge (see Table 4.6) with interactive teaching; those who did were all KS2 teachers. Kylie was an advocate of collaborative and constructive methods. She felt that the National Literacy Strategy advocated a version of 'the teacher at the front' but with the teacher engaged in presenting knowledge in an interactive way:

the teacher does the whole class presentation or whatever, into which she draws the children in. They hold up flash cards or whatever . . . or take turns to do things, come out and stick things in the book or write on the board. I think that is what the strategy means by interactive teaching.

Table 4.5 Pupil collaboration

Purposes and issues	Main tactics	Conditioning factors	Consequences
Peer support for learning	Working in pairs and groups on shared outcomes NLS and NNS methods, e.g. 'time-out' Problem-solving Use of drama	Opportunity to talk with teacher limited by NLS and NNS curriculum pressures Time for in-depth collaboration may be limited Social skills may be limited, particularly among early years pupils	More pupil collaboration Pupils more content if able to express ideas to each other
Ownership of learning			Pupils' perspectives can sometimes be more readily accessible to peers than can the teachers'
Developing listening and social skills	Teacher as facilitator Pupils need to be trained in collaborative skills Provide scaffolds	Age of pupils Especially among early years pupils, teachers perceive that social, cognitive and linguistic skills may be limited	Avoidance of pupil collaboration as teaching strategy
Pupil reflection	Mixed-ability groups Pupils need to be trained in collaborative skills Provide scaffolds	Ability of pupils. Are less able pupils able to 'pick up' understanding within peer-led discussion?	Teachers' perceptions of 'lower-ability' children's lack of skills results in them having *fewer* rather than more interactions with peers, possibly resulting in a downward spiral Less able pupils can let more able dominate

Table 4.6   Assessing and extending pupils' knowledge

Purposes and issues	Main tactics	Conditioning factors	Consequences
Assessing and extending pupil knowledge	Questioning	Teacher awareness of pupil prior knowledge and zone of proximal development	
		Time pressures to address curriculum objectives diminish opportunities for comprehensive questioning	Teachers may spend less time extending individual lines of thinking
		Careful targeting and differentiation of questions required	
	Teacher can observe pupil–pupil interaction to assess knowledge	Large class size may inhibit opportunities	Limited opportunity to assess and extend knowledge due to number of groups/ individuals to get round
	Pupil–pupil interaction can also extend knowledge		

Kylie felt that there was a place for this but also for less interactive, more didactic approaches. When she became aware of gaps in pupils' knowledge, Kylie would try to avoid didactic forms of practice and elicit the knowledge through question-and-answer techniques, drawing on the knowledge of the whole class. David, an experienced teacher linked 'presentation' with 'kinaesthetic' and 'multi-sensory approaches'. He found this beneficial because 'you're giving information in different ways; you are expecting from the pupil, you are not just producing information for them to take on board'.

Most teachers thus appeared to disassociate 'presentation' from inter-active teaching, and saw it largely as a unidirectional construct. However, one teacher, Irene, though not a focus teacher, felt that being involved in the SPRINT Project had encouraged her to refine the views expressed in her first interview in a succinct but encompassing way. In her first interview, she referred to interactive teaching as reciprocal communication. She was able to draw upon her theoretical knowledge of learning and arrived at what she termed a 'simpler' view of all the possible strands of interactive teaching. Her own use of the term 'simpler' indicates how much she had reflected upon her conceptualization of interactive teaching. She concentrated on three key features. The first was an 'assessment' need 'to know what's in their brain, what they're thinking'. The second referred to pupil engagement, to 'keep children interested'. The third drew upon her knowledge of psychology and philosophy:

> It's all to do with about what we know about how children learn. And that we know that you need, in order to learn something, you need to get your own set of pictures in your mind and you have to do it yourself. Otherwise if it's just presented and it doesn't relate you can't learn . . . They need their own concepts in order to fit it in. Now the interactive teaching I see is rather than telling the children what they need to learn, it's about getting it from them . . . And it really is like the Socratic method. You ask the questions, as a teacher you put the input in, but really you're waiting for them to put it together and make the models, and that is how we know children learn best.

Case example of one teacher's surface conceptualization

Even within this small sample, teachers indicated many different types of change, such as in their predominant type of conceptualization and in their perceptions of the appropriate foci of interactive teaching (for example, whole class, group or individual). Although many examples of teachers' thinking have been cited above, here we provide a more detailed description of how one teacher viewed her interactive teaching practice.

CASE STUDY
Surface features

Queenie, a teacher of many years experience, is confident in her practice but initially appeared more defensive than some teachers about how she construed the subject of interactive teaching. Perhaps because of this she, like several others, appeared to have given a great deal of thought to preparing for her first interview and was able to engage in quite lengthy discussion about her views. She was prepared to engage similarly with the process of the reflective dialogue about aspects of her practice. In the classroom, she was able to engage the pupils and was skilled in her practice. In her first interview, Queenie's conceptualizations were largely of a surface type, such as 'engagement' and 'practical and active involvement'. Although doubtful initially about the place of 'collaboration', she did indicate that she saw its use as beneficial and probably interactive. As was the case for many of the teachers, the only deep conceptualization stressed was that of adding to pupils' needs.

A few brief indicators of the types of comments made are included to give a flavour of her discourse, even though many have been quoted elsewhere:

> Interactive teaching is where the children are actually taking part in their own learning . . . it's children doing for themselves rather than being spoon fed . . . it's always hands-on . . . I think children learn better by doing that . . . they may follow a team leader . . . and so that sort of brings on poorer children if you like and gives them confidence and self-esteem.

In her practice, Queenie used a variety of 'standards' as recommended by the NLNS literature, such as word games and number lines. In her view, interactive teaching was justified because it aided learning retention: 'If they are actually doing it they remember actually doing that activity and they remember the content of it'.

She also referred to such learning as being 'fun'. Queenie saw interactive teaching as 'good practice' and something always done in good infant schools. She had previous experience of working in what she saw as a more didactic environment of a junior school and saw practice as exemplified by her current school as largely unproblematic. The only minor difficulties were increased organization and the need to be focused for more of the day, compared with 'the good old days, that is, pre-National Curriculum'. Though she referred to earlier times in this way, she was not critical of current practice and was largely positive about the National Literacy and Numeracy Strategies. The whole school appeared to subscribe to the same views and there were no obvious tensions or expressions of differing perspectives as found in some schools.

In her reflective dialogues, Queenie focused on the use of a standard NLS game, the use of 'hats' to teach phonics to the whole class, and in science she focused on the development of a fair test with a group of children. In the second recorded session, Queenie was teaching a large group of children history. One child and Queenie demonstrated and tried to simulate old-fashioned washing practices (without water) to the rest of the group, who sat and watched and answered questions. In the third session, the literacy hour was again the focus for the whole class. Queenies' focus of interaction could, then, be whole class, large group or small group. Queenie used pupil collaboration on standard tasks in the literacy hour. At no time did Queenie refer to individual interaction or deep interactive practice. Although initially cautious, at the end of the SPRINT Project Queenie concluded that watching the videos had helped her and she was critical of herself regarding some minutiae of her practice, such as a remark made to a child and her perceived lack of inclusion or engagement of one child in a small group. From viewing her history session, she concluded that she needed to vary her questioning technique more to keep the children engaged. Though Queenie stayed largely in the realm of surface conceptualizations, it should not be discounted that even a limited amount of viewing of videos and dialogues can make a substantial difference to practice. In her final interview, Queenie showed no sign of having altered her views at all of what might constitute interactive teaching: 'If I was being honest, no it hasn't (changed), it is just something I feel I've been doing all the time'.

She felt that her principles and practice remained largely unaltered. The only modification she appeared to recognize was that she included pupil collaboration in her views of interactive practice. Her practice was based on experience and her perception of 'what worked' with children, rather than upon any theoretical base. The National Literacy and Numeracy Strategies had encouraged her, in her view, to be more interactive, in so far as more time was spent on interactive standard activities, referred to by her as 'gimmicks'.

Summary

As we have seen, Queenie, like other SPRINT teachers, was operating at a surface level of interaction in the typology developed as part of the project. In this chapter, we have explored how surface features are apparent in both experienced and less experienced teachers' pedagogies and have emphasized that both are necessary in primary practice. A fuller exploration of the implications of the typology of interactive teaching is included at the end of Chapter 5.

5 Digging deeper
A typology of interactive teaching II

Fred Paterson and Veronica Esarte-Sarries

Introduction

The SPRINT teachers discussed their understanding of interactive teaching in interviews and reflective dialogues with their research-partners, resulting in a set of features that could be divided into two types, 'surface' and 'deep'. Following on from the surface features of interactive teaching described in Chapter 4, this chapter looks at the four deeper features that emerged. These deeper features, set out in Table 5.1, tended to be constructed in less extensive ways and to be less sophisticated in their depth than the surface features. The chapter also explores how these constructs changed over the duration of the SPRINT Project. As one teacher put it: 'you're talking about thought processes – so you're not just stating a fact, you are actually thinking about thinking'.

Table 5.1 Deep features of the typology

Assessing and extending pupil knowledge	Constructs referring to the assessment and extension of pupil knowledge
Reciprocity and meaning-making	Constructs that relate to 'two-way' communication where both teacher–pupil and pupil–teacher interaction is encouraged. Constructs that emphasize the construction of meaning through dialogue rather than didactic approaches
Attention to thinking and learning skills	Reference to paying attention to the development of pupils' thinking skills, comments that imply learning frames or attention to pupils' learning processes
Attention to pupils' social and emotional needs/skills	Reference to practice addressing the emotional needs and social interests of the pupils

It is, perhaps, worth reminding readers of the use of the labels 'surface' and 'deep'. Classroom activity, such as 'carpet time' question-and-answer, may reflect both surface practice intended to encourage broad pupil participation and the promotion of deeper thinking skills. Actions designed to encourage pupil–teacher reciprocity may also be aimed at engaging pupils. The labels 'surface' and 'deep' are not used, therefore, categorically. Rather, they reflect different aims. Surface features address instrumental interests, such as teachers' management of pupils' learning opportunities, whereas deep features reflect subtle cognitive and emotional aims. Both sets of aims are valid and important facets of practice.

In Chapter 9, we argue that messages promoted by the National Literacy Strategy have emphasized 'pace' and curriculum objectives over the slower and more reflective interaction required to enhance pupils' thinking. Galton *et al.* (1999), Mroz *et al.* (2000) and Earl *et al.* (2000) all concur with this assertion. In this chapter, we explore the impact of this emphasis on pace on the ways in which SPRINT teachers constructed various aspects of practice that contribute to pupils' higher-order thinking skills.

Assessing and extending pupil knowledge

Towards the end of Chapter 4, we referred to a comment by Irene that addressed the use of the 'Socratic' method in the surface practice of conveying knowledge. She was using the Socratic method as an example of a non-didactic practice that incorporated deep features and aimed to convey knowledge. It could also be viewed, of course, as a modelling practice to promote meaning-making and higher levels of pupil thinking. In a similar, but contrary fashion, the assessment of pupil knowledge can be seen as a surface feature as well as a deep feature of interactive teaching practice. Traditional testing procedures are clearly 'surface' practices designed to gain understanding of pupils' knowledge of particular topics. Here, we consider a variety of other activities mentioned by the SPRINT teachers that refer to deep assessment practices.

Twenty-four of the SPRINT teachers, especially the more experienced ones in both key stages, linked interactive practice with assessing and extending pupil knowledge.

Assessing pupil knowledge

'Show me' devices like whiteboards and fans were sometimes used to assess pupil knowledge, which had the benefit of being a time-efficient method of assessment. When asked whether posing a closed question followed by all the pupils holding up cards was interactive, Teresa, a less experienced KS1 teacher, reasoned:

I think yes. It's more interactive than me just saying so and so give me the answer because the twenty-one other children are not given the chance to show what they are thinking . . . it gives them all a chance . . . so then I can see if anyone has got it wrong – they've not been given the chance to look round at everybody else and see, so they're thinking of the answer themselves.

In this comment, Teresa links broad pupil participation with assessment procedures, and reflects the surface features of assessing pupil knowledge. In making the link with 'pupil collaboration', Xena responded to deeper features of assessment: 'Sometimes I would do something in a small group where the children were to ask other children questions so that I could check really, so I could check their understanding by the questions they were asking other children'.

The process makes use of 'natural' classroom interaction to provide a window into the pupils' knowledge. Ursula, another less experienced KS1 teacher, made this link within the context of teacher-led group work:

Listening and sort of assessing their learning through conversation, through watching them take part in guided text work or whatever it is . . . to assess exactly where they are and ask them questions that are going to stretch them a little bit further, so it's pinpointing their knowledge really.

It was also common for both more and less experienced teachers to link the informal assessment of pupil knowledge and its extension. Louise, a less experienced KS2 teacher, linked these themes with practice encouraged by the National Literacy Strategy:

If you are starting a book I often look at the front cover and say, 'What do you think the book is going to be about?', just so they can start using their imagination and encourage them to give their ideas and sort of extend their ideas and see what they already know, so that you know where you are starting from with that class.

Her aim was 'to gain their understanding and see what their ideas are and then try and extend it from there and use it as a starting point . . . Using it to assess where they are and then try to use it then to extend their ideas and to think even further'.

Beth noted that lack of time was a conditioning factor: 'You spend so little time with individuals, even with groups, on any one thing that you find it really difficult to know where they're at, all of them' she stated that interacting with each other might be more important 'than demonstrating to the teacher that they know the answer'. Returning to this theme later, she displayed a lack of satisfaction: 'And at the same time I want to know where they all are on everything and I find that a huge restriction, because I want to plan for them to move on . . . I just want . . . to be there for them and I don't know that that's ever going to be achievable'.

Some teachers, such as Dawn, were developing ways of getting children to assess their own knowledge:

> Finding out what the children already know and so they can evaluate what they've learned . . . We have a signal. If they are happy about what they have learned, they put all their fingers up – their hands up and wave their fingers . . . if they are not happy they keep their fists shut.

On the one hand, this strategy reflects a surface feature, similar to the NLS 'show me' techniques, in which all the class give a visual response. However, it also describes a scaffolding process that encourages the pupils to reflect on the status of their own knowledge. In turn, this could provide a platform for the teacher to explore pupils' reflection through questions like, 'What do you need to do/know to feel like you know the answer?' or 'What makes you so sure you know the answer?' In doing so, the technique addresses features that attend to pupils' thinking skills and meaning-making processes, which are discussed in the sections below.

Extending knowledge

Karen, a more experienced KS1 teacher, made remarks that mirrored what many other teachers said about the important link between the teacher's understanding of pupils' prior knowledge and its extension. She told us that it was important to use pupils' own knowledge: 'So again you're starting off with what they know and then building up from it so that they feel secure with that knowledge'.

Teachers recognized that the location of this feature may vary between individual, group and whole-class interactions. Barry and Irene were both experienced KS2 teachers. In both of his interviews, Barry referred to the use of group reading within the literacy hour as a fertile ground for interaction and 'challenging' thinking. Many teachers talked about the importance of the skilful use of questioning and, like several other teachers, he referred to the need to ask differentiated questions to include as many children as possible. While obviously central to whole-class processes, Irene was clearly aware that the use of questioning had to be very carefully targeted. She reflected that although asking questions was interactive, it might not necessarily be 'good interaction'. She speculated that sometimes teachers do 'not hear what the child is saying properly, they are only half hearing'. She implied further that teachers needed to be aware of pupils' zones of proximal development, so as not to confuse the children. This attention to theory was unusual, though when it did occur, articulating constructs with reference to theory was not the sole domain of the more experienced teachers. Dawn also talked about the need to be aware of the pupils' zone of proximal development and its variations in different subject areas.

Kylie, an experienced KS2 teacher, noted that there are problems associated with whole-class collaborative activity as a site to extend pupil knowledge: 'I'm concerned about my own way of doing things, because I often can't get round all the class and sometimes I might miss the crucial moment. I might not be there, right, when I could just "push it on" in the direction it needs to go'.

At least four teachers talked about questions extending pupil knowledge. Kylie was a keen advocate of collaborative and child-centred learning. She described how lesson materials, such as frameworks and scaffolded collaborative activity, provided a focus for talk and promoted child-centred learning. She recognized that some pupils are 'further on' than others and so encouraged some peer teaching. However, she also noted that it is necessary for the teacher to 'push it on'. Rather than providing particular knowledge or information didactically, she used questions, as the video material of her practice amply demonstrated. Her practice was an exemplar of the Socratic method referred to by Irene. This was perhaps no coincidence, as they were colleagues at the same school. When several groups of pupils had similar gaps in knowledge, Kylie would bring the whole class together to 'question the whole class about it'. Where possible, her questions were designed to draw out teaching points based on the pupils' own experience, rather than simply present information to the class. May, a year 6 teacher, echoed this point:

> I take . . . information [provided by the pupils] and ask them another question. Maybe it could be, 'right, okay, we know this. What things have we got to write down about this person?' . . . I would say to them, 'how would we find this information out?' So it's all kind of conversation with the children using group questioning and . . . questioning to get them to expand their ideas . . . I want them to organize, I want them to think about what they know already and to find out more information. I want them to find a way of finding that information [for themselves].

This highlights how questioning can be used to develop knowledge. However, it is knowledge based in the pupils' own experience, sourced by the pupils and mediated by dialogue. The teacher, in this case, strategically avoided being the sole provider of knowledge.

Table 5.2 gives a brief overview of issues reflected in SPRINT teachers' discourse about this theme. These features did not appear to become less salient for the teachers by the end of the SPRINT Project. However, as with other features, the teachers did attempt to improve their practice by paying greater attention to and thinking through these issues.

Attention to thinking and learning skills

As noted earlier, according to the literature, promoting order pupil thinking is a key aim of the National Literacy Strategy. Seventeen of the 30 SPRINT teachers referred to such thinking skills. Although teachers from both key stages and all levels of experience linked interactive practices with the promotion of thinking skills, KS2 teachers were more likely to talk about this theme, and at greater length, than KS1 teachers. Katy, an experienced KS1 teacher, reflected on the process of 'thinking about thinking': 'I suppose

Table 5.2   Assessing and extending pupils' knowledge

Purposes and issues	Main tactics	Conditioning factors	Consequences
Assessing and extending pupil knowledge Addressing deeper or implicit understanding requires extended interaction	Questioning	Teacher awareness of pupil, prior knowledge and zone of proximal development	
		Time pressures to address curriculum objectives diminish opportunities for comprehensive questioning	Teachers may spend less time extending individual lines of thinking
		Careful targeting and differentiation of questions required	
	Teacher can observe pupil–pupil interaction to assess knowledge Pupil–pupil interaction can also extend knowledge	Large class size may inhibit opportunities	Limited opportunity to assess and extend knowledge due to number of groups/individuals to get round

[interactive teaching is] a way of communicating to get the thought processes going isn't it . . . you're talking about thought processes – so you're not just stating a fact, you are actually thinking about thinking'.

Kathleen, a less experienced KS1 teacher, referred throughout her interviews to enabling pupils to 'clarify their learning' and 'giving children the opportunity to evaluate'. She and others stressed the need to create an atmosphere conducive to helping children think and develop ideas. Kathleen conducted one session using whiteboards in which her aim was for the pupils to explain their spelling strategies rather than aim for correct spellings. Having been alerted to the terms 'open questions' and 'higher-order thinking' through the process of the research, Kathleen realized the potential for deepening her interactive practice. She incorporated these concepts swiftly into her analysis of her own practice and that of more senior colleagues: 'I found myself looking for aspects of interaction you know, whether they were higher-order questions or whether they were just factual questions . . . I was watching how [a colleague] was doing what I do or did, cutting children off and answering questions'.

Beyond broad comments about the use of questions, however, teachers rarely referred to practices, such as those advocated by Merry in Chapter 1, that encourage higher-order thinking. Numeracy lessons were more commonly linked with such skills, thus adding some credence to the hypothesis that the numeracy strategy and the associated professional development opportunities have been more successful in addressing the pedagogic implications of interactive teaching. Both experienced and less experienced teachers linked the National Numeracy Strategy with thinking skills. May, a less experienced KS2 teacher, reflected: 'I ask them questions in mental maths about something and often they talk about the strategies they use. You don't say, "this is the best strategy". We talk about what THEY want . . . and I can see straight away the processes that they used'.

When SPRINT teachers considered 'thinking skills', they tended to see their role in one of two ways: either stimulating thought processes in a general sense or evaluating pupils' thinking skills. Although some said they would welcome more guidance, there was no suggestion that teachers might provide specific models or scaffold the teaching of thinking skills in the sorts of ways outlined in Table 5.3 or discussed in Chapter 1.

Reciprocal communication and meaning-making

Making meaning through dialogue is a key principle of constructivist learning theories (see Chapter 1). Sixteen of the 30 SPRINT teachers linked interactive practice with reciprocal or two-way communication. Rather than simple didactic practice, which emphasizes one-way communication from teacher to learner, reciprocal communication relies on feedback or contributions from

Table 5.3   Thinking and learning skills

Purposes and issues	Main tactics	Conditioning factors	Consequences
Enhancement of questioning, learning and thinking skills	Use of 'open', higher-order questions	Creation of conducive classroom atmosphere	May reduce engagement of non-involved pupils
	Class/group/ individual interaction	Teacher skill in accessing pupils' zones of proximal development	
	Provide models or scaffolding for development of cognitive skills		

pupils. Lisa, a less experienced KS1 teacher, described it as follows: 'Interactive teaching involves the teacher and the children being both speakers and listeners, to create an environment and sort of communication link with them where they feel they can enquire and explore'. Lisa saw the aims of interactive teaching as:

> developing their thinking skills really. And also getting away from 'teacher knows all and thou shalt do'. Again, because it's a two-way process and so their opinion is given value and credibility and worth and also that they can see a point being argued out. So they develop opinions, they develop their own ideas and can substantiate their ideas, they can see how opinions do evolve.

Similarly, Barry, an experienced KS2 teacher, described interactive teaching as 'a two-way process in which teachers listen to children, not just in a discussion, but in any lesson that they listen to children and when they talk they encourage the children to be part of the two-way process'. He emphasized that: 'the children feel that they are having a two-way communication process going on in the classroom and on a social level if they feel they want to talk to me about something [they can] . . . not just a two-way process but a quality of a two-way process'.

The quality of the process might reflect aspirations to negotiate understandings and 'dig deeper into meaning' (see below). It also draws attention to the important link, made by some teachers in this sample, between reciprocal communication and the presence of an appropriate classroom climate or environment, and thus implicitly the social and emotional needs of pupils. Several of the teachers also made the point that this aspect of inter-active teaching became more problematic as class size increased. This condition, and the perceived ability of the class, was also believed to influence teachers' opportunities to explore meanings.

At least one teacher called into question the credentials of the National Literacy Strategy in supporting meaning-making. Ewan was a less experienced KS2 teacher who had reached for a dictionary to substantiate his views: 'it is to have an effect upon each other which kind of made me think, I mean yes – that's that would be interactive teaching, with it having an effect upon me, gleaning something from what the children's understanding would be'. He continued: 'Now looking in the Strategy again, in the literacy framework I found virtually nothing that I could equate with interactive teaching'.

While a few teachers linked the construct with whole-class interactions, more teachers considered that reciprocal communication was best achieved through one-to-one or group activity. Some teachers felt that group work was the best arena for reciprocal communication and negotiating meaning. Barry said:

> It's having that almost one-to-one with each individual in the group, challenging them, challenging their intellect, challenging their thoughts and working as I said on that one-to-one basis which I believe is really the whole essence of interactive teaching when you can give children as much of your time as possible.

While initially emphasizing his work with small groups of pupils, as the project developed David, another of the teachers, shifted his attention to his interaction with the whole class. His reflective dialogues focused upon the use of non-verbal communication and how the pupils began to use specific non-verbal cues, introduced by David, in their interactions both with him and with their peers (see Chapter 7).

Although it is encouraging that 21 teachers referred either to reciprocal communication or meaning-making, only eight made explicit reference to meaning-making and interactive practice, rather than to reciprocal communication. Although this group of teachers comprised both experienced and less experienced teachers of both key stages, case analysis suggested that it tended to be the more experienced teachers who applied the construct to classroom practice. This is hardly surprising, given that constructivist notions of meaning-making are under-represented in the current NLS literature, with its emphasis on pace and covering objectives (see Chapter 9). As noted in Chapter 1, there is no extended discourse in the National Literacy Strategy about the range of methods teachers might use to make or dig deeper into meanings, or about the features of reciprocal communication like those set out in Table 5.4.

Table 5.4   Reciprocal communication and meaning-making

Purposes and issues	Main tactics	Conditioning factors	Consequences
Promoting a 'two-way process'	Both pupils and teachers are speakers and listeners Pupil involvement in the process	Class size Pupil ability	'Breeds respect and appreciation of others' Can change the course of lessons
		Little time to develop dialogue due to curriculum pressures	
		NLS structure and objectives	More likely to occur with individuals or small groups in dialogue with teacher, but possible with whole class
'Digging deeper into meanings' This was an under-conceptualized feature in teacher discourse	Challenging questions	Classroom climate	Limits opportunity for deeper communication

Attention to pupils' social and emotional needs

Interactive teaching was often associated with existing good practice, and this is reflected in the teachers' discourse on the importance of pupils' social, emotional and learning needs. The teachers never questioned the basis for these values, but some did juxtapose the literacy and numeracy strategies with what they considered to be more child-centred values. This, perhaps, reflects a Plowdenesque perspective on practice, but it was by no means only those teachers who had experience before the National Curriculum who were strongly committed to these values. The SPRINT teachers felt that pupils' social and emotional needs should form an important feature of interactive practice, and that on the evidence of training videos and other material this was under-emphasized in the National Literacy Strategy.

Using pupils' ideas was thus seen as good practice by many teachers, not only in terms of developing thinking skills, but also in fostering pupils' self-esteem and confidence. Eliza, an experienced KS1 teacher, expressed her fears that, for some children, the level of interaction with the teacher, when it took the form of persistent questioning, could be perceived as threatening and could actually cause some children to withdraw:

> I think it depends on the child sometimes. I mean interactive teaching doesn't always work for all children, some children can actually become more withdrawn and don't actually like it . . . I think that the whole idea of interactive teaching is you need to know your children.

She felt that:

> it is important for young children to actually have their ideas given a status and I feel that the children come on tremendously, they offer views on various things, if it's given a status within the class . . . because some children perhaps don't get many opportunities to actually shine at something.

Louis, an experienced KS2 teacher, also talked about the important issue of creating confidence, and concluded that 'We do need to encourage children to be risk-takers. The ability to take risks is absolutely vital'. Louis was able to use quite relaxed methods of class control to achieve a conducive atmosphere: 'We respect each other's views, we can talk to each other about feeling silly and if they do give the wrong answer, no-one's going to jump down their throat'. The views of Laura, a KS1 teacher, reflected social justice themes: 'I think that's what should come across in interactive teaching . . . children have their own rights . . . they know that they are a person and they are a being as well'. David, another experienced KS2 teacher, linked his views on promoting confidence to 'progressive' ideas: 'Learning is not just about passing exams, it's about the whole person and the life schemes that you learn. And interactive teaching *is* about learning. It's interrelationships, it's about life-skills, it's about developing your own person'.

In Chapter 1 and again in Chapter 9 we discuss how the emphasis on pace and curriculum objectives discourages teachers from pursuing pupils' interests. Although more a function of the curriculum and its structure than interactive pedagogy, lack of classroom time remained an issue for many teachers. Some teachers felt hindered by a school culture that encouraged keeping the pupils as quiet as possible. This might be attributable to external pressures, such as the need to achieve objectives, or to parental pressure, or even to the personal styles of headteachers. Several of the more experienced teachers, who were committed to paying attention to pupil needs, were also the most critical of the scope available to achieve this aim, given the time devoted to delivering the National Literacy and Numeracy Strategies. Katy, another experienced KS2 teacher, noted the difficulties of being interactive with a large class in the literacy hour: 'You can't have it child-centred as much. In other curriculum areas, however, I just think we've got more freedom, the teaching's not as intense. It is perhaps more child-orientated, they're discovering for themselves'.

By the end of the SPRINT Project, all teachers remained committed to addressing pupils' social and emotional needs. There was a general growth in confidence in their ability to meet such needs and a feeling that they were better able to balance all the demands made upon them. This was true even of those most critical of the National Literacy Strategy. Table 5.5 sets out the main features that emerged from what the teachers said about trying to meet pupils' needs.

Table 5.5 Attention to pupils' needs

Purposes and issues	Main tactics	Conditioning factors	Consequences
Developing pupil self-esteem and confidence	Praise and much non-verbal feedback	Need to provide time, especially in large classes, to promote appropriate interactions	
Enhancing progress and opportunities for inclusion of all children			Cognitive development
Promoting cognitive development through risk-taking and problem-solving	Using pupils' ideas Planning for time to use or at least consider pupil ideas Discovery methods Allowing pupil direction of areas of study Starting from pupils' ideas	Covering curriculum objectives may reduce time available NLS frameworks do not incorporate such methods beyond limited 'brainstorming' sessions	Ownership of learning Empowerment Reciprocity
Giving pupils' ideas appropriate status			
Respect for pupil rights	Praise, the inculcation of intra-class regard and communication	High level of teacher commitment to individuals and class dynamics required	Life skills and holistic development
Implicit moral/political stance or commitment to the individual	Develop the 'right ethos' or class atmosphere	Knowledge of pupils	

Change in teachers' conceptualizations

In Chapter 4 we considered Queenie's case. She constructed interactive teaching through largely surface features, which changed little during her involvement with the SPRINT Project. Both her thinking and practice remained fixed in this arena. Here, we consider Dawn, who was a less experienced KS1 practitioner in her second year of teaching, who also constructed interactive teaching largely through surface features at the start of the study. Her practice also demonstrated a variety of NLS activities that reflected surface features. As the project progressed, Dawn, a focus teacher, made a major conceptual shift in her thinking about interactive teaching to include deep features.

CASE STUDY
Deep features

Dawn appeared clearly to be a reflective practitioner. She initially saw interactive work as confined to 'carpet sessions', but had become more aware of the inherent tensions caused by lengthier interactions with individuals and, towards the end of the project, considered many of the standard practices used in the National Literacy and Numeracy Strategies to be 'peripheral'. At the beginning of the project, she viewed interactive teaching thus:

> In the literacy and numeracy hour it means involving the children individually – so it's having the children come out, putting things in a line, correcting things, writing things, using interactive displays that can be moved around. The children should be involved, interested not passive.

She became concerned that interacting with individuals might exclude other pupils and, at an early stage, was already voicing some of the difficulties found to be inherent in practice by other teachers. She referred to the literacy hour as her 'worst paced lesson' and was critical of herself in failing to live up to her own objectives: 'I aspire to it [interactive teaching] more than I actually achieve. In the literacy and numeracy hour, it affects the pace of the lesson and I feel I lose the children when one comes to the front'.

In her final interview, Dawn expanded at length upon her views of interactive practice and was one of the teachers seen to move from predominantly surface views to a deeper understanding of what interactive teaching might be. Dawn acknowledged that the reflective dialogues had helped her ruminate upon both her theory and her practice, although the relationship between the two was not clear-cut. It was she who elaborated upon the idea of 'Big I' and 'little i' interactive practice: 'I mean the juggling the concepts in the head and discussing orally. I would call it capitalized interactive'. Later this was developed further:

> I haven't appreciated before that I have felt that there were two levels of interactions, that there was the surface level of holding little cards and writing things down [on a whiteboard] or saying things at a given time, and then the real bit of teaching and learning that I, actually I the teacher, should be facilitating, checking, guiding.

As the project progressed, Dawn shifted her focus from the whole class to group work. Significantly, in view of what the next chapter will reveal about differences between KS1 and KS2 teachers, the prospect of moving to a new class of KS2 children suggested to Dawn that she would be able to develop her deeper level interactive practices:

> It may change slightly – certainly the focus on groups and individuals I hope is going to get stronger, probably the carpet work will be in the little 'i' still, for some children hopefully the big 'I', certainly if I see a glimmer of that opportunity I will go for it and, okay, for five minutes if the rest of the class are not really involved, then hopefully they will get their turn, but I am certainly hoping that I can really focus much more now on small groups and the individuals.

Although still much more critical of herself than many teachers, she did recognize that reflection was only a precursor to further developments in practice: 'I think I have got more questions than I had when I started. It has not solved any problems for me to be honest but it has certainly made me much more reflective about what I am doing'.

Unlike Queenie, who remained fixed in surface practices, Dawn was thinking deeply and critically about her own teaching and, as we have seen, this led her to consider deeper features of interactive practice. It would appear, though, that such reflection focused largely upon groups or individuals. Deeper practice with the whole class seemed to be more opportunistic and relied on interaction with more able pupils. Like many Key Stage 1 teachers, she did not articulate the possibility of using deep interactive practice with the whole class or across all abilities. Deeper interaction seemed to be linked with pupils she saw as being more able, rather than as a strategy to be applied to all. Although she articulated her thinking about deeper practice in groups, this was not apparent in the video evidence of her 'most interactive' classroom sessions. Even in group interactions, she elicited mainly short and closed responses from her pupils. Dawn herself said that information about particular strategies and techniques would have been useful, and it would appear that developments in her practice were diminished for this reason.

Table 5.6 Changes in teachers' construction of interactive teaching

Construction	No change	Movers
Predominantly 'surface' construction of interactive teaching	**Queenie** (experienced KS1) Her instrumental interests were reinforced by NLS literature. She demonstrated successful application of NLS surface strategies. Security in prior experience and curriculum constraints discouraged her development.	**Dawn** (less experienced KS1) Held reservations about NLS and had aspirations for 'deeper' interaction. She felt that SPRINT provided validation and knowledge, addressed meaning-making and thinking skills that are under-emphasized in NLS.
	'It is just something I feel I've been doing all the time . . . I don't think it has changed.'	*'Now I am more interested in more in-depth interaction . . . it popped into my mind when we were talking about the little "i" and big "I" for interaction . . . I mean the juggling the concepts in the head and discussing orally. I would call it "capitalized" interactive.'*
Incorporated 'deep' construction of interactive teaching	**Katrina** (experienced KS1) Demonstrated established interactive practice based on MA and experience.	**David** (experienced KS2) Considered deep features from start of project.
	SPRINT did not contribute anything new to her understanding.	He moved from a group/ individual focus to whole-class focus. He clarified his understanding of principles of meaning-making and thinking skills, and problematized and theorized practice.
	She was confident in her own principles, which included surface and deep constructions, and problematized and theorized her own practice.	
	Her thinking and practice reflected surface and deep features for individuals, groups and whole class.	*'I think originally, maybe at the start that was very much "Oh I've done a bit of an interactive session with the literacy hour" . . . and that's it, "tick the box", but that's not it. It impacts all. To varying degrees, but it impacts [on] all of my lessons and it impacts [on] my planning.'*

In Chapter 7, we explore Dawn's case more fully, together with several other case examples. Table 5.6 introduces some of these cases.

Summary

Some general trends in teachers' ideas about interactive teaching have emerged in this and the previous chapter. We have seen that, in the absence of much help from official literature, the teachers produced multidimensional constructs of interactive teaching. Some key features of these constructs matched closely those of the National Literacy Strategy, but others, such as children's social and emotional needs, were less emphasized in the NLS literature and video material aimed at teachers.

Given the sparse amount of information about interactive teaching provided in the NLS literature, how teachers formed and developed their views might be summarized thus:

- Initial views were influenced by assumptions about what constituted existing good practice.
- There was some development in the use of certain constructs and practices, such as greater pupil collaboration, influenced by their emphasis in the NLS literature and arguably by pressures of achieving the objectives.
- Taking part in the SPRINT Project as either a focus or a comparison teacher was beneficial in that all teachers welcomed the opportunity to scrutinize their own understanding and practice. Focus teachers all found the experience productive.
- A few teachers made substantive shifts in their understanding of interactive teaching and expressed dissatisfaction with the surface features, through their own professional interests, their experience of courses other than those promoting the National Literacy Strategy, and by contact with the SPRINT Project.
- Length of experience did not affect the types of construct used but, in some cases, was associated with an initial greater criticism of the literacy strategy.

The key issue is that teacher thinking and practice may be focused on different aspects of interactive practice, at various levels (individual, group and class) and may develop at different points. In Chapter 7, we elaborate on the idea that teacher development moves through these domains towards the situation in which both thinking and practice address surface and deep features for individuals, groups and the whole class.

In Chapter 6, we now explore the SPRINT teachers' practice of interactive teaching. Given all that was said about interactive teaching in the interviews and reflective dialogues, what did we see when teachers invited us into their classrooms to observe their most interactive practice? And how did their current practice compare with practice before the introduction of the National Literacy Strategy?

6 Teacher–pupil interaction and interactive teaching
Is there a difference in practice?

Linda Hargreaves, Anthony Pell and Roger Merry

Introduction

The previous two chapters showed the wide variety of ways in which the SPRINT primary teachers conceptualized interactive teaching and how, as they focused on this aspect of their teaching, their conceptualizations developed, becoming broader or 'deeper'. Understanding and interpreting pedagogical behaviour in words is very different, as we all know, from implementing that behaviour in practice. Systematic observation of the sort described in this chapter was developed originally to assist in training teachers to change their styles. Furthermore, as anyone who has been observed when teaching knows well, the teacher's and observer's impressions of a lesson can differ markedly. In this chapter, therefore, we consider the evidence for what the teachers actually did when involved in interactive teaching. This evidence is based on systematic coding and analysis of the sections of video that the teachers selected to illustrate their 'most interactive teaching' in the literacy hour and in other curriculum areas. To put our findings into context, we begin with a short history of classroom observation and the search for interactive teaching.

Using systematic observation in the search for interactive teaching

The search for effective pedagogical styles, which could have been labelled 'interactive teaching', has a long history, which stretches back beyond the middle of the last century. The attempt to find reliable ways of identifying such teaching in action has occupied at least three generations of educational researchers. Flanders (1970) referred to the development of systematic recording techniques from 1940 to 1970 and drew attention to a study carried out as early as 1914. The SPRINT project is, therefore, another contribution to a long line of applications of systematic classroom observation to teacher–pupil interaction.

The Flanders Interaction Analysis Categories, or FIAC, is probably the best known method of observation of classroom interaction and could be regarded as a grandparent of the more recent methods, having been developed at the University of Minnesota in the late 1950s (Flanders 1970). Observers who use FIAC classify 'classroom events' – that is, the 'shortest possible act that a trained observer can identify and record' every three seconds into one of ten categories of teacher behaviour. Flanders' aim in devising the system was to use it to train teachers to reduce the relative proportion of teacher talk, or 'direct' teaching, in favour of an increase in pupil-initiated talk, or 'indirect' teaching. Flanders' work had a political intention, namely to sustain a democratic society in the face of the perceived danger of the growth of extremist authoritarian factions as politically motivated Europeans settled in the USA after the Second World War. His concerns were allied to those of Adorno *et al.* (1950), identified in *The Authoritarian Personality*.

This link with authoritarianism led Flanders to adopt the rather extreme position of associating 'telling' with criticism and 'asking' with praise in creating his ratio of indirect to direct teaching. Nevertheless, when the individual categories were examined, some interesting patterns emerged. On the basis of ten years' research, Flanders (1970) noted, for example, that less than 5 per cent of primary teachers' talk was in response to children's ideas and that only about 15 per cent of it consisted of questions. Furthermore, 'more than two thirds of all teacher questions . . . are concerned with narrow lines of interrogation which *stimulate an expected response*' (p. 13; our emphasis). These figures are in the context of Flanders' often quoted 'two-thirds rule': 'After several years of observation, we anticipate an average of 68 per cent teacher talk, about 20 per cent pupil talk, and 11 or 12 per cent silence or confusion' (Flanders 1970: 101).

In essence, Flanders was looking for a more interactive pedagogy that would remove the contradiction between teachers' aspirations to foster the 'growth of independence and self-direction' through pupil participation in lessons and 'the current state of affairs in our classrooms [which is] . . . that teachers usually tell pupils what to do, how to do it, when to start, when to stop, and how well they did whatever they did' (Flanders p. 14).

This was the situation in US classrooms in 1970, but it resembled that in England also, even at the height of the Plowden era. Research, whether based on systematic observations of classroom interaction or analysis of teacher–pupil discourse, tended to reinforce Flanders' findings. Galton *et al.* (1980), for example, using the former, found that the 'two-thirds rule' held sway even in informal classroom settings, while Sinclair and Coulthard (1975), using the latter, found that classroom interaction that broke free from the 'initiation → response → feedback (IRF) script' was rare. A few years later, in studying the discourse of 'progressive' primary classrooms, Edwards and Mercer (1987) found that 'cued elicitation' – that is, what Flanders referred to as 'questions designed to stimulate an expected response' – was a common pattern: 'The pupil's task is to come up with the correct solutions to the problems, seemingly spontaneously, while all the time trying to discern in the teacher's cues, clues, questions and presuppositions what that required solution actually is' (Edwards and Mercer 1987: 126).

Just as Flanders had found the limited use of pupils' questions in American primary classrooms, Tizard and Hughes' (1984) found that teacher-dominated interaction with 4-year-olds was evident in nursery schools, in contrast to those same children's interactions with their mothers at home. Thus, even in the early years, there was little evidence that teachers were beginning to 'throw out limiting old assumptions and respect the flexibility, creativity, adventurousness, resourcefulness and generativity of the young mind' (David 1999: 87). By 1996, after the establishment of the National Curriculum in primary schools, Galton *et al.* (1999) found that the time teachers spent in *verbal* interaction with their classes had increased from 57 to 75 per cent of observations, and yet the relative proportion of questions to statements had remained unchanged at about one question to four statements.

The SPRINT Project gave teachers the opportunity to describe and then demonstrate their concepts of interactive teaching. Our teachers were asked to decide which part of their lesson they considered to be the most interactive. The application of the tried and tested method of systematic observation used by Galton *et al.* (1980) in the ORACLE Project has enabled us to compare our examples of interactive teaching with previous studies of teacher–pupil talk.

Systematic observation of classroom interaction

In most samples of classroom interaction in the present study, teacher–pupil interaction was taking place in almost all observations. This was perhaps to be expected because the teachers had selected 20-minute segments of lessons which showed their 'most interactive teaching'. Our impression, however, was that these 20-minute segments were not that different from the interaction rates that teachers managed to sustain throughout the literacy lessons, suggesting that teachers were now interacting with pupils for well over 90 per cent of each session.

In the remainder of this chapter, we describe how the observations were made and how the ORACLE schedule was adapted for the SPRINT Project. Then we use the results of the observations to make a series of comparisons between past and present classroom interaction, focus and comparison teachers, Key Stage 1 and 2 teachers, and interaction in the literacy hour and other curriculum areas. We will attempt also to relate the observational findings to the various forms of interactive teaching that emerged from the teachers' definitions as described in Chapters 4 and 5.

Adapting the ORACLE observation schedule for the SPRINT Project

The ORACLE system for observing pupil and teacher behaviour has been used often since the first major study of primary classrooms in the late 1970s (Galton *et al.* 1980). Different researchers have adapted it in various ways to meet their own research needs, but the basic structure and principles of the schedules have remained the same. In the SPRINT project, each teacher selected a 20-minute section of video that showed them during their most interactive teaching. While everyone in the research team learned about the observation process and was acquainted with the observation categories as part of their professional development, two members were trained to code the videos using the ORACLE teacher record. Every 25 seconds, they recorded:

- whether the teacher was interacting;
- the type of interaction they were engaged in;
- with whom they were interacting;
- the content of the interaction;
- the teacher activity if they were not interacting.

The following were coded in addition to the original ORACLE items:

- the length of pupil responses, notably those that exceeded 10 words;
- the use of phoneme fans, or whiteboards, or other techniques specific to the literacy hour;
- interactions with meta-cognitive content, such as questions or statements about *how* a child had constructed a narrative or analysed a poem.

These minor additions to the ORACLE record were made in such a way that the original schedule was preserved so that comparisons could be made with earlier studies. One advantage of the use of video was that the observers could discuss and re-view ambiguous events. Over a series of moderation trials, the inter-observer agreement, based on per cent agreement, for the categories task, task questions and task supervision was 0.8, 0.84 and 0.74 respectively, with a mean agreement across all categories of 77 per cent. A list of the observation variables is given in Appendix D.

What did we expect to find?

First, the most basic expectation was that if teaching in the literacy hour was 'discursive', 'interactive', 'ambitious' and 'pacy', as suggested in the NLS framework document, then, compared with pre-NLS observations of primary teachers, we might find:

- fewer instances of non-interaction and an increase in teacher talk;
- an increase in the use of questions relative to statements;
- more 'challenging' questions, in which children had to think out explanations, solve problems or offer answers to open-ended questions to which the teacher accepted several answers;
- more examples of teachers having sustained, uninterrupted interactions with the same child.

Secondly, if the reflective dialogues with the focus teachers were helping to refine their interactive teaching, then we expected to see more questioning and/or sustained interactions among the focus teachers than among the comparison teachers. Thirdly, since we observed the focus teachers teaching in curriculum areas in which they felt that they could demonstrate interactive teaching, we expected to see more of the features listed above in these curriculum areas. In addition to these expectations, we wished to determine whether there were any differences between the KS1 and KS2 teachers.

As soon as the teachers began to provide us with their interpretations of the term 'interactive teaching', however, the over-simplistic nature of our predictions became evident. As shown in Chapters 4 and 5, the teachers had a wide variety of definitions and interpretations of 'interactive teaching', although they had all attended NLS training sessions. For example, while our predictions were consistent with some of the 'deeper-level' conceptualizations, they did not allow for teachers whose aim was to achieve broad pupil participation, ensure active and practical participation, or encourage pupil–pupil collaboration. In fact, when all the observation data were pooled, there was a danger that these different interpretations of interactive teaching might counteract each other!

Consider, for example, three teachers. The first teacher who was encouraging active and practical participation, or pupil–pupil collaboration, might spend long periods interacting non-verbally, by demonstrating or participating in the children's practical activity, or simply observing, and be aiming to reduce her own level of verbal participation. The second, seeking two-way reciprocal interaction or probing one child's understanding, might pursue extended interactions with very few children, while expecting others to listen. The third, aiming to achieve broad pupil participation, might ask numerous short, simple, recall questions so that she could invite, and then praise, answers given by as many children as possible. Such different effects would each mask the other. Such variation between teachers has always existed and this does not invalidate the process of examining their pooled interaction patterns here, any more than it did in previous studies. Having done so here, however, in Chapter 9 we examine some individual teacher profiles and link these to the teachers' stated interpretations of interactive teaching. Before looking for differential developments in comparing our focus and comparison teachers' practice, let us look at whether all the teachers' selections of their most interactive teaching in the literacy hour differed from primary teachers' classroom interaction before the National Literacy Strategy was introduced.

How did 'interactive teaching' change teacher–pupil interaction at Key Stage 2?

To answer this basic question, we put together the KS2 focus and comparison teachers' literacy hour teaching and compared it with the observations made in the ORACLE Project of the 1970s (Galton *et al.* 1980) and 'ORACLE-20 years on' of the 1990s (Galton *et al.* 1999).

As Figure 6.1 shows, there are clear similarities and differences between the three profiles. All three are dominated by teacher statements. These increased in absolute terms after the introduction of the National Curriculum, as shown by the ORACLE 1996 figures, but have reduced slightly in the literacy hour observations. Teachers' use of questions, which had increased only slightly between 1976 and 1996, almost doubled in frequency in the literacy hour. In contrast, observations of teachers when they were not interacting with pupils (no interaction) have fallen. In the 1970s, 20 per cent of the observations found teachers not interacting with the children, but dealing with other adults, sorting out resources or putting up displays. A further 20 per cent of observations were 'silent interactions', such as non-verbal communication or gestures, reading stories aloud, listening to children read, demonstrating how to do things, or quietly marking their work. By 1996, there was less time for these kinds of activities, as teachers spent much more time talking, providing information and telling children what to do, in order to cover the content of the National Curriculum (Galton *et al.* 1999). It is important to remember that the SPRINT data refer to the teachers' selections of the 20 minutes of their 'most interactive teaching'. Thus the low level of 'no interaction' is hardly surprising, while the large increase in questioning indicates that the children were being given plenty of opportunities to interact with the teacher. Some allowance has to be made, of course, for what the

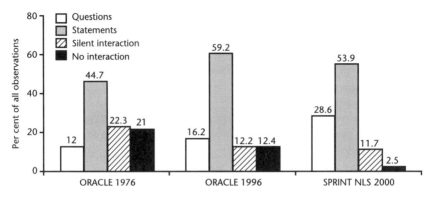

Figure 6.1 Changing teacher–pupil interaction profiles: 1976–2000.

ORACLE studies might have shown if the ORACLE teachers had been asked to select their 'most interactive teaching'.

Observations of teachers asking questions nearly doubled between 1976 and 2000 as a proportion of all observations (Figure 6.1). Sometimes, however, teachers ask questions that they go on to answer themselves before the children can respond. A key feature of the ORACLE system is that, for teacher talk to be coded as a question, it must receive a spoken answer or ample time and clear expectation that an answer will be given. In other words, the ORACLE system shows that some form of interaction really was taking place and, given how for instances of silent and non-interactions this interaction was happening with considerable intensity.

Figure 6.1 compares the literacy hour during SPRINT with observations made across the curriculum in the ORACLE projects. To make a fairer comparison, therefore, we eliminated the observations of 'silent interaction' and 'no interaction' and recalculated the ratio of questions to statements, or what we could call the 'ask to tell' ratio. We also used the observations recorded during English lessons (Figure 6.1 includes observations across all curriculum areas) in the 'ORACLE-20 years on' study. This is not to equate literacy with English, but because activities such as reading, spelling and writing were coded as English in 1996. The results of this transformation are shown in Figure 6.2. It reveals a pronounced shift not only in the quantity – up from 75 to 83 per cent – but also in the nature of teacher talk.

Whereas National Curriculum English lessons resulted in four statements to every question, the teachers' selections of 'interactive teaching' in the literacy hour revealed less than two statements per question. This suggests a better balance between teacher and pupil talk, and proportions closer to those seen in normal conversation were it not that one participant asked all the questions, while the others simply provided answers.

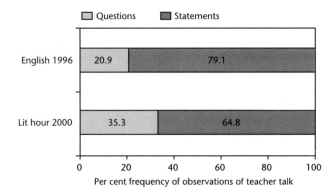

Figure 6.2 The 'ask to tell' ratio at Key Stage 2 in English and literacy lessons.

Teacher–pupil interaction at Key Stage 1

There have been few systematic studies of teacher–pupil interaction at Key Stage 1. ORACLE did not include KS1 children. Tizard and co-workers' (1988) study of inner-city young children's learning used a system that was similar to the ORACLE pupil record but did not observe teacher behaviour. One study that used a condensed version of the ORACLE teacher record was the PRISMS study of curriculum provision in small primary schools (Galton and Patrick 1990). This study was carried out in 1983–85 in a national sample of 68 schools with less than 100 children on roll. Table 6.1 shows the main types of interaction at Key Stage 1.

Compared with the ORACLE 'junior' teachers, the infant teachers in small schools in the 1980s spent much less time talking and more time in silent interaction. This suggests, for example, that they were listening to readers, reading stories aloud, showing children how to do things or singing with the class. These teachers spent less than half their time in 'conversation', which no doubt contributed to the overall conclusion that classrooms in small primary schools were relatively tranquil places in which to work (Hargreaves 1990). The second revelation in Table 6.1 is that the KS1 literacy hour figures are quite similar to the KS2 figures in Figure 6.1. The main difference between them is the greater amount of silent interaction at Key Stage 1. This can be explained by the use of special literacy hour techniques such as 'show me', and the teachers' participation in choral reading of 'big books', at Key Stage 1. This amounted to 6.7 per cent of all KS1 observations, compared with a mere 0.25 per cent at Key Stage 2. Our main interest here, however, is in verbal interaction, especially in the opportunities for children to interact with the teacher when asked a question.

Table 6.1 Teacher–pupil interaction at Key Stage 1

	Per cent of all observations	
	Small schools' infant classes in 1984[a]	KS1 literacy hour 2000
Questions	10.8	30.3
Statements	34.8	53.0
Silent interaction	49.9	14.0[b]
No interaction/not coded	4.5	2.7
Total	100	100

[a] Unpublished report, Galton *et al.* (1987).
[b] Includes interactions mediated by whiteboards, big books, flash cards and phoneme fans.

Although we have no PRISMS figures for what were referred to then as 'language' lessons, we can examine the balance of questions to statements – that is, the 'ask to tell' ratio – when verbal interaction was taking place. Whereas in the PRISMS schools the ratio was 24 questions to 76 statements, or about three statements per question, in the literacy hour at Key Stage 1 it was 38 to 62, or one question to less than two statements. Therefore, the teachers' selections of interactive teaching in the literacy hour, in both key stages, not only increased the overall amount of interaction dramatically, but also appeared to demonstrate a much more interactive pattern of classroom discourse in which children were given many more opportunities to speak. It is unclear whether this increased interaction could be regarded as interactive teaching. To do so we must look in more detail at the types of questions and statements used by the teachers and determine whether the focus teachers had developed their practice during video-stimulated reflective dialogue.

The focus and comparison teachers' questions and statements

Our initial examination of the focus and comparison teachers' observations was disappointing. Whereas the focus teachers' interaction frequencies changed relatively little from the first to the final observations of their literacy hour teaching, the comparison teachers' practice revealed several significant changes. These did not show consistent patterns, however. Table 6.2 summarizes the general interaction profiles of the focus and comparison teachers at the beginning (1) and end (4) of their video-stimulated reflective dialogues.

Table 6.2 Focus and comparison teachers' interaction profiles in the first and final rounds

	Per cent of all observations			
	Focus first	Focus final	Comparison first	Comparison final
Questions	30	27.7	35.9	28.4
Statements	53.8	56.4	49.6	54.1
Silent interaction	11.8	12.9	13.9	13.6
No interaction[a]	4.6	3.0	0.5	4.1
Total[b]	100.2	100.0	99.9	100.2

[a] Includes about 1 per cent 'not observed' when the teacher was out of sight or their speech was inaudible.
[b] Totals do not always equal 100 per cent due to rounding.

It is clear from Table 6.2 that the profiles are of similar overall shape, and the final profiles of both groups of teachers are almost identical. The changes in the observations of questions and statements from round 1 to round 4 are in the same directions for the focus and comparison teachers. The comparison teachers reduced their use of questions and increased their statements slightly more than the focus teachers, and they used 'silent interactions' (including choral reading and phoneme fans) a little more often. More importantly, when we compared these profiles with the 1996 overall ORACLE profile (Galton *et al.* 1999: 61), there was an increase in questions from 16 to 30 per cent and a slight drop in teacher statements from about 60 to 55 per cent. Silent interactions remained at about the same level as in 1996. Not surprisingly, the SPRINT teachers' selections of their most interactive teaching did not include times when they were not interacting with the class, but monitoring the children, sorting books or tidying up, or talking with colleagues. Thus the 12 per cent of the 1996 ORACLE observations labelled 'no interaction' was greatly reduced and apparently replaced by questions.

Interactive teaching with individuals, groups and the whole class

One factor yet to be addressed is the audience context for interactive teaching. The literature reviewed in Chapter 1 tends to associate it with whole-class settings (e.g. Reynolds and Farrell 1996), but the SPRINT teachers were free to use individual and group work as well as whole-class teaching. It is important to note the difference between 'audience' and organizational settings, however. Our figures refer to 'audience' – that is, the teachers' actual audience for each interaction as the lesson proceeded. Although a teacher might have organized the class to work in small groups, his or her interactions would still be with the whole class or individuals at times during the session. Table 6.3 shows the 'audiences' for the focus and comparison teachers' interactions. The first thing to note is that, despite the 'freedom' to choose the audience, the whole class was the most common choice. The focus teachers interacted with the whole class in 47 per cent of the first round of observations and 66 per cent of the final round of observations. The comparison teachers' audience preferences changed in the opposite direction, from 73 to 53 per cent whole-class interactions. Conversely, while the focus teachers interacted more often with individuals and small groups in the first round, the comparison teachers did so in the final round.

Overall, these audience figures show a clear switch from individual to whole-class teaching in primary classes. Galton *et al.* (1999) reported that the proportion of observations of teachers addressing a whole-class audience increased from 15 to 31 per cent between 1976 and 1996, whereas that for individual interactions fell from 56 to 43 per cent in the same period. As Table 6.3 shows, the audience for interactive teaching in the literacy hour in 2000 was almost a reverse image of the 1970s situation. The whole class as audience accounted for 47 and 73 per cent of all observations of focus and comparison teachers respectively, whereas those on a one-to-one basis slumped to less than 20 per cent of observations. When interactions with 'individual for class' (that is, when the teacher interacts with an individual but the whole class is the audience) are subtracted from the whole-class totals and added to the 'individual' totals, however, the switch is less dramatic. This

Table 6.3 Focus and comparison teachers' audience categories in the literacy hour

Audience	Per cent of all observations[a]			
	Focus first	Focus final	Comparison first	Comparison final
Individual (one-to-one)	20.4**	7.7**	9.9	11.9*
Group	21.9**	13.8**	11.6**	25.2**
Whole class (total[b])	47.0**	66.1**	73.3**	53.2**
Total audience interaction	89.3	87.6	94.9	90.3
Individual for class	14.9**	26.6**	35.8**	19.6**
Sustained interaction[c]	2.5	5.1	1.8	2.2

[a] These figures refer to proportions of all observations, including those times when the teacher was not interacting with the children, and have not been converted to proportions of the audience interaction totals given in row 4.
[b] Including individual for class.
[c] Uninterrupted interaction of at least 25 seconds with same individual or small group.

* $P < 0.05$, ** $P < 0.01$, chi-square raw scores.

achieves near equivalence between individual and 'pure' class interactions, with both ranging between 32 and 46 per cent of observations. Table 6.3 also shows the very low levels of sustained interaction (interaction lasting, uninterrupted, for more than 25 seconds) with any child or small group. At most, these amounted to 5 per cent of interactions, suggesting relatively few opportunities for children to develop their arguments in any depth or to engage in extended reciprocal interaction with the teacher. Since the 'deeper' levels of interactive teaching are more likely to require sustained interactions, they were either rarely used or were not selected by the teachers as their most interactive teaching.

There is clearly scope for more intricate analysis of these audience context factors, but space precludes its pursuit here. What is clear, however, is that the individualized nature of teacher–pupil interaction so typical of primary classrooms in the 1970s and pervasive right up to 1996, when 43 per cent of observations were on a one-to-one basis (Galton *et al.* 1999: 59), no longer exists. In line with the shift towards more whole-class teaching noted in the survey of teachers' perceptions by Beverton and English (2000), the National Literacy Strategy appears to have ended the focus on individual attention in the teaching of literacy in primary classrooms.

Our hope that we would find the predicted changes in the focus teachers' practice was not fulfilled. A first explanation, of course, could be that the video-stimulated reflective dialogues (VSRDs) did not work. Evidence from the interviews and the dialogues themselves (see Chapters 4, 5 and 7) suggests that this was not the case. They clearly had an impact on individual teachers' practice. A second explanation might be that any changes in practice were too subtle to be detected by the observation system, which is plausible. This type of observation system is not sensitive to infrequent forms of interaction. Thirdly, as was argued in relation to the teachers' concerns in Chapter 2, there might not have been enough time or enough rounds of VSRD for potential changes to take place. Fourthly, a few focus teachers, as shown in Chapter 2, felt that their interactive teaching was already well-developed and did not need to change. As explained in Chapters 4 and 5, however, and as shown in later chapters, most focus teachers felt that VSRD had alerted them to aspects of their practice that they wished to develop. Fifthly, as we suggested earlier, if the focus teachers were concentrating on different forms of interactive teaching, the effects might have cancelled each other out. Suppose one teacher wanted to broaden pupil participation to include more children, while another was concentrating on probing children's understanding by asking a series of questions of a small number of children. The first teacher would probably use many rapid simple recall questions to obtain short answers from as many different children as possible. The second could be asking higher-order questions in sustained interactions with a small number of children. When combined, each of these different sets of observations would cancel out the distinctive effects of the other. Lastly, though not precluding other explanations, the teachers might have been demonstrating different facets of interactive teaching in different settings, so that again the differences would mask each other in a pooled data set. All of these are plausible explanations of the lack of overall observable effect of the intervention. It could be that the teachers needed to identify much more specific aspects of teaching behaviour in their post-VSRD targets to create an effect. Meanwhile, the argument that there was not enough time is also highly plausible. Identifying and talking about teaching behaviour cannot guarantee immediate change in practice.

Key stage, however, as intimated earlier in this chapter, was emerging as a much more discriminating factor, and the lack of a systematic effect of the VSRDs allowed us to combine the focus and comparison teachers to create larger samples of KS1 and KS2 teachers suitable for an examination of the differences between the two key stages.

Does key stage make a difference to interactive teaching in the literacy hour?

The literacy hour 'ask to tell' ratios differed considerably from those before the introduction of the National Literacy Strategy; in this sense, teaching in the literacy hour was creating more opportunities for interaction than in the English lessons observed in KS2 during ORACLE 1996. We need to look more closely at the nature of these questions to assess the kinds of interactive teaching that were taking place.

The observation system divides questions into several types. First, it separates questions about the actual topic ('task') from questions about how, when or where children are going to do their work ('task supervision') or how they should behave in class ('routine'). Secondly, it classifies task questions according to the children's answers. Questions answered by recalling facts or giving an explanation which had been worked out some time earlier, and to which the teacher accepts one right answer, are called 'simple recall' or 'lower-order' questions. When a child's answer includes some on-the-spot working out or reasoning, or when the teacher accepts more than one answer to an open-ended question for example, the question is coded as a higher-order question. Figure 6.3 shows the types of questions being asked by the ORACLE and SPRINT KS2 and KS1 teachers.

Three different questioning profiles are apparent. Questions as a percentage of all observations nearly doubled in frequency to around 30 per cent; this was true in both key stages compared with pre-NLS English (15.6 per cent). Secondly, the big reduction in task supervision and routine questions, discussed earlier, was common to both key stages; these were replaced almost exclusively by a focus on task content. The most striking feature of Figure 6.3 is

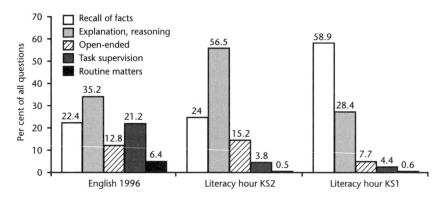

Figure 6.3   Teachers' questions in KS2 English (1996) and in literacy hour (2000).

that, at Key Stage 2, NLS 'interactive teaching' appears to have led to an increase in 'higher-order' (reasoning, explaining) questions, whereas at Key Stage 1 it has been accompanied by an increase in 'lower-order' factual recall questions. In other words, while the KS2 profile was an exaggerated version of the KS2 English profile with many more closed explanation questions and fewer task supervision questions, Key Stage 1 has turned this round so that nearly 60 per cent of all questions demanded only simple factual recall. This difference between the key stages has serious implications for literacy teaching at Key Stage 1. It suggests low expectations of younger children's ability to interpret, explain and speculate about text in literacy lessons. It raises at least two questions. The first is whether some explanation for these differences can be ascribed to the NLS objectives for the two key stages; we shall return to this later. The second crucial question is whether these profiles were simply characteristics of the SPRINT sample of teachers. We examine this, later in the chapter, by looking at what happened when the focus teachers were teaching in other curriculum areas which they had selected as particularly conducive to interactive teaching.

The lamentably low level of higher-order questions in KS1 literacy emphasizes the need for reflection on practice discussed in Chapter 1; in Chapter 9 we see how the National Literacy Strategy created dilemmas for teachers who were unhappy with its demands in this phase. On the other hand, the surprisingly high level of higher-order questions in literacy at Key Stage 2 deserves celebration. The increase in observations of explanation type questions means that the KS2 teachers *were* asking children to explain, predict or interpret text, on-the-spot. It included questions answered by children giving explanations of metaphors, or of a difficult passage, or why an author might have chosen a particular adverb. They were asked, for example, to find and justify the words and phrases poets had used to conjure up a particular mood or atmosphere. In guided writing, children might be asked to evaluate their own and others' writing, suggesting ways in which it could be improved.

Has the literacy hour discourse quashed creativity?

Another key stage difference was the frequency of open-ended questions. These were recorded when the teachers accepted, or clearly invited, more than one response to a question. So, for example, the increase in the absolute percentage of open-ended questions at Key Stage 2 resulted from teachers asking children to suggest, say, vocabulary for a poem, ideas to develop a story, or to predict what a character might do next. It also covered some very rare occasions when teachers asked children to comment meta-cognitively on their own thinking. This referred to times when they were asked to say *how* they had constructed a plot (for example, by working together) rather than simply what was in it, or, in a rare KS1 example, *how* they had worked out *how* to spell a word. On this occasion, while some managed painstakingly to explain the analysis of words into syllables, for others the strategy was 'I just thought in my head', the words accompanied by a slight frown. Even this teacher did not feel that there was time to 'dig deeper' at this stage.

At Key Stage 2, open-ended questions were slightly more frequent than in 1996. At Key Stage 1, however, open-ended questions were only half those at Key Stage 2. This limited opportunity for young children to use their imaginations and make suggestions is a matter for concern, particularly when we remember that this 7.7 per cent of *all questions* formed only 2.3 per cent of all KS1 literacy hour *observations*. Once again, it is useful to consider the ratio of open to closed higher-order questions. In 1996, 48 per cent of questions were higher-order questions. Of these, 73 per cent were closed and 27 per cent were open questions. In the literacy hour, at Key Stage 2, 72 per cent of questions were higher-order questions. Of these, 76.0 per cent were closed and 24.0 per cent were open. In other words, whereas there were more opportunities for children to answer challenging questions and suggest their own ideas overall at Key Stage 2, opportunities to 'explain' as opposed to 'suggest' were almost identical to the 1996 lessons. In Key Stage 1, challenging questions totalled a mere 36 per cent of all questions. Of these, 79 per cent were closed and 21 per cent were open. These figures are similar to the KS2 ratio, although closer to one in five, as opposed to one in four, open to closed higher-order questions. On this basis, opportunities for children to offer creative ideas or a variety of different answers to questions had not changed in relative terms. The preceding description of the changes is complicated, but shows that whereas KS2 children had slightly more opportunities to give imaginative responses, the already low level of open-ended questioning was lower still at Key Stage 1. In other words, the early experiences of literacy for these younger children could not be described as encouraging creativity.

The overall profiles in Figure 6.1, for example, show that teachers' statements still outweighed their questions, and so we turn now to focus on the nature of the teacher statements.

Teachers' statements at Key Stages 1 and 2

Figure 6.4 shows how the profiles of teacher statements have altered since the introduction of the literacy hour. At Key Stage 2, 'interactive teaching' in the literacy hour showed a decline in factual statements and an increase in the more challenging statements of ideas and problems, compared with pre-NLS English. There was less emphasis on feedback, but a sizeable increase in task supervision statements. Routine statements, including feedback on behaviour and small talk, were less frequent (11 per cent of statements) at Key Stage 2 than in 1996.

There were significant differences between the two key stages. At Key Stage 1, teachers spent more time making factual statements than posing problems or suggesting ideas. In other words, there was a reduction in cognitive challenge in Key Stage 1, but an increase in cognitive challenge in Key Stage 2, compared with before the introduction of the National Literacy Strategy. The striking feature is the pre-dominance of task supervision statements at Key Stage 1 and the finding that one in five statements were 'routine', concerning general behaviour and organization. At Key Stage 2, only one in

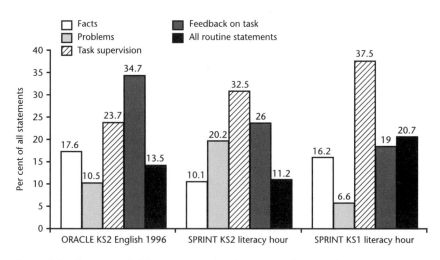

Figure 6.4 Changes and differences in teachers' statements between key stages.

ten were devoted to routine matters. If we recall that task supervision and routine *questions* were much reduced in both key stages in the literacy hour, then we can see now they have been replaced by teachers telling children what to do and how to behave, rather than giving them choices or asking them for their own suggestions. Of course, we expect teachers to direct children's behaviour and to manage their classes effectively and authoritatively. The emphasis on control rather than choice (or, at least, the illusion of choice) depicted by the SPRINT KS1 figures, particularly in relation to task supervision, has the potential to engender over-dependence on teacher direction, limit the development of self-efficacy and deprive 5- to 7-year-olds of any sense of task ownership. Meanwhile, the high levels of routine statements at Key Stage 1, particularly feedback on behaviour, might be indicative of how uncomfortable it must be for these youngsters to sit cross-legged, close together, in a large group on a carpet and give unbroken attention to the teacher for 30 minutes at a time, every day, in both the literacy hour and the numeracy hour.

One way in which KS1 teachers relieved this discomfort during whole-class shared text and word level phases of the literacy hour was to ensure interactive teaching through 'practical and active participation'. For example, they would instruct children to come out to the front and underline a word or phrase, or to write letters, on a flipchart, or hold up phoneme fans or white-boards. Games, such as 'Full Circle', were very popular in year 1 classes and involved many lower-order questions and task supervision statements. This game consists of the phoneme-by-phoneme metamorphosis of a word, such as 'sing' through a whole series of new words until 'sing' is finally reached again. The phonemes are displayed on large cards, which are held up by the children to make each word. The interaction involved in finding out which phoneme to change, the pronunciation of the new word, the reminders to children to change places and with whom, results in many factual recall questions, task supervision statements and task feedback. This game, and others like it, were clearly adored by the children, especially when played against the clock. They were a useful way for teachers to assess learning objectives. They were also 'interactive' in that they ensured broad participation, engaged children's attention, provided practical 'hands-on' activity and gave each child a moment of glory as they stood at the front to display their phoneme cards. They were simply great fun. Game formats and quizzes, with scaffolding prompts appropriated from television game shows such as 'Who wants to be a millionaire?', the skilful use of puppets, and conjuring tricks with word and letter cards were just a few of the ingenious ways in which the KS1 teachers engaged the children's attention. In addition, they reinforced previous learning and rehearsed new phonic constructions and word recognition. Use of these techniques made this otherwise context-less word-level work enter-taining and interactive, according to the definitions above, but restricted opportunities for higher-order thinking about language and literacy. They resulted also in what ORACLE termed 'silent' interactions.

'Silent interactions', as noted earlier, refer to teacher behaviours such as showing children how to do things, writing on a board or chart, participating in singing or choral reading, as well as listening to children read and reading stories aloud to them. In the literacy hour, when a teacher asked children to hold up their phoneme fans (a set of small cards, each bearing the symbol for a phoneme and joined together at one end with a butterfly clip to make a fan) to show which phoneme would fit between 's' and 'ck' to make 'sock', this was coded as a factual recall question mediated by a 'literacy hour' special technique. Since, however, the children's response did not involve dialogue, such interactions, were classified as silent interactions. They enabled teachers to assess, at a glance, the proportion of the class that had grasped a particular rule. It constituted, in essence, a form of marking. As shown in Figure 6.1, 'silent interaction' had fallen considerably between the 1976 and 1996 ORACLE studies. This drop was attributed to reductions in the time teachers spent listening to individual readers, reading stories to the class, writing on the blackboard or in 'silent marking', when children would queue at the teacher's desk to have their books marked, or the teacher would go round the class and mark work with a tick and a 'Good' or 'Try that one again' but no further interaction. At Key Stage 1, however, silent interactions appeared to have made a return, particularly in whole-class settings (see Table 6.4).

Table 6.4 shows the numbers of *all* observations, because to show 3.8 per cent of all observations as 32.8 per cent of silent interaction would present an

Table 6.4 'Silent' interaction at Key Stages 1 and 2

	Number of observations*	
	KS1 literacy hour	KS2 literacy hour
Silent interaction		
Non-verbal interaction	6.4	4.1
(e.g. show, participate)		
Listening to reading and reporting	1.4	7.3
Literacy hour techniques		
Phoneme fans, whiteboards, etc.	4.9	0.2
Choral reading, e.g. big books	1.7	0.0
Total	14.4	11.6

* To state percentages of 'silent interaction' could give a misleading impression of the frequency of these activities. Totals are given so that readers can calculate these percentages if required.

enormously inflated impression of the use of silent interaction. The difference in practice between the two key stages was marked however. At Key Stage 1, the use of phoneme fans to answer factual recall questions accounted for 2.4 per cent of all observations, with whiteboards used to answer higher-order questions (with explanations worked out on the spot, or open-ended) in 0.8 per cent of observations. The remaining 1.7 per cent of observations in this category were occasions when the teachers held up a word card, for example, and asked children to read the word on it. At Key Stage 2, silent interactions focused much more on teachers listening to children read extended passages or report on work they had done. Included in this category, for example, were times when the teacher was listening to children read out poems that they had written, or observing them dramatize or tell a story. Interestingly, and congruent with the argument above about the level of cognitive challenge at each key stage, the 0.2 per cent of all observations recorded under 'fans and whiteboards' referred to higher-order questions answered using whiteboards. Thus, although accounting for relatively little of the overall interaction, even the silent interactions exacerbated the tendency for KS1 interactions to be concerned chiefly with simple recall.

Let us now analyse focus teachers' interactions at each key stage in other curriculum areas.

Interactive teaching in other curriculum areas

As well as observing the focus teachers during the literacy hour, we observed their teaching in curriculum areas of their own choice, in which they felt able to demonstrate interactive teaching. These observations were made at the beginning of the project and again midway through the fieldwork. When the literacy hour and 'other curriculum' interactions were compared for the full sample of focus teachers, there were few differences. Clearly, they used similar interactive techniques in the literacy hour as when teaching history, science or numeracy. Interestingly, several teachers told us that the numeracy hour provided them with more opportunities to demonstrate what they called 'interactive teaching' and they chose the numeracy hour as their other curriculum area. Having identified the key stage differences reported above, we split the 'other' curriculum observations up by key stage to establish whether the literacy hour findings would be replicated here. In fact, a much more encouraging picture emerged for Key Stage 1, but one which raises questions for Key Stage 2. The results are shown in Figure 6.5.

Line graphs are used to accentuate the crossover – or 'interaction', in a statistical sense – between cognitive demand and curriculum area at each key stage. The graphs reveal that the literacy hour apparently exerts a depressing effect on challenging questions (closed explanation plus

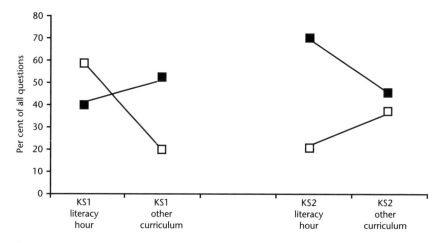

Figure 6.5 Cognitive demand of teachers' questions at Key Stages 1 and 2. □, low cognitive demand; ■, high cognitive demand.

open-ended questions) at Key Stage 1, while promoting greater use of lower-order (factual recall) questions. At Key Stage 2, the reverse is true. The literacy hour appeared to have raised the number of interactions to promote challenging questions. When the KS2 teachers were working in their chosen curriculum areas, the relative values of higher- and lower-order questions were almost identical with those observed during the ORACLE projects. In the ORACLE 1996 history and geography lessons, for example, lower-order questions made up 35 per cent of all questions, with higher-order questions accounting for 40 per cent in history and 46 per cent in geography. Of course, these overall figures do not apply to individual teachers. Although the KS1 teachers used many recall questions, some of them also asked challenging questions. Similarly, at Key Stage 2, some teachers asked many challenging questions both in literacy and other curriculum areas. In Chapter 9, we present individual profiles of such teachers.

Our figures suggest some effect of the literacy hour on cognitive challenge. Perusal of the objectives in the NLS framework document tends to confirm this. It could be argued that the objectives for year 1 term 2 and year 5 term 2, for example, lead to these outcomes. Table 6.5 lists the verbs within each objective. While neither key stage has exclusively higher- or lower-order objectives, there is a preponderance of verbs associated with lower-order activities such as 'identify', 'use', 'reinforce' and 'practise' in the KS1 list and more demanding verbs and those which invite open-ended activity in KS2, such as 'investigate', 'understand' and 'explore'. The lists in other terms and years follow a similar pattern. In other parts of the literacy framework, such as word level or sentence level work, the differences are arguably more concrete and factual at Key Stage 1 and allow more scope for interpretation, discussion and imagination at Key Stage 2. On the other hand, there is some scope for higher-order interactions among the KS1 objectives. The second objective listed invites 'working out' and 'predicting', for example, and there are potential discussions and comparisons in subsequent objectives.

Teacher–pupil interaction and interactive teaching – one and the same?

In this section, we consider the above question. Throughout this chapter, evidence has been presented that the teachers selected segments of their lessons that involved high levels of interaction, which would probably have been difficult to sustain throughout the complete school day. These high levels of interaction were undoubtedly achieved through the 'explosion' of questioning used by the teachers, especially at Key Stage 1. The hoped for changes in the focus teachers' practice were not significant, despite their participation in the video-stimulated reflective dialogues. The comparison teachers made more significant changes in their practice, reduced their use of

Table 6.5 Examples of literacy hour text level objectives at Key Stages 1 and 2

KS1 year 1 term 2	KS2 year 5 term 2
1 Reinforce and apply word level skills	1 Identify and classify
2 Use phonological knowledge to work out, predict and check meanings . . . and make sense	2 Investigate versions, identify similarities and differences; recognize change over time and place
3 Choose and read, discuss preferences . . . give reasons	3 Explore similarities and differences
4 Re-tell, sequence . . . and notice differences; compare, refer	4 Read
5 Identify and record, practise reading and using	5 Perform
6 Identify and discuss range of story themes, collect and compare	6 Understand terms . . . identify typical features
7 Discuss reasons for or causes of . . .	7 Compile – with commentaries
8 Identify and discuss, speculate, discuss, compare	8 Distinguish between, investigating viewpoint . . .
9 Become aware – by role-playing	9 Investigate features of . . . different genres . . . discuss appeal of
10 Identify and compare	10 Understand differences . . . through discussing effects of imagery
11 Learn and recite, re-read	

lower-order interactions and increased their use of higher-order questions. Explanations for these findings were offered earlier, but it is possible that the comparison teachers were working to a definition of interactive teaching that fitted our initial notions, whereas the evidence in Chapters 4 and 5 suggests that the focus teachers' definitions had diversified. A key stage analysis, however, rendered the differences between the focus and comparison groups somewhat meaningless in the face of major key stage differences in the literacy hour. The KS1 teachers used significantly more lower-order interactions and significantly fewer higher-order interactions than the KS2 teachers. This became a greater cause for concern when tested against teaching in other curriculum areas. This indicated that the literacy hour itself was probably responsible for the emphasis on low cognitive demands at Key Stage 1 and higher cognitive demands at Key Stage 2. It suggests that the KS1 teachers as a whole tended to select surface forms of interactive teaching, whereas the KS2 teachers asked more challenging questions, which might be congruent with the deeper forms. Despite the challenge of their questions, however, the expected developments – such as more sustained interactions – did not occur. This suggests that children are having few opportunities for extended discussion with teachers, or time to reflect on and develop an argument, in the way that the deeper conceptualizations suggest.

These important findings are supported by those of Hardman *et al.* (2001), who investigated the impact of the literacy hour on pupils with special educational needs in mainstream schools. Their observations, using a format derived partially from the ORACLE system, are congruent with the SPRINT findings. Although they classified question types slightly differently, they found that KS1 teachers asked significantly more closed questions, fewer open questions and directed children more than KS2 teachers. Although this was not the intended or expected outcome of our study, the research has revealed an important issue.

Summary

In summing up, we must address our opening question – namely, is there a difference in practice between teacher–pupil interaction and interactive teaching? Our results indicate some dramatic changes in the quantity and types of teacher–pupil interactions. There has been an overall increase in teacher–pupil interaction, meaning more opportunities for children as well as the teacher to speak, a prerequisite for interactive teaching. There has been a major, though not unexpected shift away from the erstwhile individualized nature of primary teacher–pupil interactions to whole-class interactions. The children in SPRINT teachers' classrooms were more likely to experience their individual interactions with the teacher in a public rather than a private setting. There were differences in the nature of teachers' questions in the two key stages, with an emphasis on simple recall at Key Stage 1; at Key Stage 2, challenging questions were much more common. At the same time, when teaching in other curriculum areas, KS1 teachers presented more cognitively challenging questions, whereas KS2 teachers reverted to more typical proportions of higher- and lower-order interactions. The opportunities for children to have a say in how they would do their tasks have been severely reduced, with teachers in both key stages having increased the time spent directing and prescribing tasks and activities. The implications for a generation of children made over-dependent on their teachers for direction require consideration.

So, is there a difference between teacher–pupil interaction and interactive teaching? Our observations can be interpreted as strong evidence of the forms of interactive teaching defined as 'surface' level in Chapter 4. The increase in task questioning and slight drop in teacher statements, although the dominant mode of interaction, support this. Evidence of interactive teaching that probed children's understanding, or of reciprocal meaning-making, was more difficult to find. At Key Stage 2, the higher-order interactions, which might indicate the deeper features of interactive teaching, showed a significant increase in the literacy hour compared with previous studies or other curriculum areas. We did not find corresponding increases of longer teacher–pupil interactions, of children being given time and space to offer extended responses, to enter into a genuine dialogue with their teachers, or to ask exploratory or higher-order questions of their teachers.

The conclusion here must be that the upturn in questioning is the beginning of a process that is essential for in-depth, two-way reciprocal interactivity, or real discussion, to occur. In other words, the SPRINT teachers' examples of interactive teaching mark a first and vital step on the way to realization of all its forms in practice. They demonstrate the surface features of interactive teaching but many steps remain to be taken to establish the deeper forms in practice. As we have seen in Chapters 4 and 5, individual teachers did use the video-stimulated reflective dialogues to explore, articulate and experiment with their thinking and practice of interactive teaching. For evidence of dialogue that indicated real engagement with children's thinking and understanding as described in the deeper forms, we need to look more closely at individual teacher's practice. This we do in Chapters 7 and 9.

7 Teachers' voices
Case studies from the SPRINT Project

Fred Paterson and Morag Hunter-Carsch

Introduction

Chapters 4 and 5 have shown how an important dimension of interactive teaching emerged during the project, derived both from the literature and from teachers' own constructions of interactive teaching. This dimension took the form of a distinction between what might be called the 'surface' features and the 'deep' features of interaction, the former referring to observable behaviour and the latter to unobservable cognitive and emotional processes. Although the data do not offer conclusive evidence, we hypothesize a developmental progression from the former to the latter in interactive teaching pedagogy.

By comparing and contrasting case examples, we explore teachers' constructions and uses of interactive teaching and examine the complex influences of experience, attitudes, knowledge, thinking and practice. Through the comparative case studies, we draw attention to four broad themes in teachers' discourse about interactive teaching:

- their philosophical/theoretical basis for practice;
- the implicit/explicit principles employed;
- reflection upon their principles, practice and theory;
- their application of strategies and techniques.

The cases explored in this chapter reflect the variety of contexts, key stages, experience, attitudes, knowledge, reflection and practice found among the SPRINT teachers.

Comparative case study 1

In this first case study, we compare Dawn and David. Although an inexperienced teacher, in her second year of teaching, Dawn was a highly reflective teacher. She problematized her practice, demonstrating an awareness of Piagetian and Vygotskian theory, and reflected on the impact of her interactive practice on the pupils. She used her background in psychology as a foundation to develop her own personal theory about interactive practice; namely, the idea that interaction can be either 'surface' (little 'i') interaction or 'deep' (big 'I') interaction. She surmised that there were:

> two levels of interactions, that there was the surface level of holding little cards and writing things down or saying things at a given time, and then the real bit of teaching and learning that I, actually 'I', the teacher should be facilitating, checking, guiding and also to pick up on misconceptions there as well if possible. I mean [how the pupils are] juggling the concepts in the head and discussing orally I would call it capitalized interactive.

Although Dawn articulated this attention to thinking skills, it was not reflected in her classroom practice. The ORACLE analysis of the video of her self-selected most interactive practice revealed that most of her interactions with the pupils elicited closed or short responses. The pupils' attention span in her lessons appeared to be short and, subsequently, led to frequent disruptions. Dawn's chosen focus for the video clips moved from class 'carpet time' to small groups. Even though she considered that the 'best quality' interaction was within teacher-facilitated small groups, her interactions still mainly elicited short pupil responses. Dawn was clearly caring and had the pupils' needs at the forefront of her mind. She tried to engage the pupils with visual and interactive props such as puppets, but in whole-class sessions, for some reason, appeared not to engage many members of the class, and most of the interactions were at the 'surface' level.

In contrast, David, an experienced KS2 teacher, was very successful at engaging his class in such depth. His class had a high percentage of special needs pupils, many of whom had social and behavioural difficulties. Usually two or three support staff were also in the classroom. David engaged his pupils through active and collaborative strategies that encouraged broad participation. In terms of depth, there was collaborative group work to encourage the interchange of ideas and explicit attention to meaning-making and thinking skills. David was the only SPRINT teacher whose discourse reflected all nine features of interactive teaching outlined earlier. The ORACLE analysis of his 'most interactive' sessions showed that David elicited more extended responses from pupils as the SPRINT Project progressed.

Like Dawn, David problematized his practice, recognizing the possibility of multiple responses to pedagogic problems, and sought challenge through contact with the higher education community. He also referred to public knowledge relating to accelerated learning, emotional literacy and special needs practice that influenced his teaching (although how these interests impacted were not expressed specifically).

Apart from the obvious differences in experience and key stage, Table 7.1 allows us to make some interesting comparisons. Before their involvement, neither teacher had read about nor received professional development that addressed interactive teaching, and both linked interactive teaching with existing 'good practice'. Both were initially positive about the literacy hour, although by the end of the project both revealed reservations. Dawn talked about 'subverting' the literacy curriculum to pursue pupils' interests, and David described it as 'prescriptive'. This might suggest both a growing confidence in their understanding of the literacy curriculum and a deepening awareness of interactive teaching practice as developed through the SPRINT Project.

David's construction of interactive teaching shifted from a focus on class surface activity and deeper group interaction to incorporate deeper whole-class interaction. Dawn's focus moved from whole-class activity to stress the importance of group activity for 'quality' interaction. Although both expanded their construction of interactive teaching, their widening understandings were dissimilar. We return to this again below.

In the SPRINT interviews and reflective dialogues, both teachers were reflective about their own interactive teaching practice. Both public and personal knowledge provided foundations for various broad principles that were the basis for these teachers' construction of interactive practice. These were sometimes clearly espoused. For example, David's comment that, if children's 'interest is engaged, they are more likely to be involved in the lesson', highlights his construction of the feature 'engaging pupils'. Sometimes features were implicit within teacher discourse. In one session, for instance, David asked his pupils: 'Why is that guess so good? . . . What are you doing in your head?' Implicit in this is, of course, not only an interest in pupils' thinking skills, but also an attempt to encourage pupils to reflect on these skills for themselves, promoting metacognitive awareness.

Initially, the key features mentioned by Dawn related to pupil engagement, practical and active involvement, assessing prior knowledge and attention to pupil needs. Through her involvement with her research-partner, Dawn linked practical involvement with 'surface' interaction and 'deeper' conversations with group work. She also noted that, before her involvement in the SPRINT Project, 'I was really only thinking whole class for interactive teaching, but what it has really brought home to me now is that it is not whole class, it is the whole class, group and individual as well'.

The video clips of her practice demonstrated the use of a whiteboard, fans, a puppet and 'get up and go' cloze procedure activities that address the themes of pupil engagement, active and practical involvement and broad participation. Nevertheless, as noted above, Dawn recognized problems with

Table 7.1 Case Study 1: David and Dawn

Teacher	Attitudes	Knowledge	Theory	Principles (implicit/explicit)	Reflection	Practice
Dawn KS1 Less experienced Focus teacher	Positive towards literacy hour and numeracy period. Later talked about 'subverting' the literary curriculum	'Not read anything' about interactive teaching Expanded from class focus to include group	Referred to Vygotsky and Piaget	Engagement Active/practical Broad participation Assess knowledge Pupils' needs	Problematized her practice	Recognized little deep interaction in video clips Problems with engaging pupils
David KS2 Experienced Focus teacher	Positive towards interactive teaching and the literacy hour and numeracy period Saw interactive teaching as 'good practice' Later saw literacy hour as 'prescriptive'	'No definition' of interactive teaching Expanded focus from group to class	Referred to accelerated learning, emotional literacy and SEN	Engagement Active/practical Broad participation Collaboration Knowledge Pupils' needs Thinking skills Reciprocal communication Meaning-making	Problematized his practice	Attention to pupils' thinking Well-paced sessions that engaged pupils

pupil engagement with the material. With the support of her SPRINT research-partner, she recognized that group work was the site of 'deeper conversation'. She was not explicit, however, about why this was important or how she might achieve these deeper interactions. Although Dawn identified a difference between 'deep' and 'peripheral' interactions, her construction of interactive teaching remained focused on the teacher–pupil interaction, de-emphasized the value of pupil–pupil collaboration and remained inexplicit about the requirement to address pupil thinking skills. Dawn limited the scope of 'deep' interactive practice to group activity, while through his contact with the SPRINT Project David recognized that 'deep' interactive practice could also be applied to whole-class activity.

David was less prone to using 'gimmicks' in the literacy hour, such as whiteboards and fans, although he did make good use of 'big book' texts as visual stimuli and as a focus for pupils. David's discourse with his research-partner addressed all nine features identified by the SPRINT typology. At the start of the project, David focused on his work with small groups. In one small group scenario, David asked pupils to close their eyes to build mental images, share these verbally without opening their eyes, and later to explore how effective the tactic was for helping creativity and remembering a narrative. This and the earlier cameo highlight his interest in developing the thinking and metacognitive skills of pupils and the process of meaning-making around themes addressed in the activities. Like Dawn, he sought to engage pupils actively and practically, and each lesson on video included collaborative activities for the pupils. From the start of the project, however, David demonstrated well-paced lessons that successfully engaged the pupils, many of whom had special needs. By the end of the project, David was inter-ested in developing more interactive whole-class practice, with a particular emphasis on non-verbal interactions and the pupils' ability to incorporate this into their own peer interactions. While David himself would recognize the scope for further development in his interactive teaching, his practice was demonstrably and qualitatively more accomplished than Dawn's. So what were the reasons for this?

Neither teacher was aware of a specific knowledge base for interactive practice, and both expanded their construction of interactive teaching through their involvement in the SPRINT Project. Both teachers were positive about literacy teaching and interactive practice. Both teachers linked theory or public knowledge with their interactive practice and both based their actual practice on principles that they were able to articulate in the research inter-views and reflective dialogues. Maybe their differences simply reflected a difference in experience. Of course, experience will always be an important influence, but as we shall see from the case study below, an inexperienced teacher who demonstrated little reflection was, nevertheless, able to engage and involve her pupils broadly and collaboratively.

Although both Dawn and David expanded their construction of inter-active practice and both reflected upon public knowledge and their own per-sonal theories, the breadth and depth of their reflection provides a clue to their differences. Dawn only briefly alluded to the practical process that would facilitate the development of pupil thinking. David was much clearer about how pupil thinking and meaning-making might happen initially in group situations and later in whole-class contexts. A key factor appeared to be his ability to apply theory, knowledge and principles and translate them into practice.

The importance of the 'surface' interactive practice of engaging the pupils was also highlighted. Although Dawn showed clear intentions to engage her pupils, she was not completely successful in this. David, on the other hand, was successful in engaging his pupils. This allowed him and them, initially in small groups, to engage in 'deeper' and more subtle interactive practices that addressed reciprocal communication, meaning-making and thinking skills. In widening his construction of interactive practice, David expanded his interest in pupil thinking and meaning-making into the arena of the whole class. He achieved this by 'applying' his own principles in clear and specific ways. For instance, in both small group and whole-class contexts, he expected and encouraged pupils to stop and think, to ask questions and to reflect on their own thinking. One technique he used was a non-verbal cue, which involved putting his fingers to his temples and bowing his head to indicate to the children that they should stop and reflect for a while. The children seemed both to understand and enjoy this technique.

In contrast, the video evidence for Dawn showed that most of her inter-actions with the pupils elicited closed or short responses. Even though she recognized the importance of 'deeper' interaction, this appeared not to be happening. The reasons for this were perhaps related to other aspects of her teaching. However, the analysis shows that being motivated, knowledgeable and reflective was not a sufficient condition for this inexperienced teacher to operationalize her own principles. We might hypothesize that engaging pupils is a necessary 'surface' requirement for this. A more experienced teacher may have a store of methods, techniques and strategies to address the various 'surface' aspects of interactive practice. It is perhaps understandable that, like Dawn, inexperienced teachers need examples of teaching techniques and methods that address these key practices. Indeed, Dawn expressed a desire for a catalogue of techniques from which she might choose, and newly qualified teachers such as Patricia also expressed this view. This highlights, perhaps, a pragmatic need of teachers with limited time or energy who, nevertheless, continue to aspire to improving practice. It should be stressed, however, that we are not advocating such pragmatic and instrumental support in isolation from the need to develop and pursue reflective practice.

Comparative case study 2

The next case example describes the practice of a less experienced KS1 teacher (Patricia), which shows the support that a 'significant other' provided. It also shows how practical tips were successfully implemented with neither a public knowledge base nor much reflection upon practice. Patricia is contrasted with an experienced and reflective KS1 practitioner, Katrina.

Patricia, a less experienced KS1 teacher in her first year of teaching, was positive about interactive teaching, linking it with 'good practice'. She had a positive attitude to both the literacy and numeracy strategies. Although Patricia did not initially feel knowledgeable, she considered that both her teacher mentor and numeracy training opportunities had contributed to developments in her practice. She also noted the positive impact of the SPRINT Project on her understanding of interactive teaching.

Dialogue with Patricia suggested that her construction of interactive practice was primarily based on three overlapping key principles. The first was to engage the pupils by ensuring that they had 'fun' and enjoyed activities. The second was the principle that there should be broad involvement of as many pupils as possible, while the third was that this involvement should be active and practical in nature. She did not refer to pupil thinking or learning processes, or meaning-making processes that characterize 'deeper' interactive practice. Although she was happy with her own understanding of interactive teaching, Patricia said: 'I've had no guidance on [interactive teaching]. I don't know if I'm doing it right'. In spite of this uncertainty and lack of reference to 'depth', the lessons videoed for the SPRINT Project were competently taught and included various literacy hour techniques, such as 'get up and go', 'time-out' and 'show me' activities, which matched the 'surface' principles espoused by Patricia.

She described a supportive relationship with her mentor that helped generate strategies and activities to use in the classroom. Patricia wanted 'guidance' in areas in which she lacked confidence, and although she valued the teaching ideas that the National Literacy and Numeracy Strategies videos offered, she did not feel these were explicit about interactive practice. Like many beginning teachers, including Dawn, Patricia's concerns were with the strategies and techniques required to perform appropriately in the classroom, defined in her terms by the level of enjoyment experienced by the pupils. Thus, it was these instrumental interests in approaches offered by colleagues and professional development materials that dominated. The data provide no evidence of Patricia problematizing her practice and she found self-questioning during the reflective dialogues extremely diffi-cult. She said, 'I found it easier . . . if you started off a question and then I answered it and could lead on from that. I found it difficult to pinpoint

Table 7.2 Case study 2: Patricia and Katrina

Teacher	Attitudes	Knowledge	Theory	Principles (implicit/explicit)	Reflection	Practice
Patricia KS1 Less experienced Focus teacher	Positive about interactive teaching and felt that the literacy hour and numeracy periods adapt well to interactive teaching Interactive teaching is 'good practice' Gained confidence in interactive teaching through being part of SPRINT	Did not feel knowledgeable about interactive teaching Felt more knowledgeable through SPRINT Project Later added emphasis to pupil–pupil interactions	Did not refer to theory specifically Referred to accelerated learning late in project	Pupil fun and enjoyment were key orientating themes Engaging pupils Active/practical Collaboration Broad participation Assess knowledge Pupils' needs Reciprocal communication (implicit only)	Found self-questioning difficult in unproblematic contexts Needed considerable support from researcher during RDs	Actual practice emphasized 'surface' interaction

Katrina KS1 Experienced Focus teacher	Positive about interactive teaching Negative about the literacy hour Happier with numeracy period than literacy hour	Katrina felt knowledgeable but wanted to know how to be more effective within literacy and numeracy hours SPRINT offered theoretical background Constructed interactive teaching as teacher–pupil plus pupil–pupil, class, group and individual from outset	Refers to 'social constructionist' theory	Broad participation Collaborative Reciprocal communication Pupil thinking Thinking about thinking	Problematized practice Sought multiple viewpoints to problems Considered her understanding of interactive teaching was different to the government's view	Not altered by literacy hour Demonstrated methods that encouraged 'deep' interaction Slow pace and question and answer apparent

specific questions. Easier, more so, later on [when] I understood your ex-pectations of the process'. This comment highlights the point that it took several dialogues before Patricia accepted that her research-partner would not take a 'tutor style' guiding role, and that it was an important aspect of the reflective dialogue process for her to take ownership of the development process.

Patricia made no specific mention of educational theory or philosophy underpinning her practice until the very end of the project, when she made links between 'accelerated' learning, interactive teaching and her own practice following a professional development course. This indicates, perhaps, a developmental progression for Patricia, in that she was beginning to link her own personal knowledge and practice with principles and theory. At the end of the project, however, it had not resulted in specific attention to 'deeper' levels of interactive practice. Her focus for the video clips of her 'most inter-active' practice shifted from small groups to a whole-class session and included more open questions.

Patricia discussed the difference between her experience of literacy and numeracy practice, saying that she was much more confident in the former than the latter. She explained that she taught a less able group for numeracy and that she found teaching at the appropriate level for these pupils prob-lematic. She felt the children struggled with the work and she 'was continually questioning' herself. She said, 'I would struggle to watch a video of me teach-ing numeracy and then ask questions about it, because I'm CONTINUALLY asking questions about it and I'd be cringing because I just think it's useless because the children still can't do half the stuff they're meant to do'. Patricia's lack of reflection on literacy practice was, therefore, perhaps a reflection of her own contentment; a view that was mirrored by her teacher-mentor, advisory staff and an education inspector.

Katrina presents a clear contrast in many ways. She held a negative attitude towards the literacy hour, felt knowledgeable about interactive teaching and reflected on both practice and theory. She also demonstrated practice that addressed the 'deeper' issues of pupil thinking and learning skills, reciprocal communication and meaning-making.

Currently teaching a year 1 class, Katrina had close to 20 years experience in Key Stages 1 and 2. Her master's dissertation on collaborative learning paid attention to interactive teaching methods, and Katrina also talked about other professional development focused on collaborative teaching methods that helped her 'out of a rut' and to 'see the light'. She also referred to 'social constructionist theory'. Based on this experience, it is unsurprising, perhaps, that at the start of the SPRINT Project Katrina already felt knowledgeable about interactive teaching. She wanted to know, however, how to be more effective in her own practice within the NLNS strategies. Katrina argued that class size was a constraint within the structure and curriculum of the National Literacy

Strategy. Although her negative attitude to it had been tempered somewhat by recent professional development experiences, she did not feel that
the structure of the literacy hour was suited to early years provision and considered the NLS view of interactive teaching to be quite different to her own.
She felt that her construction of interactive practice involved more participation and involvement of the pupils. She explained the importance of pupils
and teacher informing each other, constructing meaning and understanding
together, and argued that the NLS videos omitted to show input and feedback
from pupils. Nor did she feel that the National Literacy Strategy and associated
videos addressed pupils' social and emotional needs or the issue of the quality
of learning outcomes.

Katrina demonstrated a reflective approach in the way in which she linked
her theoretical knowledge with practical application of 'deeper' levels of interaction. She looked up 'interactive' in the dictionary as a precursor to dialogue
with her research-partner and, following her first video-stimulated reflected
dialogue, Katrina constructed two graphical models of literacy hour practice as
a basis for further discussion.

Katrina constructed interactive practice in terms of both 'surface'
principles (including collaboration) and 'deep' principles that attended to
pupil thinking, reciprocal communication and meaning-making. She talked
about one video clip of her practice:

> I actually said to them at the beginning we're going to look at medial
> vowel sounds in the middle of words. They went away and did an
> activity and they came back and talked about what they'd found
> and we actually found that the 'key' and 'tea' word didn't have a
> 'eh' in the middle, so something that didn't fit the pattern was
> brought to light. We talked about it. I feel my plenary sessions are
> more interactive because it's things that actually come from the
> children. Sometimes on the [NLS] videos when I've watched them the
> plenary sessions are not as deep. They've sort of been guided towards
> what [children] should have found out.

Katrina also addressed the practical issue of providing pupils with the skills
required to interact reciprocally, stating that she needed to engage in 'training
them to listen to somebody else and to take on board other people's opinions
and ideas, which is quite hard for some children'.

Reflecting on her own understanding, she noted how interactive teaching
went beyond reciprocal, two-way, open-ended discussion and involved communication that attended to thinking processes: 'you're talking about thought
processes – so you're not just sort of stating a fact, you are actually thinking
about thinking [with the pupils]'. Not only was such practice espoused by
Katrina, but she also provided evidence of it in the lessons and group work

videoed for the project. She used slower paced question-and-answer sessions that addressed how pupils came to their conclusions in order to provide models of thinking for the remainder of the class. In considering a shared text, Katrina asked the children to 'think in your head' about an aspect of the plot, and continued by asking 'What happened at the beginning [to a character]?' Children who responded were then prompted to ask themselves 'How do you know that?' in order to illuminate how they worked this out from various clues. This provided a model for other pupils to respond to similar questions, and offered a simple practical example of how Katrina addressed year 1 pupils' thinking skills.

In her construction and practice, we saw Katrina paying attention to both surface and deep features of interactive practice for individuals, groups and the whole class. There was little change through the SPRINT Project for Katrina. There appeared little that she needed to change.

Discussion

From this analysis of case studies of SPRINT teachers, we can derive various hypotheses, which ultimately will need to be tested against further cases. It appears that these teachers constructed interactive teaching in a variety of ways, sometimes singly and sometimes in combination. We have seen how these teachers' constructions of interactive practice were influenced by their attitudes to curriculum and pedagogy; their instrumental interests in strategies, methods and tactics; implicit and explicit principles rooted in personal experience and educational acculturation; and explicit educational theory or philosophy.

Reflection upon practice in dialogue with their research-partner helped reveal which of these 'strategies for construction' were used by individual teachers, and the breadth or level of thinking and understanding within each of these. Patricia, for example, was heavily influenced by her instrumental interests, whereas Katrina's construction was influenced by all four interests listed. Teachers' principles may only attend to procedural themes, and it is apparent that both the focus and depth of construction will be an important consideration. We also suggest that teachers might be concerned with both 'surface' and 'deep' features of interactive teaching, where the former are explicit and observable and the latter are subtle, implicit and qualitative. The locus of these features is also an important consideration. The National Literacy Strategy concentrates on whole-class teaching and, in this sample of teachers, surface features were often associated with teaching the whole class. In contrast, very few of the SPRINT teachers associated deep features with whole-class practices.

Patricia did not utilize theory, was mainly unreflective and constructed a diminished set of principles that emphasized pupil activity and engagement over pupil thinking and meaning-making. She was, however, successful in applying surface-level interactive practices. Dawn, in contrast, made explicit reference to educational theory, reflected upon practice and constructed a set of principles of practice that referred to both surface and deep forms of interaction. She was, however, not as successful as Patricia in applying either surface or deep interactive teaching methods. The reasons for these differences are complex, but the example of these two less experienced KS1 teachers does suggest that constructing and manifesting sophisticated, yet ill-defined, teaching practices relies on a number of factors. These factors include both public and personal aspects: public knowledge, in terms of available theories and approved techniques, needs to be balanced with the teacher's personally constructed principles and practice mediated through reflection (see Chapter 3). Despite indicating contradictory attitudes to the National Literacy Strategy, the case examples of David and Katrina showed that attention paid to instrumental interests, principles and theory, combined with reflectivity and longer teaching experience, were sufficient conditions for applying both surface and deep interactive teaching practices to individuals, groups and the whole class.

The analysis also suggests that the conditions for 'skilful' interactive practice are not fulfilled merely through positive attitudes, public knowledge, rich principles or reflectivity. Some teachers who had positive attitudes to the literacy hour and interactive teaching espoused theoretical underpinning, described principles of practice, were reflective and still showed no application of 'deep' interactive strategies. It was apparent, though, that more experienced practitioners who reflected on theory, principles and their own practice were the teachers who were *explicit* about the importance of addressing reciprocal communication and pupils' thinking, and were more likely to demonstrate this in practice.

Our work with the SPRINT teachers, did suggest a conceptual matrix that helped us to make sense of the progression that the teachers were making. The matrix in Table 7.3 consists of four domains that reflect teachers' attention to surface/deep features and individual/group/whole-class activity.

We can use the matrix in Table 7.3 to highlight the differences between the four teachers discussed in this chapter. It is apparent that Katrina constructed interactive teaching in all four domains and her practice, fully attending to surface and deep features of interactive teaching through individual, small group and whole-class activity. This was true of both her thinking and her practice. During the course of the SPRINT Project, David shifted his attention to the deep whole-class domain, so that his thinking and practice developed to cover each of the four domains. Patricia's practice addressed the surface domains and almost inadvertently had begun to address deeper

Table 7.3 Four domains that reflect teachers' attention to surface/deep features and individual/group/whole-class activity

	Surface features	Deep features
Individual/small group		
Whole class		

features, even though there was little in her discourse to demonstrate this as an explicit construct. Dawn's thinking ranged over many of the domains, but her practice appeared ineffective in all but the group surface domain.

David and Katrina appeared to be more successful for several reasons. Like Resnick (1987), they recognized the complex nature of higher-order thinking and, like Sternberg and Spear-Swerling (1996), they sought to make thinking explicit through dialogue. The role of questioning is, of course, important and David and Katrina employed questions skilfully. However, through the support of an experienced mentor, so did Paula. Without a great deal of knowledge, theory or reflection, she engaged her class and encouraged some considered and extended responses from her pupils. In comparison with the dearth of this in the Key Stage 1 group as a whole, this is a notable achievement.

Given that the ORACLE analysis highlighted an increase in questioning compared with before the National Literacy Strategy, it would appear imperative that the nature and focus of these questions be explored in teacher professional development opportunities. To reach the level of practice demonstrated by Katrina and David, not only should teachers be reflective and have positive attitudes, they also need a knowledge base such as that outlined in Chapter 1. In addition to the development of explicit principles based on this knowledge, what these case studies reveal is the requirement for teachers to 'practicalize' their principles. This requires practical techniques and strategies to address both surface and deep features of interactive practice, which, as we have seen, can be developed successfully with the assistance of an experienced mentor to great effect.

We would also argue that the contemporaneous NLS literature and accompanying training materials were deficient in their theoretical or philosophical grounding, offered an inexplicit and diminished set of principles and emphasized an instrumental view of interactive practice based on a limited set of techniques and strategies. While the routine application of methods and strategies is an important part of teachers' busy schedule, this analysis suggests that, if an underlying aspiration of the literacy hour is to enhance pupil thinking (Beard 1999), teachers need to make reflective links between theory and their own principles of practice. In effect, they need to become explicit about the 'deeper', more subtle aspects of interactive practice and address these directly in their teaching. We must therefore encourage teachers both to reflect and act in all four domains described above.

Summary

Through this analysis of cases, the SPRINT Project offers the basis for an enhanced model of interactive practice. In earlier chapters, we described our typology of features that describe principles for interactive teaching practice. In this chapter, we offer a framework through which teachers can develop these principles for themselves. We suggest that, to develop and apply the full range of interactive practices (as denoted in the domains described above), teachers will need to reflect upon:

- their own attitudes to curriculum and pedagogy;
- implicit and explicit principles that drive practice;
- explicit educational theory and public knowledge;
- implicit personal knowledge that underpins their principles;
- the methods and strategies that will allow them to apply these principles;
- their own instrumental interests in strategies, methods and tactics;
- the conditions that mediate the application of these practices in the classroom.

The involvement of a research-partner, mentor or 'significant other' colleague is clearly one way to support this process. The use of video-stimulated reflective dialogue, as used in the SPRINT Project, provides another method through which teachers, their mentors and trainers might achieve these aims (see Chapter 8). It is also hoped that the work of the SPRINT Project will ultimately help develop a database of knowledge, methods, strategies and tactics that teachers can consult in their efforts to enhance their interactive teaching practice.

8 It wasn't as bad as I thought!

Learning from reflective dialogues

Janet Moyles, Fred Paterson and Neil Kitson

Introduction

Geraldine, a young teacher on the SPRINT Project, talked about her experience of using videos and reflective dialogue to develop her practice:

> I found it helpful actually. The second video we did was the lesson I thought . . . was the 'lesson from hell' really. When I actually watched it, it wasn't as bad as I'd thought it was and it was useful to *see* that because you don't often get the chance to sit and watch . . . and you cringe and then you start thinking, 'Oh yeah, *that* was a good idea,' or 'I didn't like *that*' and then, of course, you start seeing children who are floating off and then you start seeing the same children respond-ing all the time and thinking, 'Oh yeah, we've heard your voice about six times, let's have a think about somebody else'. So you do, you start looking at it in quite a critical way, You get a bit blasé [about your practice] and you think, 'Well I do this, that and the other and it works for me, so I'm not going to try anything else', whereas I think that's why it's been good being videoed because you think, 'Well, that *does* work for me, so how can I move it on from that', rather than thinking, 'Well that works for me – stop – no more – let's leave it at that. Just carry on doing that exactly the same as I've been doing for years and that's always going to work'. I think you're more likely to think a bit more deeply about how you've done something and how you can move on from it.

What Geraldine shared with other teachers was an excitement in the pro-cess of deconstructing and reconstructing practice with a research-partner through observation of a video of her own teaching and learning. Within the SPRINT Project it became clear that reflective dialogue – or, more fully, video-stimulated reflective dialogue (VSRD) – is both an effective professional development strategy and a potentially valuable research tool for drawing out from practitioners their knowledge and informed perceptions of their daily practices and stimulating cognitive and metacognitive processes. The reflectve dialogue, as perceived by teachers, tutors and researchers, is a tool for professional development that is the basis for evidence-informed and reflective practices. A key element of the process is that the practitioner controls both where attention is focused and the direction and pace of enquiry. This chapter outlines the VSRD process and explores the actions and reactions of the teacher and tutor research-partners, the underlying theory and how the process informed the outcomes and findings of the SPRINT research. First, we provide an explanation of the process as used within this project.

Looking more closely at reflective dialogues

Facilitating meaningful and lasting teacher development is highly problematic. Joyce (1992) suggested that as many as 20 repetitions are required before new skills become embedded in practice. This highlights the limitations of standard inservice education formats, particularly short-term modular structured courses. Reflective dialogue, on the other hand, is a process that can help sustain the focus and motivation required to persevere with particular innovations or developments in practice over a period of time. It is essentially a two-way discussion between collaborators or critical friends – as we have used it, between a teacher and a research-partner. The dialogue aims to uncover significant thinking about day-to-day practice through the process of scaffolded discussion about images of that practice. In a video-stimulated reflective dialogue, the two research-partners (teacher and tutor/researcher) draw on each other to extend and develop their pooled thinking about practice using a shared source of information – a video. The dialogue then focuses on thinking about aspects of that practice by the practitioner, scaffolded and supported by the tutor research-partner.

Before the video-stimulated reflective dialogues, the teachers received documentation outlining the process (see Appendix E) and offering them some suggestions for thinking through the issues in preliminary viewing of the video. These were intended to provide a 'transparent' process through which the teachers could share and value the professional development goals of the process. The documentation also reinforced the team's commitment to a grounded and constructivist approach to the research, and the importance of the teacher's role. It explained that the intention was for the teacher to direct the focus of questioning about the lesson on video using a series of questions drawn from the literature on reflective practice (see Table 8.1). The role of the tutor-researcher was to support this and to draw attention to further questions or themes that might be applicable. Where teachers found it difficult to choose questions, the tutors modelled the process by choosing and asking questions from the options suggested. The ultimate goal within the SPRINT Project was that teachers would develop their reflective thinking about interactive teaching and develop their practice of 'interactive' teaching.

Appointments were made in advance with the focus teachers to 'capture' on video aspects of interactive teaching that teachers wanted to discuss. In the classroom, the teachers were exhorted to 'ignore the video camera' as much as possible. In practice, some teachers immediately felt at ease, whereas others continued to feel 'very self-conscious' about the presence of the research-partner and the video camera. To maintain a viable focus and to

Table 8.1 Theoretical basis for framework and bibliography

Intentions and purposes	Technical reflection
The object is to explore your intentions and goals to review what they are based on. What are your criteria for effectiveness? It is important to recognize that change is a personal process influenced by your previous experience, current school and classroom	Technical reflection involves identifying the educational basis for intentions and providing reasons for action. It aims to assess the effectiveness of practice used to attain defined educational goals
Self-awareness	**Perceptual awareness**
The object is to bring your attention to yourself in the moment of teaching. What do you sense about yourself – physical feelings, emotions, thinking and attitudes 'in action'	The object is to help you focus on *perceptions*, not your thinking. Where is the focus of your attention? What is noticed from the video that was 'un-noticed' in action? What additional foci might be developed 'live'?
Dialogic reflection	**Critical reflection**
Educational ends and means are viewed in terms of the value commitments underlying them. The aim here is to explain and clarify the assumptions and predispositions underlying teachers' practice. Dialogic reflection seeks out alternative assumptions, claims, perspectives and solutions and weighs competing practices	Both the ends and the means of teaching and its context are seen as value-governed selections from a range of possibilities. Critical reflection aims to question and critique the goals and practices of the profession; to raise awareness of the impact of unsurfaced professional aims and ideology; and take account of social, cultural and political forces in teachers' practice. Based on the desired and potential outcomes for students and other stakeholders; critical reflection questions the ethical and moral justification for educational ends and means

encourage multiple reviewing of sections, it was important to identify only about 20 minutes of the most interactive teaching, as focus teachers perceived it. In practice, this often meant 'dipping into' different parts of the literacy hour and teaching within other curriculum areas. This video footage formed the focus for subsequent dialogue between research-partners. In their communications with teachers, the research team emphasized that teachers should *not* plan a 'model' lesson: the aim was to focus on the everyday reality of busy classrooms and provide the opportunity for potential changes in practice that would last beyond the project. This method:

- recognized the teacher as a stakeholder in research;
- offered teachers co-control of the process;
- represented the tutor research-partner as facilitator of meaning-making and professional development;
- recognized that dialogue is an important precursor to making meaning from practice, which in turn, helps make teachers' tacit/implicit understanding explicit.

The questions derived from Table 8.1 that were used during reflective dialogues are shown in Table 8.2.

Table 8.2 Questions derived from the reflective dialogue theories

---

Intentions/purposes

- What were your intentions/aims/purposes in using this teaching strategy?
- How far were you successful in this?
- How did you come to this view?
- What did you expect the pupils' response to be?
- How/why was it different?
- What does this tell you?
- On what basis were your purposes formed?
- Did the context (school policy/time of year, etc.) influence your purposes?

Technical reflection

- What were you doing/aiming for here?
- How did you decide what outcomes were appropriate?
- Why did you choose this strategy/subject matter?
- What evidence/information did you base this choice on?
- Can you break down what you were doing into different aspects/elements
- What's significant about the different elements?
- How might different/individual children perceive/respond differently to the strategy/activities?
- How did your prior experience of the class influence your actions/thinking?
- How might your actions be improved?
- What kind of learning was promoted? How do you know that?

Self-awareness

- What were you thinking in this moment?
- What were you feeling in this moment?
- What are the roots of this feeling?
- What do you learn from viewing your self?

Perceptual awareness

- What were you aware of in the classroom at this moment?
- Where was your attention focused?
- What do you notice now that you weren't aware of during the lesson?
- What alternative foci might there be?

Dialogic reflection

- What assumptions are you making about teaching and learning?
- What are these assumptions based on – personal experience, teacher training, other professionals, school/professional culture, research evidence?
- What alternative actions/solutions/views might be appropriate?
- How might you decide which is appropriate to your situation?
- What source of new/alternative knowledge/ information might be useful?
- What values are represented in the teaching?
- What other values might be applicable to the teaching?

Critical reflection

- What does 'being professional' mean to you?
- What ethical/moral choices have been made here?
- What alternative professional/moral/ethical positions are there?
- What wider historical, socio-political, cultural forces/constraints apply here – interpersonal, classroom, school?
- How are pupils affected by your actions beyond the classroom/in subtle ways?
- What covert messages might be conveyed?
- Does the practice offer equality of opportunity? Is it just? Judged by what criteria?

By providing a repertoire of reflective questions (the sources of which will be examined in the next section), the aim was for teachers to enhance their reflective thinking skills. This questioning framework could also be used on an ongoing basis for professional development purposes. However, it is also possible that adherence to a 'rigid' framework might limit teachers' own inherent creativity, a point to which we will return later.

In summary, the VSRD process operates as follows:

1   Before involvement in the research partnership, the teacher is given a written explanation of the method.
2   The practitioner identifies about 20 minutes of practice exemplifying the use of interactive teaching strategies in the literacy hour; this can

be in one sequence or over a number of different episodes within the particular teaching sessions.

3 The research-partner takes video footage of this activity and the tape is handed immediately to the practitioner.

4 He or she then identifies (over the next few days) several key points or interesting passages from the footage taken.

5 At a mutually convenient time, the practitioner and the research-partner view – and review – the video together. The practitioner stops the tape at points of interest and, from the framework of reflective questions, selects a question with which to examine the action. If in the early stages the practitioner finds difficulty in selecting appropriate stimuli, the research-partner models the questioning and response process.

As the VSRD process involved a number of meetings over several months, the research-partners also set up to three action points – ideas on potential changes or adaptations to practice intended to bring about improvement. These, in themselves, formed the basis of the subsequent VSRD.

From the above description, one can see how video-stimulated reflective dialogue might fulfil all or some of the following purposes:

- to bring to the surface practitioners' personal knowledge and professional theories;
- to highlight the assumptions practitioners make in their thinking about teaching;
- to help practitioners critique their own thinking and practice;
- to provide a model of reflective practice and to encourage practitioners to think reflectively;
- to develop practitioners' awareness of their learners and of themselves as practitioners;
- to support developments in practice;
- to provide practitioners with meta-cognitive opportunities – that is, opportunities to think about their own thinking processes in relation to their teaching.

The theoretical background to reflective dialogues

The VSRD method draws upon various established methodological arenas, in particular action research, stimulated recall, cognitive interviewing, reflective and evidence-informed practice. Video-stimulated reflective dialogues also build upon a growing body of educational literature focusing on the use and efficacy of the combination of video evidence and professional dialogue as research methods. The reflective questions above were specifically based on the conceptual framework of reflective thinking developed by Hatton and Smith (1995), which, in turn, was rooted in the work of Habermas (1973).

The aims of action research, as advocated by such eminent scholars as Stenhouse (1985) and Carr and Kemmis (1986), are three-fold:

- to improve practice;
- to improve practitioners' understanding of practice; and
- to improve the context in which practice occurs.

Reflective dialogues are aligned with action research in all these aims and in the ethical position that practitioners should guide this process.

The method also has similarities with processes followed in interpersonal process recall (Kagan 1979) used for training mental health professionals. In interpersonal process recall, an 'inquirer' guides professionals or students via a given set of prompts as they review a video- or audio-recorded session with clients or colleagues. Various research studies have reported the benefits of this process. Reflective dialogue is, however, different from interpersonal process recall in one crucial detail – it is the practitioner who controls the focus and pace of the prompts, rather than their researcher-partner.

Responses of SPRINT teachers to reflective dialogue

One might imagine that the VSRD process could be intrusive and challenging. What was the reaction of those involved? What pitfalls and benefits were described? As indicated previously, 15 focus teachers were involved. With their research-partners, they were engaged in three reflective dialogues each over three terms. These teachers linked several aspects of professional development to the use of video and reflective dialogues, including:

- enhancement of awareness of classroom practice;
- developments in their thinking and reflection about interactive teaching;
- enhancement of self-awareness;
- greater awareness of the dynamics of classroom interactions;
- greater awareness of the learners.

Many aspects of the project outcomes were informed by the video-stimulated reflective dialogues, including the typology (see Chapters 4 and 5) and the case studies of teachers that are included throughout this book. Above all, the reflective dialogues gave us qualitative data to support and triangulate the quantitative data collected through the ORACLE and CBAM processes (see Chapters 2 and 6).

The following analysis of the video-stimulated reflective dialogues is based on responses to the final interview questions addressing the process itself at the end of the fieldwork. It mainly represents teachers' views but also includes views from the tutor research-partners.

Reflecting on reflective dialogues and interactive teaching

Although discomfort, anxiety and difficulty were expressed by many of the participants initially, all 15 teachers were ultimately positive about the use of video and professional dialogue (even those who initially described themselves as 'terrified' by the prospect). One teacher, Kylie, was extremely uneasy about the reflective dialogues and unsure about the various feelings that surfaced throughout the project. She was very committed to collaborative learning and felt that the reflective dialogue had called into question much of her educational philosophy and practice. Although she was highly sceptical about the National Literacy Strategy and had considered leaving teaching altogether at the time of its introduction, she attended the final teacher conference to express her view that although the process had been extremely uncomfortable, with the benefit of six months hindsight she realized that the video-stimulated reflective dialogue had been an important and powerful learning experience for her. Many teachers felt that the combination of video evidence and structured professional dialogue was a useful professional development tool, and some of the schools involved decided to encourage staff to use video as part of their continuing professional development programme.

Reflective dialogues were considered variously to be 'enjoyable', 'very useful', 'a very good tool', 'helpful', 'a valuable resource', very good' and 'interesting'. David said, 'Reflective dialogues, well, they've just been wonderful'. Teachers' evaluations endorsed the view that the reflective dialogues had enhanced self-awareness, refined insights into classroom practice, supported recognition of the dynamics of classroom interactions and prompted changes in thinking. How far these were apparent in practice by the end of the project are discussed below.

Impact on teachers' awareness

The following comment from Kylie shows how viewing the video helped modify her perspectives and revealed the nature of one difficulty in her classroom:

> When I watched [the video], I began to feel sorry for *me*! I thought, 'You mad woman, you're running about from table to table', you know. You're trying to listen to everyone's conversation; you can't possibly do it, and then when they've finished, they're 'acting up' because they've finished and you're not ready for them because you're . . . trying to help someone with some sums.

When asked in the final interview about specific changes she had noted in her practice, Dawn linked changes with the reflective dialogues.

> Interviewer: Can you actually think back to what prompted the changes?' [teacher contact with pair/small group work and peer tutoring]
> Dawn: I think really it is probably the reflective dialogues. To actually see my own practice and then to discuss it with you has changed the way I view things.

Interesting here is the use of the word 'view'. Dawn's comment suggests that changes in practice are associated with changes in awareness or a perspective shift. However, the visual metaphor may not imply a change in perceptual awareness, so much as a new way of constructing her understanding of what is happening in the classroom. David also spoke about being more 'lucid' and having more clarity in his practice, and related this to the support offered by his research-partner: 'You've enabled me to be clearer in what's going on in my class, and as part of an inclusion project, you need clarity. You need someone to keep you focused or to just, you know, remind you of certain things'.

Geraldine talked about her awareness of the impact of literacy hour objectives on the needs of children, as we saw in the opening comments to this chapter. These remarks highlight how the opportunity to review practice in combination with dialogue facilitated shifts in perspective that motivated the SPRINT focus teachers to reconsider their practice.

Impact on teachers' understanding and thinking

As we saw in earlier chapters, several teachers made substantive shifts in their conceptualizations of interactive teaching. In several cases, they acknowledged their debt to the VSRD process for enabling them to examine their views. Ewan noted how his involvement in the reflective dialogues had encouraged him to think about interactive teaching for the first time: 'I think my attitude [before] was one of, to be honest, not even thinking about it really'. Paula added, 'It gets you to think about your own practice. How can I make it better? It gets you to reflect on different parts of your teaching, doesn't it?' Paula also talked about increased confidence in her practice.

Kylie noted that she was able to take something positive from a lesson that she had considered unproductive: 'I found it [VSRD] helpful actually. The second video that we did which was the lesson I thought . . . was the 'lesson from hell' really. When I actually watched it, it wasn't as bad as I thought it was and it was useful to *see* that because you don't often get the chance'. Dawn added:

> It is very useful to see yourself actually teaching but then to look at it again with the reflective dialogue criteria it really has made me so more aware of what I am doing, what I could be doing and what I am not doing and with your support things that you feel I am doing well or could develop further.

An enhancement in the reflection upon her practice seems to be implicit in this comment, although we are unclear whether this continued after the project. Additionally, unlike some teachers, Dawn's professional thinking was not confined to the pupils. She also reflected on her own practice, its aims, intentions and reasoning. Thus, Dawn demonstrated that video-stimulated reflective dialogue had helped her to reflect at more sophisticated levels of reflection (Hatton and Smith 1995). In the following remark, she demonstrates reflection on the tacit reasons for practice and the implications of holding only partial perspectives on classroom dynamics:

> To actually view it objectively, it was so useful, even just from a classroom management point of view . . . and then moving onto what am I actually doing? What was I trying to do there? What was my reasoning behind that bit? To see the children's reactions, because you think you can see them all but obviously you can't, you miss some at some times, so that has been really useful.

Impact on teachers' practice

A fundamental aim of the SPRINT Project was to facilitate development of teachers' practice in the literacy hour. No significant changes were found in the focus teachers' (about 650 observations) use of questions and statements, or task and routine interactions, but there were significant changes in the audience categories. Reductions in one-to-one interactions and group audience settings were replaced by increased use of 'individual for class' and whole-class audience. The results for comparison teachers appeared to reflect moves in the opposite direction; that is, more individual and group audience. There was a non-significant increase in focus teachers' encouragement of extended pupil responses to questions.

It was perhaps optimistic to identify substantive changes in such a short time and, as described in Chapter 2, measurable changes in attitude were only just evident. The failure to find significant effects among the focus teachers might be explained by the short time-scale and also by their differing personal aims. Thus, if teacher A attempted to increase 'broad pupil participation' across the whole class, whereas teacher B was concentrating on developing reciprocal communication and meaning-making with a few pupils, the observed effects would counteract each other in a pooled data set. However, individual changes were found in practice, based on the evidence of teachers' practical application of action points. These issues continue to be explored by the SPRINT team.

Opportunity for reflection

Several teachers valued the opportunity that the video-stimulated reflective dialogues provided for thinking about their practice and some teachers wanted more time for reflection: 'It's been quite nice to be videoed and you can literally have a chance to reflect on what you've done'. Several teachers suggested that there was little time in the usual hectic world of the primary phase teacher for reflection. David talked about the dialogue with his research-partner making him stop, think and unpick his own thinking. It might be argued that, in primary teaching, taking (or indeed having) the opportunity for reflection has been perhaps one casualty of recent reforms and initiatives. Paula commented, 'You just don't do it 'cause you just don't have the time to do it. And [the SPRINT Project] gave me the time to reflect on [my practice] really'.

Katrina noted the significance of the timing of the reflective dialogues. Certain stages of the year and term were 'horrendous' for finding appropriate time for videoing and dialogue. This highlights the point that the time-tabling of the process, like other focused professional development, needs to be undertaken with the needs of the teacher, their pupils and colleagues in mind. The pragmatic concerns about the availability of time and space for the reflective process are under-explored in the professional development literature (but see Elliott 1991: 66–7). Eraut (1994) and van Manen (1995) both recognize the importance for teachers of the availability of time, or lack of it, in facilitating reflective practice. However, writers in the field have tended to avoid the pragmatic requirements of this aspect of reflection. The use of video alongside a framework for a reflective dialogue, as exemplified in the SPRINT Project, can provide a useful tool for teachers. This is especially true in busy school contexts where ongoing contact with mentors or advisors is problematic.

The tutor-researchers' views on the VSRD method

Six higher education tutors and two researchers (both teachers) constituted the research-partners and all reported their growing allegiance to the process. Shedding their 'normal' role of raising open-ended questions (usually with initial teacher training – ITT – students) was difficult but not impossible and all agreed that the teachers had a greater autonomy over the process of reflection that encouraged metacognition. In the opinion of the higher education research-partners, the reflective dialogues resulted in shared rich data that constituted a 'comfortable' challenge for both partners and also increased the learning of both.

The tutors were uncertain about the level of 'detachment' or otherwise required to conduct a fully effective reflective dialogue and about the nature of discussions that were specifically focused on one behaviour – interactive teaching – as opposed to teaching in general. The framework of reflective questions (as outlined above) was seen by the tutor research-partners on the one hand as a useful scaffold, but on the other as rather too detailed. The least experienced tutor-researchers found that the breadth of questions tended to divert their attention from the actual dialogue with the teacher partner.

Most of the tutor research-partners held their own ideas about what constituted interactive teaching and when such aspects were not included by teachers in their responses, the tutor research-partners reported a tendency to try to draw the teachers' reflection in specific directions. They recognized that they needed to resist focusing only on those questions that might bring out what they themselves wanted to hear rather than a balanced exploration of interactive teaching. Some confusion was also expressed by tutor research-partners as to the level of 'detachment' required to conduct a fully effective reflective dialogue. Initially, the teachers had asked their tutor research-partners to present 'the right answer'. The tutor research-partners were confused about the appropriate response to these questions, but as readers can imagine, we all developed our skills significantly over a period of time (see Chapter 10). Although they were aware of several perspectives on 'interactive' practice, they remained uncertain about the 'validity' of research data if their views about interactive practice influenced the teachers. This, perhaps, reflected insecurity in the role of the video-stimulated reflective dialogues as an 'intervention' strategy and the two-way nature of the dialogue, as compared with the project interviews that were designed to ascertain teachers' initial and final conceptualizations of interactive teaching. The Concerns-Based Adoption Model (CBAM) offered a framework of teacher development and advice on appropriate interventions (see Chapter 2). This advocated offering teachers a range of applicable 'knowledge or information' about the innovation in question when asked. This problem was perhaps exacerbated by the fact that interactive practice had been so poorly defined in the teacher-focused literature, and the tutor research-partners felt poorly qualified to offer what they perceived as their own personal knowledge rather than academically validated perspectives.

Tutors experienced challenges in operating in a changed role, in that most were used to supporting student teachers on school-based placements. They were, therefore, like the teachers, used to analysing others' 'teaching' behaviours rather than their own. Tutors had to shed their 'normal' role of raising open-ended questions, which were nevertheless intended to 'lead' a (student) respondent in certain directions. This proved difficult to achieve. Yet, as a group, we were adamant that the tutor-researchers must allow the teachers maximum autonomy over the process of reflection. This parallel-partner relationship with the teachers meant that the tutors also reported some conflict between being the camera holder – and, therefore, having some measure of control over what was photographed at what time – and trying to be genuinely open in exploring different facets of interaction identified by the teachers. Interestingly, tutors and teachers rarely agreed on the questions that should be raised about the video clips of interactive teaching.

As researchers we had set the agenda and in effect controlled the focus of interactive teaching. While teachers who were involved had an interest in the area, the original idea came from us and, at any time, the teachers could have called a halt. The fact that they didn't might, in itself, say something about the VSRD process and the shifting controls. One area for development of the VSRD process is in encouraging participants to add to, or re-define, the framework of reflective questions. As mentioned above, the framework offered a particular theoretical perspective. Offering participants the opportunity to re-define this or develop their own would be a natural progression towards a more truly equitable collaboration. This, of course, leaves aside the problem of finding the time to devote to such an exercise.

Summary

What must by now have struck readers, as it did the tutor research-partners, are the similarities between the VSRD process and dimensions of interactive teaching as outlined in Chapters 4 and 5 – in other words, the medium was in itself the message! The process also brought to mind the notion of 'scaffolding' as a pedagogic tool within the VSRD process because, as researchers, we felt that we were often working from the basis of teachers' zone of proximal development (Vygotsky 1978). It also provided a 'comfortable challenge' (as pointed out by Merry 1998) for both partners from which both were able to learn about interactive teaching and pedagogic practices. The two-way process of posing and responding to questions is very rare in research interview contexts but, as we have seen above, led to shared, rich data becoming available to support deeper analysis and interpretation. A bonus to the whole process would appear to be that, once practitioners become familiar with the process, they can readily become an advocate and a supporter for other colleagues, and hence the process can be cascaded efficiently through an entire group of teachers who wish to analyse dimensions of their own practice.

We began this project with a focus on interactive teaching within the literacy hour. As we have seen thus far, the project has encompassed much more, particularly in relation to teachers' reflections and, with them, dilemmas and confusions. In chapter 9, we return to the issue of literacy teaching and to some of the conflicts felt by SPRINT teachers, expressed during interviews and reflective dialogues, in fulfilling the demands of the NLS.

9 Can we talk about that later?

The tensions and conflicts of teaching interactively in the literacy hour

Eve English, Jane Hislam and Linda Hargreaves

Introduction

Ellen, an experienced SPRINT Project teacher, reflected on some of her frustrations in teaching the literacy hour:

> We're just trying to keep them going, trying to achieve our learning objectives, trying to actually work through the strategy – they [the children] may come in with something exciting that happened, or whatever, that they are desperate to actually share with you and sometimes it sounds very cruel, but sometimes you have to say, 'Can we talk about that later?', because you're very aware of your timetable.

This chapter explores some of the dilemmas facing teachers as they have tried to act upon the pedagogical advice, sometimes contradictory, contained within the National Literacy Strategy (DfEE 1998). English (2000) reported teachers' perceptions of the changes to their practice in the teaching of reading in the last decade. Here, however, we examine evidence of teachers' confusion as they have been making changes, attempting to reconcile the requirement for 'high quality oral work' and 'interactive teaching [where] pupils' contributions are encouraged, expected and extended' with the parallel requirement for 'well-paced lessons' and 'a sense of urgency, driven by the need to make progress' (DfEE 1998: 8).

The National Literacy Strategy was introduced into schools in September 1998 as a non-statutory but strongly recommended programme with the explicit intention of raising standards of literacy nationally:

> Our presumption will be that the approach to teaching we set out, based on the National Literacy Project (NLP), will be adopted by every school unless a school can demonstrate, through its literacy action plan and schemes of work and its performance in National Curriculum (NC) Key Stage tests, that the approach it has adopted is at least as effective.
>
> (DfEE 1997: 19)

The NLS Framework for Teaching (DfEE 1998) prescribes objectives for the teaching of literacy and sets down how these objectives are supposed to be achieved in terms of classroom management and organization. The first section of the framework contains a rationale that describes successful teaching as being:

- *discursive* – characterized by high-quality oral work;
- *interactive* – pupils' contributions are encouraged, expected and extended;
- *well-paced* – there is a sense of urgency, driven by the need to make progress and succeed;
- *confident* – teachers have a clear understanding of the objectives;
- *ambitious* – there is optimism about and high expectations of success.

(DfEE 1998: 8)

Contradictions are apparent here, notably between the second and third characteristics. Although the aim of 'high quality oral work' and 'interactive teaching (where) pupils' contributions are encouraged, expected and extended' are compatible, they appear to be in conflict with the recommendation for 'well-paced lessons' with 'a sense of urgency, driven by the need to make progress'.

The beginnings of a rationale for interactive teaching appeared as part of a review of relevant research underpinning the literacy hour (Beard 1999). This retrospective review described how the National Literacy Strategy had drawn on several strategies from school effectiveness research, including, for example, the use of direct, interactive teaching with an emphasis on higher-order questioning and discussion. At this time, there was still little practical advice on the nature of interactive teaching or how teachers should use it. The first set of 'NLS fliers' in 1999 gave more specific and practical guidance on teaching strategies, including the use of interactive teaching. These were distributed by local education authorities, whose differing distribution criteria meant that, at the time of our research, these fliers had been received by some but not all of our teachers. The first flier, 'Talking in class' (DfEE 1999a), suggested that teachers should stay open to unexpected ideas, use pupils' answers, show an interest in what children think (and not just what they know), ask for clarification of an answer, encourage pupils to elaborate on their answers and let what children say affect the course of the discussion, but 'only as long as you don't lose sight of the objectives' (DfEE 1999a: 4). Thus this flier advocated interactive teaching in which children's contributions were to be encouraged, *on condition* that they did not interfere with the achievement of the learning objectives.

The second flier, 'Engaging all pupils' (DfEE 1999b), provided an explicit description of interactive teaching and outlined four interactive teaching techniques: namely, 'time-out', 'show me', 'get up and go' and 'drama'. It stated that 'whole class teaching should involve plenty of interactivity, with a balance of contributions from teacher and pupils' (p. 1). In 'time-out', for example, it is recommended that children are allowed 30 seconds to gather their thoughts, perhaps in discussion with a partner, before responding to a teacher's question. This, too, was accompanied by a cautionary note: 'Beware though – if overused, Time Out can reduce the pace of teaching. And it can be abused as an opportunity to gossip!' (DfEE 1999b: 1). Similarly, a highlighted section entitled 'Interactive Techniques' exhorts teachers to 'Choose the technique because it serves the objective, not for cosmetic reasons' (p. 4). In sum, the use of these techniques, which might increase pupil contributions, was discouraged if they were likely to limit the meeting of short-term objectives.

Together with written advice and guidance for teachers, the Office for Standards in Education (OfSTED 1997) produced a series of videos of NLS practice in which teachers demonstrated 'well-structured lessons' with 'high expectations, resulting in a good pace and challenging work' (p. 1 of 'Teacher notes') and a 'strong emphasis on *instruction* with intensive teacher–pupil interaction' (p. 5). These training videos gave a vivid visual modelling of literacy teaching through rapid, intensive question-and-answer sessions and, viewed by a large section of the profession, probably exerted a much greater impact on classroom practice than any reading of the NLS literature could.

This chapter focuses specifically on whether teachers spontaneously perceived the possible conflicts within the NLS advice and, if they did, whether this affected their practice. We were interested also in whether the National Literacy Strategy has had a discernible effect on teacher–pupil interaction since its introduction.

In previous chapters, we have examined teachers' classroom practice, concerns about and conceptualization of interactive teaching. Here we bring together the perceptions of conflict and sense of confusion expressed by teachers during their interviews and reflective dialogues. These parts of the research process had allowed teachers to raise their own concerns about interactive teaching as revealed by their practice. The teachers were not specifically prompted by their research-partners to comment on, for example, conflicts between 'interactive teaching' and meeting teaching objectives. These issues have emerged through examination of the data.

In the following section, we show how four teachers – Geraldine, Kathleen, Ellen and Kelly – identified the dilemmas posed by the literacy strategy and gradually changed their practice or their attitudes to ease the resultant tension.

The teachers

Geraldine

Geraldine, in her second year of teaching, was one of the least experienced teachers in the sample. She taught a year 6 class and had responsibility in her school for history and geography. Geraldine was enthusiastic from the outset about her involvement with the SPRINT Project and was happy to articulate her views both in the interviews and reflective dialogues in a confident and assured manner. She showed no reluctance whatsoever at being filmed in action and welcomed the whole process of viewing the video and engaging in reflective dialogue.

In her first reflective dialogue, however, Geraldine became aware of what she described as her teaching 'pace'. By this she appeared to mean the energy and speed with which all her teaching, her movement around the classroom and even her speech took place. Without prompting, she selected this as a target and wrote for herself: 'PACE – speed of delivery – allow space/time for pupils to think and answer questions/respond to ideas. Time allowed for unexpected input by pupils'.

In considering what she meant by 'allowing space', she wondered whether smaller groups might facilitate this more. Whole-class teaching suited her and she was clearly pleased with aspects of her own performance, remarking on how surprised and interested she was to observe herself. She described herself as 'very physically present in the classroom'. She drew attention in particular to the way she moved around the classroom, used gesture, eye contact and an animated tone of voice. She felt that all of these contributed to a 'repertoire' of interactive behaviour, which were referred to in the reflective dialogue as 'interactive prompts', because they appeared to act as signals to the pupils that they were invited to respond in the whole-class setting. However, other aspects of the video caused her concern. She said, 'I need to slow down my speech'. She felt that by allowing more time for pupils to talk she would be able to involve children more fully. In particular, she identified pupils who might not be able to follow the speed of her talk and the language that she deliberately pitched at an 'adult level', for example, in her use of linguistic terminology. Subsequent discussion in the reflective dialogue focused on how Geraldine might vary the patterns of discourse in the classroom, which were seen to be almost exclusively of the initiation → response → feedback (IRF) type.

Geraldine was not alone in raising concerns about pace. In other interviews teachers raised similar concerns. Dawn, for example, in her initial interview, remarked: 'It is very difficult to use interactive teaching with children with behavioural difficulties – the pace of the lesson is difficult to sustain – difficult to sustain all pupils' attention – difficult to give them all a fair chance'. Another teacher's interpretation was that 'They were saying it meant teachers being very up front – doing delivery teaching, whereas you can teach in other ways'.

Geraldine, however, appeared to be very comfortable with the idea of 'up front' delivery and, although other strategies, such as the use of talk-partners, were discussed, it was noticeable that in the next recorded lesson none of these were adopted and the IRF pattern remained dominant. Interestingly, despite this, Geraldine did not perceive that the literacy hour created any conflict between her wish to involve all 35 of her pupils, giving them space to think and the need to move at speed or to deliver the objectives. In all her interviews and discussions, she remained positive that the National Literacy Strategy allowed her to work as she would anyway wish to teach. Instead, she appeared to see the problem as one of 'personal style'. The video and reflective dialogue had raised her awareness of this classroom style, which she had never noticed in her practice before.

Unfortunately, for reasons beyond her control, Geraldine withdrew from the project before the final round of observations, but we can compare her initial teaching profile with the pooled Key Stage 2 teachers' first set of observation data, as shown in Figure 9.1. Geraldine's profile differs from the round 1 norm in two ways. First is her frequent use of higher-order cognitive inter-

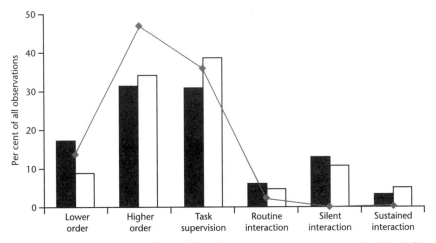

Figure 9.1 Key Stage 2 first (■) and final (□) literacy hour profiles and Geraldine's first round profile (◆).

actions – that is, those which involve explanations, problems or new ideas. Second is the complete absence of any 'silent' or 'no interaction' categories. Silent interaction refers to interactions without any conversational components, such as marking, reading aloud (including reading in chorus from a 'big book') or demonstrating without a spoken component. In other words, Geraldine was interacting at speed for every moment of the 20-minute video. Geraldine's lesson was devoted to planning for poetry writing and involved creativity rather than recall, hence the unusually high frequency of higher-order interactions in her profile. The lesson began with a whole-class section, in which Geraldine was giving the children ideas for what they might do. She then moved to using open-ended questions (defined as questions to which the teacher accepts more than one answer) after the children had moved to their tables and were brainstorming rhyming words. At this stage, Geraldine was interacting on a one-to-one basis with them. The observation profile corroborates Geraldine's reflective comments about the pace of her teaching as she responded to individuals. She used no silent interaction, but appeared to be involved in verbal interaction almost every second of the 20 minutes. It is not surprising that she was impressed by her 'teaching pace'.

Kathleen

We turn now to consider Kathleen, who taught a year 1 class in a high achieving school for children aged 5–7 years. She was a mature, recent entrant to the profession, and was a highly conscientious teacher who felt concerned to do everything demanded of her. Despite her school's good achievement record, Kathleen and her colleagues were constantly aware of pressure from parents for their children to succeed. The school's response was to plan meticulously around clear objectives in every aspect of the curriculum. The teaching was 'ambitious' in that the literacy objectives were those set for the next year group. At the time of the first interview and for most of the project, Kathleen had not seen the NLS fliers but had attended all the initial NLS training.

Kathleen identified 'time' as a critical issue and explicitly voiced her concerns about what she saw as mixed messages being given by the National Literacy Strategy. She was very positive about the possibilities of interactive teaching and wanted to comply with the NLS recommendation to develop interactive teaching. She felt that it could encourage children to 'become more confident, to clarify their learning'. At the same time, however (and with uncanny closeness to the wording quoted earlier of flier 1, which had not been distributed to KS1 schools in her authority), she was concerned that 'it might encourage idle chit chat', which would interfere with the achievement of the 'learning objectives that [teachers] must cover'. She felt that, 'In an ideal world, interaction is good but I don't always have the time'.

Even when Kathleen felt she had given adequate time for the children to talk to partners and reflect on part of a lesson, 'interacting with one another and sharing their thoughts . . . [she found that] when I look at it on video, I don't think I've given them time to fulfil that activity . . . I think I have done it too quickly, I haven't given them time, I am forever thinking of pace'. Kathleen was not alone in her thinking. Katrina, a KS2 teacher also expressed concern about the need to extend pupil thinking:

> If it's sort of a one-word response from the child, it has to be the right response, then to me that isn't interactive teaching . . . We've got such a pressure of time that we're just waiting for the right answer because it's much quicker to go on to the next page, and you don't always have time to go through explanations.

Kathleen, however, began to relax about interactive teaching after ascertaining that her class had already met most of the objectives. Her reflective dialogues had led to two consciously implemented strategies to allow children more time. The first was to import a method from the National Numeracy Strategy and ask children to explain their strategies for remembering how to spell certain words. She thus introduced a meta-cognitive dimension in her class of 6-year-olds. Secondly, again as a result of observing the children's reactions in her videos, she made a point of allowing children a couple of minutes to 'settle' into their group work before joining her target group. This she felt enabled them to think about their tasks without the initial counter-productive pressure of her presence. In her final interview, she expressed her feeling that it was perhaps more important to give the children more time to reflect and to respond: 'to listen to what someone's got to say [instead of] cutting them off straight away [as if to say], "Yes, that's the answer I want but I'll finish it off for you". That's what I felt I was doing'.

Kathleen was concerned about responding to children's needs, not only intellectually, but also socially and developmentally, and she worried about whether the needs of the 5-year-olds in her class were being met appropriately. She commented during the reflective dialogue:

> I had asked S. a question. I had asked him to respond to a question, which he did do but he didn't do it correctly. He jumped ahead and then I asked someone else to help him and I noticed that I didn't go back to S. I left S. in limbo and . . . so I noticed there I interacted with S. and then I just abandoned him and moved, which is quite bad really and it's giving out the wrong vibes altogether, kind of, 'yes I'll listen to you for a bit, but I'm not coming back to you'.

Despite Kathleen's concerns, her initial and final observation profiles (see Figure 9.2) reflected changes in her practice that she was able to meet her own

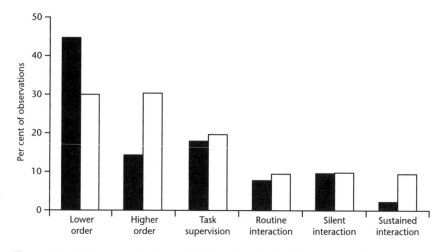

Figure 9.2   Change in individual profiles: Kathleen. ■, first literacy profile; □, final literacy hour profile.

pedagogical teaching objectives and allow children time to think and respond. Her profile shows considerable use of sustained interactions. Teacher–pupil interactions sustained beyond 25 seconds are unusual (see Galton *et al.* 1999), but Kathleen's use of sustained interactions in her final video were at the extreme end of the range for the project's Key Stage 1 teachers (see Figure 9.3). In addition, she had reduced the use of low cognitive level (simple recall) interactions and increased her use of higher-order interactions to be well above the norm for the KS1 teachers. Her pupils had the highest frequency of extended responses (over 10 words) in either key stage. These amounted to 20 per cent of observations in her final video. Kathleen's informal comments after the lesson, concerning what she had learned about the children's thinking, showed the value of the exercise. One 6-year-old had needed over 90 seconds to explain the relative complexity of attempting a word as a whole, 'whereabouts in half', as he put it, the task was relatively simple. It was unusual for him to volunteer to answer questions. Thus Kathleen, by asking the children *how* they tried to remember their spellings and *giving them time to reply*, instead of merely asking them to spell the words, was asking more challenging questions and engaging the children in what we defined as higher-order thinking.

However, we are left with important questions. Would Kathleen have had the confidence to do this if her class had not already met their assigned learning objectives? Would the development of children's thinking, under-standing and oracy have been compromised by seeking to meet concrete short-term objectives? We turn now to a teacher whose main concerns were

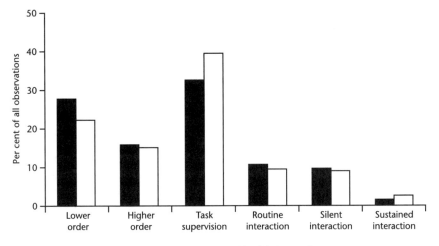

Figure 9.3 Key Stage 1 literacy hour first (■) and final (□) rounds.

to ensure broad participation and protect children's social and emotional personas.

Ellen

Ellen, a teacher with over 20 years teaching experience, felt that the National Literacy Strategy was prescriptive and was acutely aware that learning objectives had to be delivered in a limited amount of time. This, she felt, precluded the kind of interaction with her class that had been possible in the past. She was deputy head of a high-achieving infant school where she taught 5- to 6-year-olds. Although the catchment area from which the school drew was similar to that of Kathleen's school, there was less evidence of the high level of parental pressure in Ellen's school. Like Kathleen, Ellen had received all of the early NLS training but had not seen the NLS fliers at the time of the project.

Ellen stated, perhaps more clearly than anyone, her frustration with what seemed to her to be conflicting requirements. She expressed concerns about meeting the objectives within a limited time while still encouraging the children to contribute what was relevant and meaningful to them. Her concerns appear to epitomize how difficult it is to put into practice the recommendation in flier 1 (DfEE 1999a) to 'let what the children say affect the course of the discussion as long as you don't lose sight of the objectives'. Ellen said, 'I am trying to give opportunities for interactive teaching within the literacy strategy, although I do feel again that time's ticking on and that . . . you've got your learning objective'. She went on to describe her policy when a child wanted to pursue a dialogue that was moving away from the identified learning objective:

> I think it has to be pursued if the effect of pursuing it is to the benefit of the children in the class. If it is something that really you can see as getting absolutely nowhere I think you just . . . say that was wonderful or whatever, but perhaps actually pursue it at another time so you don't lose the impact.

The effects of the reflective dialogues on Ellen had been to help her feel more relaxed about the literacy strategy. She had reconciled her initial concerns by allowing limited flexibility within the framework, while, at the same time, emphasizing the importance of the hour and the need to sustain the pace:

> The literacy hour is not a literacy hour and a half, so it still has to be a pacy hour session . . . I don't think I am unduly aggrieved if perhaps ten minutes goes into 13 minutes in one session because I may be able to catch up on the time, but I do feel the hour is critical; it is an hour not an hour and a half. So I think, yes, the interaction is great . . . but you have to watch it.

The relative lack of change in Ellen's interaction profile (Figure 9.4) can be explained in part by her change of attitude and in part by her concerns to ensure broad participation and foster children's self-esteem. She made a

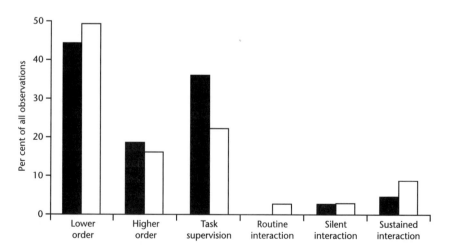

Figure 9.4 Change in individual profiles: Ellen. ■, first literacy profile; □, final literacy hour profile.

point of naming children to answer so that responses were not restricted to the most eager children. Her frequent use of lower cognitive, simple recall interactions (twice the mean KS1 level) was more likely to ensure success for the targeted child. At the same time, perhaps the considerable reduction in her task supervision interactions (telling children what to do) allowed time for longer responses from the children. In both her first and final literacy hour videos, 9 per cent of observations involved medium length responses of 5–10 words, but in the final round an additional 5 per cent were responses of over 10 words.

Kelly

Kelly, a year 2 teacher with more than 20 years experience, was the literacy coordinator for her school. She had begun her working career as a speech therapist but had taken to her teaching career, especially the teaching of English, with great enthusiasm. She was a comparison teacher within the context of the research and so did not participate in the video-stimulated reflective dialogues. On the other hand, she expressed concern in her first interview about the conflict she felt, as a literacy coordinator who had to advocate to her colleagues a strategy with which she was uncomfortable. In this interview, Kelly described her perceptions of interactive teaching as being when 'the children have an opportunity to contribute to the lesson spontaneously with their own ideas and those ideas should then be shaped and refined following interaction with either the teacher or other children in the class'. She was very clear about the difference between what was and what was not an interactive lesson:

> The one that's not is the one where the child is giving you the right answer that was in your head, the child who can finish your sentence, that sort of thing, whereas a truly interactive one I would regard as one that is actually progressing the learning and the child is maybe going to get it wrong and you're going to have some sort of opportunity.

She talked about her concern and frustration that her teaching was not as interactive as she would like it to be: 'I would dearly love to say that I was one of those marvellous teachers who manages to do everything, but I must say that I feel myself torn in many directions and continually frustrated by my ability to do it [interactive teaching]'. She felt 'happier with it' when she 'genuinely wanted to know what the children know at the moment . . . or genuinely want to know what they think', such as at the beginning of a science topic. Her frustration centred around the fact that '80 per cent of my time is spent in situations where there is a right answer and the children need to have it'. She went on: 'I feel utterly challenged by the concept of interactive teaching and I think that you end up either catering for one group's interactive needs and you have to disregard the rest or you just dispense with anything you think is interactive'.

The main constraints on her being able to teach in a more interactive way were the timetable and meeting objectives.

> your problem is the time it [interactive teaching] takes. You know, interactive teaching takes a lot longer than you modelling or you choosing a child that you know very well has got a very good idea to model. And there's the problem that maybe they won't get it right and then if they don't get it right, you have to do a big circuit to make sure they do get it right.

Although Kelly was not a focus teacher and so had not taken part in reflective dialogues throughout the year of the project, she was a teacher who considered her practice carefully and, by the final interview, she had come to a compromise about teaching interactively but meeting objectives at the same time: 'I think I am increasingly aware of a different type of interactive teaching in a way of meeting teachers' objectives or framework objectives – I am pleased with it, although it doesn't come close to the more basic ideal that I hold'. She described this change as moving from child initiation to interacting with a child's response: 'the teacher can interact with [the child's] response to move forward as opposed to the more idealistic notion of the initiation coming from

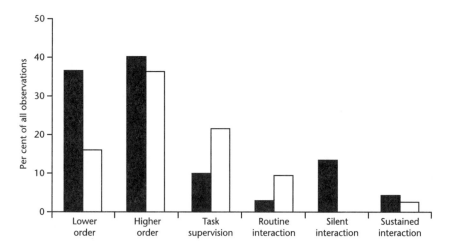

Figure 9.5 Change in individual profiles: Kelly. ■, first literacy profile; □, final literacy hour profile.

the child'. Kelly seemed to have taken a pragmatic approach to the challenge and frustrations that she had felt earlier in the year, but there was a sense of loss as she described the move away from her ideals.

Kelly's profile in Figure 9.5 shows a consistently high level of higher-order interactions (see the KS1 mean in Figure 9.3). Kelly reduced her use of lower-order interactions but increased her use of task supervision. In other words, since task supervision consisted overwhelmingly of statements, she was directing the children more, perhaps, to ensure that they achieved the objectives.

Conflict resolution or resigned compromise?

We have presented case studies of four teachers who found different ways to respond to the pedagogical dilemmas posed by the National Literacy Strategy. As we showed in Chapter 3, all of the SPRINT teachers were positive about interactive teaching and described its value and importance in terms of children's learning, yet over half of them revealed spontaneously their aware-ness of pedagogical conflicts associated with the literacy strategy. The focus teachers, however, were able, to varying extents, to articulate and resolve these dilemmas through the VSRD process. The constraints they recognized on being able to teach in an interactive way included the time available, the focus on identified learning objectives and the tension between teaching in which 'pupil responses are expected, encouraged and extended' and the demand that lessons should be 'well-paced – with a sense of urgency' (DfEE 1998: 8). The case study teachers appeared to see the use of interactive teaching as something of a luxury.

Kathleen permitted herself to implement strategies designed to extend pupil responses and increase higher-order interaction, only after ascertaining that the class had met most if its learning objectives. All four teachers, and others in our sample, acknowledged the value of interactive teaching, but felt that it should not get in the way of the pace and objectives of the lesson. Geraldine identified a need to 'give children more time', but did not see the contradictions between her style and her pedagogical aims. She was satisfied that her practice represented appropriate fast-paced interactive teaching. Had she completed the full set of reflective dialogues, she might have gone further in articulating a conflict. Kelly, a comparison rather than a focus teacher, also completed only initial and final reflective dialogues. Her period of unsupported reflection seems to have resulted in her compromising her ideals of what she initially saw as interactive teaching to ensure the meeting of NLS learning objectives. Ellen, whose profile was more typical of the KS1 teachers, completed the VSRD process and resolved her feeling that the literacy strategy denied the kinds of interaction she had encouraged before its introduction by allowing a margin of flexibility within its rigid time frame. She did not change her classroom practice significantly, however. Kathleen, having checked that she could afford to relax her pace, reflected critically and constructively on her teaching. By doing so, she not only increased her use of higher cognitive interactions, and allowed children more time to make extended responses to her questions, but also encouraged her class to engage in meta-cognitive activity.

As we saw in Chapter 6, the 'most interactive' sections of literacy hour teaching represented a transformation of the more typical, and seemingly 'fossilized', patterns of teacher–pupil interaction charted by Galton and colleagues' (1980, 1999) ORACLE studies, by raising the ratio of questions to statements from about one in four to one in two teacher utterances and by drastically reducing the use of silent interactions and periods of no interaction. As shown in Chapter 6, the time that teachers used to spend in silent inter-action, such as marking, reading a story, listening to readers; tidying up, setting up displays or doing routine administrative tasks, has been redistri-buted to time spent constantly talking and listening to children. This tells us that the pace of interactions, if not increased, was certainly relentless. While our observation system cannot record pace as 'utterances per minute', we can see plainly that if questions and statement have increased from 75 to 84 per cent of the time since the introduction of the National Literacy Strategy, then pace is likely to have increased as well. It is our impression also, that although the teachers had chosen the most interactive sections of the lessons, inter-action rates were remarkably high throughout the observed lessons. The increase in the questions to statements ratio has increased pupil participation rates, but as Ellen and others pointed out, persistent questioning, as one aspect of interactive teaching, doesn't always work for all children: 'Some children can actually become more withdrawn and don't actually like it. I think . . . you need to know your children'.

Our observations suggest that teachers had been very successful in making their literacy teaching more interactive. Pupil contributions were expected and encouraged twice as often as they were before the introduction of the National Literacy Strategy. The crux of the 'pace' versus interactive teaching dilemma, however, is rooted in whether pupils' contributions are 'extended' or whether they have been shortened by teaching that has 'a sense of urgency, driven by the need to make progress'. There is no doubt that Kathleen, Ellen and Kelly felt that they were forced to 'cut off' children's responses if they were taking too long to answer. As we saw in Kathleen's story, sustained interactions were rare, and had declined from 27 to 5 per cent of interactions in KS2 English compared with 1996 (Galton *et al.* 1999) and to only 2 per cent at Key Stage 1 during the literacy hour. The high level of sustained interaction in English lessons in 1996 included teachers listening, without interruption, to children read, an activity that has been changed considerably in nature by the literacy strategy. A final measure, related to the pace of interaction, is the length of pupil utterances. The more single utterances were extended, the more the pace would be slowed down. We found, however, that only about 10 per cent of observations included children's responses of more than three words and only 5 per cent were longer than 10 words. These figures contribute to the impression that the pace was rapid in most classes and that pupils' contributions were not 'extended'. In other words, as long as nine out of ten pupil contributions are of only two or three words in length, the literacy strategy's recommendation that successful teaching is 'discursive – characterised by high quality oral work' (DfEE 1998: 8) seems unlikely to be fulfilled. As Mroz *et al.* (2000: 389) pointed out, classroom discourse is unlikely to begin to 'resemble discussion . . . [where] . . . teachers interweave pupil initiations into the topics so as to promote thematic coherence and higher order thinking'.

Summary

In this chapter, we set out to determine whether teachers spontaneously perceived the potential conflicts in the NLS literature. Our initial interviews suggested that over half of them had noted the conflicts and felt confused by demands on them. Our observational data indicated that the effects of the National Literacy Strategy on practice have been to increase the rate of pupil contributions but reduce opportunities for extended interactions. The process of video-stimulated reflective dialogue allowed some of the teachers to identify their confusions, try to make sense of the NLS demands and refine their understanding and use of interactive teaching. Their unanimously positive attitudes towards the reflective dialogues and the intention, in some cases, to adopt the method within their schools, suggests that, over a longer period, the method would have helped Ellen, Geraldine and Kathleen to analyse their practice further.

Some key messages emerge from the perceptions and experiences of our four teachers and others within the sample. In an educational climate driven by inspection, test results and parents as customers, interactive teaching, in all forms suggested by the SPRINT teachers (but particularly those referred to in Chapter 5 which were concerned with understanding), was regarded as an optional extra, permissible once the learning objectives had been met.

All four teachers described here were ambitious for their pupils and critical of 'delivery modes' of teaching, but their awareness of their accountability to parents and anxiety to implement government-dictated strategies created tensions for them that made it difficult to hold to their pedagogical principles. All four remained firmly focused on the learning needs of their pupils. Geraldine and Ellen tried to resolve the issue by interpreting interactive teaching as the need to involve as many pupils as possible, and hence pace was not only justified but essential. Kelly extended her understanding of the meaning of 'objectives', while Kathleen actually changed her practice. They certainly perceived the conflicts, but resolved them only by devaluing their own values. Although their schools might have maintained or improved their SAT results and satisfied the parents, fulfilment of these short-term goals are unlikely to satisfy the SPRINT teachers, in particular those like Kathleen and Kelly, or David and Katrina, who challenged children's understanding and sought longer-term, deeper level outcomes. As Pollard (2001) said in his 'fuzzy generalisation' from the apocalyptically named Primary Assessment Curriculum and Experience (PACE) Project, 'If teachers are strongly con-strained in their professional work, they are likely to become disenchanted and this probably affects recruitment and retention' (p. 16). Referring to research carried out before the imposition of the National Literacy and Numeracy Strategies, he continued: 'where the individual teacher, or the school as a whole, lacked the confidence to engage in the "creative mediation" of external policy directives, or where individual or personal circumstances made this difficult, the picture was likely to be one of conflict, stress and disillusion' (p. 18). The PACE Project identified confidence as a crucial factor in combating these perils. We would like to argue that the SPRINT teachers' professional conflicts were at least reduced by the feedback from the observa-tions and the opportunity, through the reflective dialogues, to engage in a form of 'interactive peer tutoring' with their research partners.

Note

Parts of this chapter are based on work published in the *Cambridge Journal of Education*, 32(1): 9–26.

10 Interactive teaching
Digging even deeper into meanings

Janet Moyles, Linda Hargreaves and Roger Merry

Introduction

As will have become evident throughout this book, the processes of the SPRINT research have, in themselves, been an interactive journey. We have been struck by the parallel processes in which we have engaged while trying to engage teachers interactively and about interaction. What we were asking teachers to do in their practice, we were also doing, that is interacting with 'learners' – in the case of teachers, with children and, in the case of researchers, with their teacher research-partners. The intention was that all those involved should learn through interaction about interaction and its effects upon learners and teachers. Just as teachers try to understand children by empathizing with their ways of learning, so we were trying to 'see inside' the teachers' heads to understand better their perceptions and approaches to interaction. Throughout the book, we have tried also to interact with you, the readers, to convey to you our enthusiasm for the research, its processes, findings and close relationship to primary classroom practices.

The research project was not without its unforeseen challenges in other ways: foot and mouth disease restrictions at that time, in parts of North Yorkshire and County Durham, restricted not only the movement of cattle, but also the movement of the research team, rendering attendance at some meetings almost impossible. Half-way through the project, two of the co-directors were promoted to posts in other institutions with consequent challenges to communication as two participating institutions became four, and meetings demanded even more geographical flexibility and tolerance. The strength of the team, however, and their commitment to each other and to the project meant we continued with unabated enthusiasm – most of the time!

In this final chapter, we first present a summary of the research findings to bring the whole picture into view for readers. Then, we suggest several implications of the research for policy-makers and politicians, teachers and

their professional development and those related to extending and furthering
the SPRINT research. We also introduce one more concept, that of the tutor-
researchers' own professional development in relation to the project, as yet an
unrevealed objective of the research.

Interactive teaching, the National Literacy Strategy and SPRINT

Although the research and the book have been about the relatively early days
of the literacy hour, at that time in its second year, the National Literacy
Strategy is a continuing process and interactive teaching is receiving more
rather than less attention. Other research is being developed in the area
(see, for example, Fisher *et al.* 2000; Hardman and Smith *et al.* 2001). Therefore, the findings from the research have ongoing implications that are likely
to reverberate throughout primary schools for some time to come, and must
be taken into consideration in the implementation of the KS3 strategy for
literacy in secondary education. This is particularly so in relation to teachers'
understanding of the meanings behind our typology of interactive teaching
and the extension of their own and the children's thinking from surface to
deeper features.

Before we present the key findings and discuss their implications, it
is worthwhile reiterating what we set out to achieve so that readers can judge
for themselves how successful the outcomes of the research, presented in this
book, have been.

The research aimed to:

- develop research on pedagogy – to define interactive teaching in
  collaboration with teachers;
- generate an accessible model(s) of skills involved in interactive
  teaching;
- enhance teachers' professional development by carrying out for-
  mative and summative evaluations of the implementation of the
  interactive teaching model through a process of video-stimulated
  evidence-based dialogue.

A further aim, not yet highlighted, was to support four initial teacher-training
tutors in their own development of research skills and methodology.
This was somewhat innovative and became a crucial and interesting part
of the research because the tutors were themselves, like the teachers, learning
about the research and its processes as the project developed. This was also
extremely useful for the team as a whole, because the 'novice' tutors were able
to perceive the situation from the perspective of the teachers and researchers

and contribute significantly to the development of the various elements of the research.

The objectives included our desire to:

- construct a working definition of interactive teaching to share with primary teachers and to generate further thinking about interaction;
- observe experienced teachers at work over a period of a school year when implementing and evolving their constructs of interactive teaching in the literacy hour and in one other area of the curriculum;
- provide evidence-based feedback and dialogue with teachers to foster their critical reflection on pedagogical skills;
- convene teachers' workshops and conferences to refine and disseminate the emergent models of interactive teaching in an ongoing, interactive way.

These aims and objectives, once achieved, were capable of having an impact upon a range of different people, not least those involved in the project as teachers and researchers and primary teachers in general. It was intended, also, that the outcomes of the research would inform policy-makers, teacher-educators and researchers and influence in a significant way the continuing development of DfES strategies.

The earlier chapters in the book have shown the various direct and indirect ways in which we met these aims and objectives. A fundamental example of the way we had to change our thinking was the early evidence that the attempt to identify a single, common 'model' of interactive teaching was untenable. The wealth of variants of interactive teaching provided by the teachers in the first phase of the research made this clear. Our initial expectations moved, therefore, towards the concept of a typology of interactive teaching. This, too, went through several metamorphoses, with seven, eight and then nine 'types' of interactive teaching as the researchers searched, sifted, synthesized and debated the growing quantity of qualitative data. Numerous cycles of analysis, reformulation and re-analysis took place in our attempts to construct a typology of interactive teaching that would represent the teachers' descriptions and demonstrations as faithfully but economically as possible. Gradually, the typology divided into the 'surface' and 'deep' forms that seemed to encapsulate better the teachers' personal theories and their practical interpretations of interactive teaching. The resultant typology remains as much a starting point for further research as a conclusion to the SPRINT Project. Further research is required of how teachers integrate their attention to each child's social and emotional needs with other purposes of interactive teaching. We have begun to explore how they assimilate prescribed learning objectives and teaching methods and accommodate these into their personal pedagogical principles but, more specifically, focused research is required.

In addition to the typology, we have generated substantial and significant qualitative and quantitative evidence of various forms of interactive teaching in literacy and other areas of the curriculum throughout Key Stages 1 and 2 in two geographical regions of England. We have few doubts that the findings are applicable to England as a whole. In brief, our findings show that:

1 Interactive teaching is a complex pedagogical form. There is no single clear picture of what constitutes interactive teaching in primary schools. It was interpreted and practised differently, often intuitively, and in several guises by individual teachers.

2 Teachers themselves were very unsure about interactive teaching in their own repertoires of teaching strategies. Some felt they were doing 'it' already and that it was part of everyday practice. Some did not like to admit that they had no 'formal' knowledge or understanding of what it constituted, feeling that they ought in some way to know. Teachers exhibited significant craft knowledge of interactive teaching as good practice.

3 Initial concerns among the 'focus' group of teachers, as defined within the Concerns-Based Adoption Model (CBAM) questionnaire, concerning lack of knowledge about interactive teaching, decreased significantly as they articulated and gained confidence in their own understanding of interactive teaching through the video-stimulated reflective dialogues (VSRDs). Having reduced their concerns about practical managerial aspects of interactive teaching with their research-partners, they were moving towards concerns about and consequences of more sophisticated interactive strategies after three reflective dialogues. Some teachers also engaged in greater critical evaluation.

4 Instead of the 'model' of interactive teaching originally anticipated, the typology we developed defines teaching and its associated contexts and conditions, which teachers and others reading this book can draw upon in considering their own and others' interactive teaching practices. The typology is grounded in the teachers' own terminology and validated by the teachers at the mini-conferences. It generates a repertoire of effective practice for teachers and indicates, in broad terms, both surface and deeper features of professional practice and thinking. At a surface level, teachers can involve pupils in broad ways, for example, with whiteboards, fans or quick question-and-answer sessions. However, if teachers want to foster pupils' self-esteem, to support the co-construction of knowledge or to develop higher-order thinking skills in pupils, they need a slower pace of teaching in which individuals' learning styles and strategies can be addressed. These features, moving well beyond the NLS

framework, were emphasized consistently by many teachers in the research.

5 Teachers have shown themselves to operate, as they should in our opinion, from a basis of certain pedagogical principles – that is, those things which they will not compromise for themselves and their pupils within their own values and beliefs. In the face of massively imposed, prescriptive strategies, they are left with significant dilemmas as to how they can respect those (and be 'true' to their professional thinking) and practise them appropriately.

6 Changes in teacher–pupil interaction since the introduction of the literacy hour suggest that the pace and intensity of interactions have increased, while their quality needs further investigation. During the literacy hour, teachers have greatly increased the amount of verbal interaction, the frequency of questions and the ratio of questions to statements. The KS2 teachers were more likely to pose higher-order questions, which were answered by an explanation or imaginative idea, than KS1 teachers. At Key Stage 1, a predominance of lower-order, factual recall questions raises questions about cognitive challenge in literacy tasks for young children. Statements, however, remain the dominant form of teacher–pupil interaction, accounting for over 50 per cent of all observations.

7 Despite the increase in higher-order questions at Key Stage 2, the children were still responding in relatively few words and were not engaging in long interactions with teachers, in which the teacher might probe and challenge their thinking. Thus although interaction between teachers and pupils has reached a level of one question to two teacher statements, compared with one in four before the introduction of the National Literacy Strategy, it remains heavily teacher-dominated. It is almost exclusively the teachers who were asking the questions. This situation is a considerable distance from the two-way reciprocal communication envisaged, and attempted, by some of the teachers.

8 The major differences found between the teachers of the older and younger children suggest that the teachers of the younger children tended to use more of the surface types of interactive teaching. In other words, they were keen to engage pupils' attention, ensure broad participation and foster pupils' social and emotional well-being. In addition, tasks within the literacy strategy appear to be much more directly teacher-controlled for KS1 children than studies have suggested previously.

9 In areas other than literacy, the SPRINT teachers were teaching in ways that are closer to interactive teaching (as we have defined it in

the typology) but not all were by any means operating at the deeper level or using a full range of potential strategies. While at Key Stage 1 teachers used more lower-order questions in the literacy hour and fewer higher-order questions, in other curriculum areas, such as science, history and mathematics, the reverse was true: higher-order questions were more prevalent than lower-order questions, and the overall rate of questioning was less inflated. At Key Stage 2, however, the high incidence of cognitive challenge found in the literacy hour, but not in other curriculum areas, may be indicative of low expectations in the foundation subjects. This underestimation of children's thinking is a potential cause for concern.

10 Video-stimulated reflective dialogue is a useful tool for the professional development of teachers and teacher trainers. Most teachers during the course of the SPRINT Project made some alterations in their definitions and reported use of interactive teaching; the majority of the focus teachers also felt that the experience of reflecting on the videos enabled them to make more substantive shifts in practice. It allows teachers to consider both the art and the craft of teaching and encourages analysis and critique of practice in ways that support professional development (Ghaye and Ghaye 1998). This is a new methodology in the way we have used it – attributable directly to the SPRINT Project – which is capable of wider use in research and teacher development.

All of these dimensions have been elaborated in earlier chapters, which should be consulted for the source of our findings. At this point in the book, however, we want to extend the argument further through exploring the *significance* for teachers, trainers, policy-makers and academics of some of these findings.

The significance of the SPRINT Project's key findings

The emphasis on the 'surface' interactive features of teaching in NLS training materials has had a considerable effect on teachers, and teaching of this type seems to dominate literacy hour practices. However, it remains heavily teacher-dominated. The two-way communication and reciprocal exchanges envisaged by the SPRINT teachers as 'deeper' forms of interactive teaching have yet to be widely realized in either of the key stages. Undoubtedly, the SPRINT teachers conceived interactive teaching to be far more complex and to be subject to specific conditions and contexts than is implied by the NLS definition. Many of the teachers refined and/or expanded their interpretations during the project, and changes in their attitudes, knowledge, thinking and practice emerged. These would, we feel, certainly have become more extensive had the project continued for longer.

The typology reflects a conceptual distinction in the teachers' thinking between five 'surface' (explicit and observable) and four 'deep' (more implicit and qualitative) practices. Reference was made to these by one focus teacher as 'little i' and 'big I' interactions; the former were considered 'gimmicky things', such as the phoneme fans and whiteboards introduced by the National Literacy Strategy. One of the four 'deep' elements in the typology – attention to pupils' social and emotional needs or skills – appeared in both surface and deep senses and so straddles the surface/deep distinction. Teachers used it in a 'surface' sense when they were referring to their concern that children experience success and enjoyment, but also engaged in complex processes of decision-making when contemplating individual children's needs for experiences that would support, or at least not undermine, their self-esteem.

We have discussed in Chapter 1 the variety of educational theories and philosophies that might underpin interactive practice (Merry 1998). If, however, one of the aspirations of the National Literacy Strategy is to enhance pupils' thinking, as promoted by Reynolds (1998) and Beard (1999), teachers need to address the 'deeper', less explicit aspects of interactive practice, by making reflective links between their own principles of practice, theory and knowledge, and through greater access to the theories of learning and pedagogy. However, only a few teachers, typically those who had pursued or were pursuing a higher degree, referred to educational theory. Our evidence suggests that the process of video-stimulated reflective dialogue showed signs of success in promoting reflection on practice, but that more time might be needed for a greater effect.

Given the emphasis on surface and deep features, the typology is significant because of its ability to enable teachers to dig that little bit deeper to understand the effects of their interaction with pupils and with the curriculum. At the final workshop, the teachers specifically commented on three aspects:

- understanding the issues about interactive teaching (and the development of the typology) from a wider base than just their own schools;
- having the chance to step back and observe their own practice;
- being offered a 'safe challenge' to professional thinking.

This has implications for the training of teachers, particularly at continuing professional development level, where they can build on their experience and expertise to exploit opportunities to analyse and critique their practice more fully. Furthermore, these are the very opportunities teachers need, rather than a sustained diet – as in the past few years – of learning how to deliver packages of pre-determined learning and teaching tasks, which has considerably reduced professionalism within professional development.

For example, as we have shown in Chapter 9, teaching that is 'pacey' tends to inhibit interactions that are challenging to primary age children because there is no time for contemplation about responses or for developing higher-order thinking. Therefore, the means of teaching as prescribed in the National Literacy Strategy do not match the overall aims of the strategy. In any case, the strategy lacks what we have described as 'deeper' features of teaching and learning, concentrating as it does at a surface level only. We feel that the literacy strategy needs to be revised to ensure that all those aspects within our typology are covered effectively and that their implications are explored in detail by teachers.

Beard's (1999) three-phase framework of questioning (cited in the Introduction) appears to reflect some aspects of the different ways in which questioning should be used (that is, to problem solve, to assess pupils and to develop higher-order thinking). The literacy hour militates against this happening, especially for KS1 children. For example, although more challenging questions were prominent in KS2 classes, teachers rarely extended pupils' responses or challenged their thinking in ways previously promoted in DfEE-funded research (McGuinness 1999). That such cognitive challenge is even less likely in other areas of the curriculum within KS2 classes is worrying, given the need for such skills as problem-solving and analysis and synthesis of information in the twenty-first century. Similarly, we question what the impact is likely to be within the literacy hour as children move from Key Stage 1 to Key Stage 2. Will KS2 teachers see the effects of the diet of quick-fire simple factual recall questions and decreased opportunities for higher-order thinking in literacy in young children transferring into Key Stage 2? If higher-order thinking for pupils is the objective, then knowledge of how to promote it through interaction between teachers and pupils needs to be embedded through the strategies. This certainly did not appear to be occurring at Key Stage 1 in our analysis of observations and interviews with teachers. Moreover, many conflicts and confusions are perceived by teachers, as we have shown in Chapter 9. Teachers are aware of the contradictions within the National Literacy Strategy, but feel somewhat powerless to change anything in ways that would be significant to teaching and learning. Policy-makers need to realize that these contradictions are leading teachers away from the very focus of what is being promoted through the English strategies.

Higher levels of cognitive demand upon children also require sustained time for teachers and children to interact. In their research, Gipps et al. (2000) found that interactions between learner and teacher needed to be sustained and accompanied by feedback or 'debriefing'. In Siraj-Blatchford et al.'s (2002) research, the key feature of adult contacts with children that generated greater cognitive demand upon the latter was 'sustained shared thinking'. Bruner (1986) calls these 'joint involvement episodes'.

The KS1 teachers' use of higher-order questions in curriculum areas other than literacy suggests that the children are, in the teachers' eyes, quite capable of responding to challenging questions. In the literacy hour, it appears that policy-makers and teachers alike are more concerned to promote children's completion of tasks and complete programmes than to extend thinking. It certainly seems that the literacy hour at Key Stage 1 may be seriously under-estimating young children's thinking skills. There is some support for these findings in the recently published work of Hardman *et al.* (2001), who also report key stage differences in teacher-initiated behaviour. In particular, they found that KS1 teachers used significantly fewer open questions and twice as many closed questions in the literacy hour than KS2 teachers. Fortunately, this is not the case in other areas of the curriculum. If it were, we should all be rightly concerned at the failure of education to develop young children's higher-order thinking skills at this early and crucial stage in their schooling. As some of our case studies show (reported, for example, in Chapter 8 and in English *et al.* 2002), video-stimulated reflective dialogue has the potential to enable teachers to identify and reflect on such issues.

There are also significant longer-term implications for the development of decision-making skills in pupils. For example, the literacy hour, which appears to be more teacher-directed, limits young children's choices and restricts their independence and sense of ownership. Potentially, this may not only be significant when children move into Key Stage 2, but also in the longer term, for their motivation and dispositions towards learning.

As the National Literacy Strategy moves into Key Stage 3, we are left wondering whether teachers in that phase of education will be given more opportunity to take on board some of the issues we have raised to avoid the pitfalls and contradictions experienced by KS1 and KS2 teachers. Perhaps equally importantly, the emphasis within the Curriculum Guidance for the Foundation Stage (DfES/QCA 2000) on reception year children as young as 4 years of age being subject to literacy hour style teaching should be challenged. If such teaching is resulting in significant increases in telling what and how rather than in asking children to think things through for themselves, then this will merely promote 'learned helplessness' and will disempower both children and teachers. It could result in a generation of children waiting to be told what to do rather than using their initiative and also in some very unhappy and unmotivated young learners as they move progressively through their schooling. The value of child-initiated, play-based learning for young children has been well documented and researched (see, for example, Moyles and Adams 2001; Moyles *et al.* 2002). Similarly, in terms of pace and speed, Elkind (2001) has warned of the dangers of taking a 'too much too soon' approach to young children's learning. Key Stage 1 teachers have, on the whole, been unhappy about the levels of prescription in the National Literacy Strategy and in the literacy hour in particular – perhaps our findings indicate that they have good professional reasons for feeling this way. No thinking teacher likes to work within a context that has such low expectations of children, who have so much to offer (Eraut 2000). Policy-makers within the government should take note of new research (much of it encapsulated within Bowman *et al.* 2001), which points to the capacity of young children to learn. The Eager to Learn Report emphasizes what it suggests is the 'one clear message to emerge from the explosion of knowledge', which is the 'prodigious enthusiasm and competence for learning shown by young children' (p. vii). The writers also express concern that this potential is not realized 'in many – perhaps most – early childhood settings', a sentiment with which we might concur in England at this time.

The issue of promoting higher-order thinking should not be seen in a vacuum, however. There has been for some time a growing awareness of the importance of understanding how children learn, as well as creating lists of required curriculum content, to the extent that the government commissioned a report on the effectiveness of thinking skills programmes (e.g. McGuinness 1999). Moreover, many psychologists and educators believe that we are about to witness a breakthrough in our understanding of learning, as the findings of neuroscience and psychology are finally beginning to come together (see, for example, Bransford *et al.* 1999). In such a context, it is a pity that the opportunities for such thinking in the National Literacy Strategy are not being exploited.

While the research focus was essentially on the teaching, teachers often drew us and themselves back to the children. It is interesting to speculate why this happened and whether teachers were deliberately trying to divert attention from their own role because of anxieties about being videoed or concerns that what they were doing was not adequate. Because teachers were, in the main, volunteers in the research and, especially in the case of focus teachers, were partners in the process, we doubt that this was a significant issue. What instead we suggest is that, in England, the last decade has witnessed such a rate of educational innovation that concern about the effects on children has become a constant anxiety for teachers. Added to this, teachers are aware that the social conditions under which increasing numbers of children live have changed perceptibly over the last two decades for both good and for bad. Hence concerns for children's welfare dominate how teachers perceive teaching and learning and frustrate both practitioners and policy-makers who strive to improve standards and outcomes.

Policy-makers, on the other hand, perceive primary pupils as future citizens who must acquire certain skills through schooling to justify public expenditure on the process. As David Blunkett's Foreword to the NLS

Framework for Teaching states (DfEE 1998: 1): 'All our children deserve to leave school equipped to enter a fulfilling adult life. But if children do not master the basic skills of literacy and numeracy while they are at primary schools they will be seriously disadvantaged later'. The next page pointed out, however, that 'The government has committed over £50 million of funding in 1998–99 to training and support for schools . . . and will give further support as they work towards the national target' (DfEE 1998: 2). It would appear that practitioners and policy-makers need to meet half-way to promote both the affective and cognitive domains of teachers' and children's school lives. Social and family policy cannot be divorced from educational policy, anymore than teachers can be – or should be – divorced from their professional thinking and opportunities for 'real' professional development. Prescribed teaching methods and curriculum content pressures have reduced significantly many teachers' sense of ownership over teaching and learning decisions, particularly within the context of literacy. An inevitable consequence of this is that reflection on professional practice has been reduced to those aspects that ensure survival rather than those that extend and advance effective practice – the 'just tell me what to do and I'll do it' type of response. Similarly, many teachers were not sure whether they were 'allowed to' adapt practice within the literacy strategy, yet came under criticism from NLS officials for complying too closely with the guidance. Professional development for teachers is not about telling them how to carry out their teaching, but about building on their already substantial skills and knowledge about teaching and learning and supporting them in developing these into new arenas. The Concerns-Based Adoption Model (CBAM) showed that offering new knowledge to teachers is important. The skill of the supporter is knowing when to throw in adjuncts that educate rather than merely 'support' (McIntyre and Hagger 1996; Moyles *et al.* 1998).

The CBAM also offered some justification for considering the emotional and affective development of teachers – teaching does not happen within a vacuum of emotions and experiences and many primary teachers, as we have seen, are very concerned about their pupils' well-being as well as education. This was also evidenced within the reflective dialogues. In fact, teachers rarely talked about the content of the literacy hour and other teaching without putting it in the context of children's responses. As one teacher remarked of interactive (and other forms of) teaching, 'I've said it repeatedly, if it doesn't have an impact in the classroom on the children, what's the point of doing it?'

Teachers also, it seems, underestimate their *own* skills: witness the fact that interactive teaching was seen as 'good practice' and very much taken for granted. Teachers don't deliberately ignore their own skills, but rather they expect that certain of them will come readily and not need specific thought day after day. It is a truism that if we thought about every action and behaviour each day, it would render all of us incapable of doing anything! (Claxton 2000). Teachers appeared more at ease and less anxious about situations that were capable of greater interaction. For example, these include those in less prescribed, more pupil-centred curriculum contexts, such as the Arts and the Foundation Stage, which depend more on spoken interactions.

The relevance of reflection, and in particular the influence of dialogue as part of reflection, is well established in the literature (Carr and Kemmis 1986; Handal and Lauvas 1987; Zeichner 1994; Hatton and Smith 1995). Similarly, the relevance of evidence-based practice, including the use of visual representations of practice, is also acknowledged (Hargreaves 1996; Davies 1999). The evidence from our typology suggests that, to develop and apply a full range of interactive practices from a reflective stance, teachers need opportunities to explore and challenge:

- their own attitudes to curriculum and pedagogy;
- implicit and explicit principles that drive practice;
- explicit educational theory and public knowledge;
- implicit personal knowledge that underpins their principles (Atkinson and Claxton 2000);
- the methods and strategies that will allow them to apply these principles;
- their own instrumental interests in strategies, methods and tactics;
- the conditions that mediate the application of these practices in the classroom.

These aspects are also reflected in what teachers suggested to us at the mini-conferences, when asked what they had appreciated from the research processes. However, reflection alone does not make teachers change practice. As Atkinson (2000: 71) suggests, 'Reflection on practice may lead to better understanding but not necessarily to better practice'. Carol, one of the SPRINT focus teachers, made a similar comment:

> I think I have got a view of more strategies and of different strategies now. I think I have got more questions than I had when I started. It has not solved any problems for me to be honest, but it has certainly made me much more reflective about what I am doing. I am not sure it has made me more effective.

McIntyre (1993) argued that reflection is more relevant for experienced practitioners for three reasons:

1   With experience, actions become fluent and intuitive, so an on-going process and attitude of reflection is required to surface and

articulate underpinning assumptions before any conscious changes or developments can be made. A novice practitioner, on the other hand, will still be at the stage of deliberating and establishing aspects of expertise.

2   Experienced practitioners have a rich repertoire of experiences on which to draw, offering opportunities for creative reflection in and on their experiences (Schön 1983).

3   Experienced practitioners are more likely to have had opportunities to develop the skills of reflective practice.

The reflective dialogue process in itself appeared to empower teachers – it provided a focus for analysis of practice and self-analysis in terms of teachers' hearing and articulating what they were able to say about their own practice. As such, it is a meta-cognitive process that promotes professional thinking at a deeper level. In addition, it challenges but also supports teachers in terms of their emotional responses to teaching, not least in feeling that someone else is interested in talking with them about their particular classroom issues, problems, challenges and practices at a professional level.

The effects of researchers and higher education tutors as research-partners

The research team, as noted in the Introduction, consisted of three research co-directors, two part-time research assistants and four tutors from initial teacher education courses. All nine operated during the project as research-partners to individual teachers. Our achievements are slightly different from those of teachers as we, in a sense, deliberately set ourselves a challenge and the process inevitably led to much questioning of our roles as researchers.

The team were aware of several challenges likely to occur within the project, for example, how they would:

- facilitate teacher development without apparently promoting particular theoretical or conceptual models of interactive teaching;
- respond when teachers asked for information or 'academic perspectives' on interactive teaching;
- ensure teachers benefited from the skills and experience of their tutor research-partners, all of whom were experienced education tutors, mentors and advisers, while retaining a democratic partnership.

Participants initially thought we had the answer to what interactive teaching actually is. We clearly had a notion, indeed several notions, but not a unified concept that we all shared. There was a dilemma in trying not to pre-empt what teachers thought. The concept of being a 'research-partner' also generated anxiety in tutors in offering 'theory' that might have implied superiority. There was inevitably a reticence to offer comment on content in an arena where we were drawing out teachers' own meanings. But in many cases, the process seems to have worked for the teacher involved, as the following quote from David shows:

> The literacy hour was *so* prescriptive, and I think as I've gone through this year on this project, I can see lots of merits in the literacy hour, I still *do* see merits, but I think this project has given me the confidence to say we *can* cover this material but, we can cover it in a different way, which is not necessarily following the literacy hour letter by letter . . . you've sort of given me that confidence, which is good because it means that this project isn't just a project for project's sake.

As research-partners, the research team found that the process of working with teachers within the VSRD process (see Chapter 8) generated many challenges to thinking and practice in a variety of ways, many of which have since infiltrated our work, albeit as researchers or teacher-educators. Initially, concerns were raised by individual tutors that we, the research team, had set the agenda (and, therefore, held the locus of control) on the focus of interactive teaching. While teachers who were involved had an interest in the area, the original idea came from us and, at any time, the teachers could have stopped. The fact that they did not might say something about the VSRD process and the engagement they fostered with their research-partners. We have already mentioned the parallel learning opportunities in the early part of this final chapter.

Tutors found themselves operating in a changed role – that is, most were used to working with teachers as tutors supporting student teachers on school-based placements and were, therefore, like the teachers, used to analysing others' pedagogic behaviours rather than their own. As we also supplied continuing professional development courses to teachers, we were seen as having some 'authority' in terms of various theoretical and practical issues, including providing the content of programmes. The expectation that we would tell teachers what interactive teaching was is, therefore, understandable. Shedding their 'normal' role of raising open-ended questions, albeit those intended to 'lead' the respondent in certain directions, proved difficult to achieve, yet, as a group, we were adamant that the tutor-researchers must allow the teachers greater autonomy over the process of reflection. This parallel, partner relationship with the teachers meant that the tutors also reported some conflict between being the camera holder – and, therefore, having some measure of control over what was photographed at what time – and trying to be genuinely open in exploring different facets of interaction identified by the teachers themselves. Occasional confusion was expressed by tutors about the amount of 'detachment' or otherwise required to conduct an effective reflective dialogue and about the nature of discussions that were focused specifically on one behaviour – interactive teaching – as opposed to teaching in general. Such is the nature of focused investigations!

Neutrality also presented challenges, in that most tutors had their *own* ideas about what constituted interactive teaching and, when such aspects were not included by teachers in their responses, the tendency was to try to take the teacher's reflection in specific directions. The questions, outlined in Chapter 8, were, on the one hand, helpful in this regard and, on the other hand, represented an opportunity, which needed to be resisted by the tutors, of focusing only on those questions that might bring out what they themselves wanted to hear rather than a real professional exploration of interactive teaching. To the tutor-researchers' credit, they were able to overcome this challenge, partly because there were others in the research team who offered support. All deemed the process to be one of reflecting back to teachers in words, often in précis style, their own comments and using this as a check on both definitions and understandings. Yet the process was deemed to be beyond the act of simply 'mirroring' and involved much more pro-active engagement between the two partners.

Initially, it was difficult to conceive of the reflective dialogues as something beyond and different from 'normal' research interviews, except that the two-way process of asking and answering questions is not a usual process in standard, schedule-based interviewing. The benefits, however, of shared, rich data were also different from those achieved in standard interviewing procedures and, if for no other reason, this alone was a source of inspiration to the research-partners. Getting to know the teacher-partner and having someone with whom to genuinely share this professional enquiry offered a 'comfortable challenge' for both partners (Merry 1998).

Working from a grounded stance meant having the joys, on the one hand, of generating unique and interesting rich data but, on the other hand, also created some uncertainties among the tutor-researchers as to exactly what interactive teaching really looks like in practice. The process supported a good deal of open-ended discussion, but also frequently resulted in debate with the teacher about whether there were any 'answers' to the problem of what is interactive for example, is child–child interaction suitably placed under the heading of interactive teaching?

The tutors were all asked to keep a diary of their own professional development, and to fill in a questionnaire reflecting on it at the end of the project. Not surprisingly, comments covered a wide spectrum, including:

- As expected, we had many discussions about our own ideas of what we thought interactive teaching might mean. Apart from reading widely around the area, we often had 'academic' discussions with other team members which refined our own ideas. Brainstorming sessions gave place to a host of lists, diagrams, typologies and hierarchies that were hotly debated.

- Other discussions focused more on the methodology. One tutor, for instance, in discussion with a colleague not involved in the project, discovered some interesting similarities with the methodology used by this colleague in a previous piece of research (Cooper and McIntyre 1996). Similarly, it was invaluable for colleagues who had not used systematic observation schedules before to learn about their use in classrooms.

- On a more personal level, we frequently compared notes about what it was like to carry out a reflective dialogue from the researcher's point of view. One member of the team, for instance, wryly noted the number of times he had said 'I don't want to put words into your mouth, but . . .'.

- Another area of discussion was the use of video as a research tool. At least one member of the team was not used to this method, and several questions arose about what to do if the children 'played up' for the video, or where to focus when the teacher gave them some time for discussion, for instance.

These brief examples indicate the range of professional development experiences which we encountered during the project, deepening not only our own ideas about interactive teaching, but also our skills and experience as researchers engaged in what was, in some ways, radically different from 'traditional' research.

Critique of our research design and methodology

It would be inappropriate to conclude without reflecting on the original design and methodology, for the validity and reliability of our findings rest on the suitability of the methods and tools we used to collect the data. Interpretation of findings was supported through our teacher conferences and also through having a range of researchers and tutors engaged together in the research. It was difficult for anyone to make an independent (and potentially rash) decision or interpretation with eight others potentially challenging it during our team meetings and continual e-mail dialogues. Through this team method, it was also possible for us to do initial trials of all our instruments and validate evolving analyses and interpretations.

Working as a team was not without its challenges. We've already identified the problems of distance and time, but team members' familiarity with, and understanding of, the research processes varied considerably, and so aspects that are often taken-for-granted in projects were regularly scrutinized. On the one hand, this ensured the 'groundedness' of the evolving thinking but, on the other hand, could be regarded as inefficient in terms of the time needed for all responses to be gathered and considered. From the point of view of raising research awareness and expertise, however, this was an investment of time and effort in the professional development of the whole team. The continual questioning by those unfamiliar with certain methods, of the value of certain procedures, or the relevance of seemingly disparate, meaningless quantities, kept us focused on the validity and authenticity of the data we were collecting as well as the consistency or reliability of the collection process.

Two adaptations of the ORACLE Teacher Observation Record (Galton *et al.* 1980) were examples of this process. These concerned the inclusion of additional categories. There was lively debate within the team between systematic observation sceptics, agnostics and believers about the adequacy of the ORACLE teacher observation record to present a valid picture of interactive teaching in the literacy hour (see Chapter 6). At issue was the extent to which the addition of new categories to produce a finer grained and, ultimately, more valid instrument undermines the reliability and 'usability' of the basic instrument, as observers have to be able to select from even more categories. On the other hand, observer frustration at not being able to record what they see as significant features threatens both validity and reliability. In particular, the tutor-researchers expressed concern that new techniques such as phoneme fans and whiteboards represented a distinctive form of interactive teaching that should be recorded independently. These methods, however, could be subsumed under existing categories of the ORACLE such as 'silent interaction' (see Chapter 6). As Table 6.1 reveals, in the end both sides 'won'. Phoneme fans and other 'gimmicks' found a place in the schedule as sub-categories of silent interaction, and had a useful explanatory function in the interpretation of the observations. The second example is the inclusion of meta-cognitive content as a sub-category of higher-order interactions. Whereas the phoneme fans were added on the basis of initial observations, the recognition of meta-cognitive interactions had an *a priori* theoretical foundation, as detailed in Chapter 1 (e.g. Adey and Shayer 1994; McGuinness 1999). In the final analysis, we found that talk about meta-cognitive processes was extremely rare, despite Medwell *et al.*'s (1998) research on effective teachers of literacy.

The 'lively debate' thus served not only as a vehicle for extension of the whole team's understanding of the use of systematic observation, but also increased the authenticity of our findings. Two particular features of the methodology are significant for other researchers: our use and development of the Concerns-Based Adoption Model (CBAM) and the video-stimulated reflective dialogue methodology; we expand on these below.

The CBAM Stages of Concern Questionnaire is part of a tried and tested approach to the measurement of innovation adoption developed by Gene Hall and his colleagues at the University of Texas at Austin in the 1970s. As Hord *et al.* (1987) explain, the CBAM consists of three diagnostic instruments that can be used by a 'change facilitator', such as an advisor, headteacher or curriculum leader, to monitor progress as teachers take on a new programme, scheme or, indeed, a National Literacy Strategy. It combines data about teachers' concerns about the innovation, their use of the innovation and developments in their conceptual understanding of it through 'innovation configurations'. The change facilitator uses this information to diagnose what approach to take, or support to provide, for each member of the group during the change period. Chapter 2 explains how SPRINT adapted the 35-item Stages of Concern Questionnaire to examine the teachers' concerns about using 'interactive teaching'. Rather than simply using Hall and Hord's original analytic structure, which had been developed in the late 1970s with hundreds of Texan teachers, however, we carried out a new analysis of the SPRINT teachers' responses and compared this with the original Stages of Concern model. The reliabilities of five new 'scales of concern' were considerably higher than those obtained using the original version. These good reliabilities, and the greater ecological validity of using a structure derived from contemporary English primary teachers, led us to develop and use the 'SPRINT five scales of concern' in our analyses. At the same time, the considerable overlap between the original seven stages and SPRINT's five scales indicated a high degree of construct validity – that is, the two versions were measuring the same basic constructs. As we point out in Chapter 2, given the cultural, geographical and historical differences between Texas in the 1970s and England in 2000, as well as the massive educational reforms in England during the 1990s, we expected some redistribution of teachers' concerns. The SPRINT sample consisted of only 30 teachers, however. There is an urgent need, therefore, for larger samples to test the validity and stability of the five SPRINT scales.

Video-stimulated reflective dialogues

While not without its challenges, as we have seen in this chapter and Chapter 8, the SPRINT teachers found viewing their own practice and reflecting upon it both stimulating and demanding. Their tutor research-partners were also challenged to move beyond their usual repertoire and together forge new meaning and understanding from dialogue about the visual evidence. There were various reasons for this.

Unlike many research methods, the control of the VSRD process is mostly in the hands of the teacher. It is likely that this encourages deeper reflection and richer dialogue about the themes in focus. This, in turn, enhances research validity. It could also be argued that it may equally lead to limited perspectives. The skills of the research-partner are paramount here, and the soundness of the method will be enhanced with appropriate experience and training in the VSRD method. As we noted earlier, the framework of questions used in the process will be subject to continual review in terms of both scope and content. Fortunately, video-stimulated reflective dialogue is being used in various other contexts and the validity of evidence resulting in the use of the question frame will inevitably be enhanced with further enquiry. However, both the SPRINT teachers and their research-partners were ultimately extremely positive about the method and its potential. For the researchers it provided 'instant' triangulation – as the teachers' thoughts were reviewed in dialogue within sight of 'concrete' visual evidence. In the hectic life world of the teachers involved, reflective dialogue provided both time and interaction that they found helpful. Such dialogue is, therefore, opportune at a time when reducing the disparity and distance between research and practice is an important goal of the profession. There is clearly more work to be done on the method but its future looks promising. We would be interested to see the development of video-stimulated reflective dialogue in others' research.

Where to now?

There are many issues within SPRINT that deserve to be pursued. The following are just a few examples, in no particular order:

- Teachers have expressed the view that the National Numeracy Strategy promotes greater focus on interactive teaching and a wider range of teacher and pupil strategies, a claim that needs to be investigated using parallel approaches to those used in the SPRINT Project.
- The SPRINT research has shown clearly that teachers respond thoughtfully to images of their own teaching. More sophisticated use of images of practice in determining quality might allow teachers to re-view and re-evaluate their practice, revisit their experiences and reflect on those experiences with knowledgeable others, together drawing out commonalities and differences.
- Feeding back to teachers the outcomes of video-stimulated reflective dialogue was begun during this project and led to action points being decided. This proved a helpful strategy and one that would be worth pursuing; for example, giving teachers full transcriptions of their reflective dialogues for comments and follow-up.
- Tomlinson (1999: 541) has argued that different forms of visual data allow practitioners to step outside their own practice while simultaneously providing an opportunity to review, draw awareness

and reflect upon action as precursors to meaning-making. This is vital because of the apparent contradictions in the National Literacy Strategy.

- The efficacy of the combination of visual evidence and professional dialogue as research methods (Jaworski 1990; Laycock and Bunnag 1991; Copeland and Decker 1996; Wilkinson 1996; Hutchinson and Bryson 1997; Fletcher and Whitehead 2000; McNamara *et al.* 2000) and a smaller literature on the use of still images for educational research (Walker and Weidel 1985; Preskill 1995; Prosser 1999; Hall and Powney 2000) appears to provide a way forward in promoting and developing both practice and reflection on practice.

- As many teachers felt that the National Literacy Strategy provided more opportunities for interactive teaching, similar research needs to be conducted in the numeracy period in primary schools to extend the typology and allow further investigation of surface and deep constructs of interactive teaching.

- No-one appears yet to have asked pupils how they feel about being subjected to 'interactive teaching'. It is vital that research be conducted on pupils' perceptions of interactive teaching, their experience of and attitudes to the high rates of interactivity found here, and the demands on them to be 'interactive'. After all, developing pupils' reflective skills – perhaps even through a simplified VSRD process – would certainly support the notion of not underestimating them!

Final comment

The SPRINT Project has generated several new data sets and has potential for significant replication, as well as implications for practitioners, policy-makers and teacher trainers. Our evidence suggests teachers' conceptions of interactive teaching in our typology of interactive teaching are more sophisticated than those offered in the NLS documentation and indicate various surface and deep interpretations. At the same time, teachers' knowledge and understanding of the pedagogical principles involved needs to be developed further to foster pupils' higher-order thinking. Video-stimulated reflective dialogues are an effective means of professional development. Teachers' talk in interactive sections of the literacy hour is considerably different from pre-NLS teacher–pupil interactions and major differences were found between Key Stages 1 and 2 in terms of cognitive demand.

Despite the difficulties for teachers in dealing with so much innovation and change in their daily work – and the bureaucratic and prescriptive nature of many of these – the SPRINT teachers were hard-working, committed and enthusiastic. They were keen to think about their practices and to spend time reflecting with their research-partner on promoting teaching and learning activities that supported their pupils' development and learning. However, the political foci on, for example, speed of delivery and the urgency in meeting ever-increasing targets for themselves and their pupils is antithetical to sustained pedagogic reflection. Exciting discoveries in the field of neuroscience are telling us that 'The child's thinking (and, therefore, development of connections in the brain) should be expanded not narrowed through learning experiences' (Moyles 2002) and emphasize the sustained time needed if vital thinking skills are to be developed and enhanced. If policy-makers really aspire to a primary teaching profession that supports high-quality teaching and learning, time for sustained and deeper reflection by both teachers and young children must be created.

The final comments on the outcomes of SPRINT will be left to two of the teachers' reflections on the research and its methodology:

> Well, my general classroom practice *has* changed and I think the evidence of that is within the videos. I employ interactive strategies, I think, more frequently within the curriculum and I think that's partly because the children have learned different methods of learning.
>
> (David)

> I mean just to view a video . . . it's very useful to see yourself actually teach, but then to look at it again with the reflective dialogue and the criteria, it really has made me so much more aware of what I am doing, what I could be doing and what I am not doing and, with your support, things . . . I am doing well or could develop further.
>
> (Kim)

References

Adey, P. and Shayer, M. (1994) *Really Raising Standards: Cognitive Intervention and Academic Achievement*. London: Routledge.

Adorno, T.W., Frenkel-Brunswik, E., Levinson, D.J. and Sanford, R.N. (1950) *The Authoritarian Personality*. New York: Harper & Row.

Alexander, R. (2000) *Culture and Pedagogy: International Comparisons in Primary Education*. Oxford: Blackwell.

Alexander, R. (1995) *Versions of Primary Education*. London: Routledge/Open University.

Alexander, R. (1996) *Other Schools and Ours: Hazards of International Comparison*. Centre for Research in Elementary and Primary Education Occasional Paper. Warwick: University of Warwick.

Alexander, R., Rose, J. and Woodhead, C. (1992) *Curriculum Organisation and Classroom Practice in Primary Schools: A Discussion Paper*. London: DES.

Anderson, G. with Arsenault, N. (1998) *Fundamentals of Educational Research*, 2nd edn. London: Falmer Press.

Atkinson, T. (2000) Learning to teach: intuitive skills and reasoned objectivity, in T. Atkinson and G. Claxton (eds) *The Intuitive Practitioner: On the Value of Not Always Knowing What One is Doing*. Buckingham: Open University Press.

Atkinson, T. and Claxton, G. (eds) (2000) *The Intuitive Practitioner: On the Value of Not Always Knowing What One is Doing*. Buckingham: Open University Press.

Barnes, D. (1976) *From Communication to Curriculum*. Harmondsworth: Penguin.

Beard, R. (1999) *National Literacy Strategy: Review of Research and Other Related Evidence*. London: DfEE.

Beverton, S. and English, E. (2000) How are schools implementing the National Literacy Strategy?, *Curriculum*, 21(2): 98–107.

Biggs, J. (1994) What are effective schools? Lessons from east and west, *Australian Educational Researcher*, 21(10): 19–40.

Bowman, B., Donovan, M. and Burns, M. (eds) (2001) *Eager to Learn: Educating Our Preschoolers*. Washington, DC: National Academy Press.

Bransford, J., Brown, A. and Cockign, R. (eds) (1999) *How People Learn: Brain, Mind, Experience and School*. Washington, DC: National Academy Press.

Brown, A.L and Palincsar, A.S. (1989) Guided co-operative learning and individual knowledge acquisition, in L. Resnick (ed.) *Knowing and Learning: Issues for a Cognitive Psychology of Learning*. Hillsdale, NJ: Lawrence Erlbaum.

Bruner, J. (1986) *Actual Minds, Possible Worlds*. Cambridge, MA: Harvard University Press.

Bullough, R.V., Jr. and Gitlin, A.D. (1991) Educative communities and the development of the reflective practitioner, in R. Tabachnich and K. Zeichner (eds) *Issues and Practices in Inquiry-Oriented Teacher Education*. Lewes: Falmer Press.

Carr, W. and Kemmis, S. (1986) *Becoming Critical, Knowledge and Action Research*. Lewes: Falmer Press.

Claxton, G. (2000) The anatomy of intuition, in T. Atkinson and G. Claxton (eds) *The Intuitive Practitioner: On the Value of Not Always Knowing What One is Doing*. Buckingham: Open University Press.

Cooper, P. and McIntyre, D. (1996) *Effective Teaching and Learning: Teachers' and Students' Perspectives*. Buckingham: Open University Press.

Copeland, W. and Decker, D. (1996) Video cases and the development of meaning making in preservice teachers, *Teaching and Teacher Education*, 12(5): 467–81.

David, T. (1999) Valuing young children, in L. Abbott and H. Moylett (eds) *Early Education Transformed*. London: Falmer Press.

Davies, P. (1999) What is evidence-based education?, *British Journal of Education*, 42(2): 108–21.

Day, C. (1999a) Researching teaching through reflective practice, in J. Loughran (ed.) *Researching Teaching: Methodologies and Practice for Understanding Pedagogy*. London: Falmer Press.

Day, C. (1999b) *Developing Teachers: The Challenges of Lifelong Learning*. London: Cassell.

DfEE (1997) *The Implementation of the National Literacy Strategy*. London: Department for Education and Employment.

DfEE (1998) *The National Literacy Strategy: A Framework for Teaching*. London: Department for Education and Employment.

DfEE (1999a) *NLS Flier 1: Talking in Class*. London: Department for Education and Employment.

DfEE (1999b) *NLS Flier 2: Engaging all Pupils*. London: Department for Education and Employment.

DfEE (1999c) *The National Numeracy Strategy: Framework for Teaching Mathematics from Reception to Year 6*. London: Department for Education and Employment.

Earl, L., Fullan, M., Leithwood, K. and Watson, N. (2000) *Watching and Learning: OISE/UT Evaluation of the Implementation of the National Literacy and Numeracy Strategies*. London: DfEE.

Edwards, D. and Mercer, N. (1987) *Common Knowledge: The Development of Understanding in the Classroom*. London: Routledge.

Elkind, D. (2001) *The Hurried Child: Growing Up Too Fast Too Soon*, 3rd edn. Cambridge, MA: Perseus Publishing.

Elliott, J. (1991) *Action Research for Educational Change*. Buckingham: Open University Press.

English, E. (2000) The teaching of reading – a decade of change, *Curriculum*, 21(3): 126–33.

Eraut, M. (1994) *Developing Professional Knowledge and Competence*. Lewes: Falmer Press.

Eraut, M. (2000) Non-formal learning, implicit learning and tacit knowledge in professional work, in F. Coffield (ed.) *The Necessity of Informal Learning*. Bristol: Policy Press.

Fisher, R., Lewis, M. and Davis, B. (2000) Progress and performance in National Literacy Strategy classrooms, *Journal of Research in Reading*, 23(3): 256–66.

Flanders, N. (1970) *Analysing Teacher Behaviour*. Reading, MA: Addison-Wesley.

Fletcher, S. and Whitehead, J. (2000) The 'look' of the teacher: using digital video to improve the professional practice of teaching, Paper presented to the BERA Annual Conference, University of Cardiff, September.

Foster, P. (1996) Ethical issues in observational research, in *Observing Schools: A Methodological Guide*. London: Paul Chapman.

Fuller, F. (1969) Concerns of teachers: a developmental conceptualization, *American Educational Research Journal*, 6: 207–26.

Galton, M. and Patrick, H. (eds) (1990) *Curriculum Provision in the Small Primary School*. London: Routledge.

Galton, M., Simon, B. and Croll, P. (1980) *Inside the Primary Classroom*. London: Routledge.

Galton, M., Hargreaves, L., Comber, C., Wall, D. and Pell, A. (1999) *Inside the Primary Classroom – 20 Years On*. London: Routledge.

Ghaye, A. and Ghaye, K. (1998) *Teaching and Learning through Critical Reflective Practice*. London: David Fulton.

Gipps, C., McCallum, B. and Hargreaves, E. (2000) *What Makes a Good Primary School Teacher? Expert Classroom Strategies*. London: Falmer Press.

Habermas, J. (1973) *Knowledge and Human Interests*. London: Heinemann.

Hall, G.E. and Hord, S.M. (1987) *Change in Schools: Facilitating the Process*. New York: State University of New York Press.

Hall, G.E., Wallace, R.D., Jr. and Dossett, W.A. (1973) A Developmental Conceptualisation of the Adoption Process within Educational Institutions. Austin, TX: Research and Development Centre for Teacher Education, University of Texas.

Hall, G., Archie, A. and Rutherford, W. (1979) Measuring Stages of Concern about the Innovation: A Manual for Use of the SoC Questionnaire (reprinted 1998). Austin, TX: Southwest Educational Development Laboratory.

Hall, S. and Powney, J. (2000) Photographs in educational research, Workshop presented at ECER, University of Edinburgh, September.

Handal, G. and Lauvas, P. (1987) *Promoting Reflective Teaching: Supervision in Practice*. Milton Keynes: The Society for Research into Higher Education and Open University Educational Enterprises.

Hardman, F., Smith, F. and Wall, K. (2001) An investigation into the impact of the National Literacy Strategy on the literacy learning of pupils with special educational needs in mainstream primary schools, Report for the Nuffield Foundation. Newcastle-upon-Tyne: University of Newcastle-upon-Tyne.

Hargreaves, A. and Fullan, M. (1998) *What's Worth Fighting for in Education?* Buckingham: Open University Press.

Hargreaves, D. (1996) *Teaching as a Research Based Profession: Possibilities and Prospects.* London: Teacher Training Agency.

Hargreaves, L. (1990) Teachers and pupils in small schools, in M. Galton and H. Patrick (eds) *Curriculum Provision in the Small Primary School.* London: Routledge.

Harrod, P. (2002) Teaching children to read: a vision for the future, in J. Johnston, M. Chater and D. Ball (eds) *Teaching the Primary Curriculum.* Buckingham: Open University Press.

Hart, S. (2000) *Thinking through Teaching: A Framework for Enhancing Participation and Learning.* London: David Fulton.

Hatton, N. and Smith, D. (1995) Facilitating reflection: issues and research, *Forum of Education,* 50(1): 49–65.

Hord, S. (1987) *Evaluating Educational Innovation.* London: Croom Helm.

Hord, S.M., Rutherford, W.L., Huling-Austin, L. and Hall, G.E. (1987) *Taking Charge of Change* (reprinted 1998). Austin, TX: Southwest Educational Development Laboratory.

Hutchinson, B. and Bryson, P. (1997) Video, reflection and transformation: action research in vocational education and training in a European context, *Educational Action Researcher,* 5(2): 283–303.

Jaworski, B. (1990) Video as a tool for teacher's professional development, *British Journal of Inservice Education,* 16: 60–5.

Joyce, B. (1992) Cooperative learning and staff development: teaching the method with the method, *Cooperative Learning,* 12(2): 10–13.

Kagan, N. (1979) *Interpersonal Process Recall: A Method of Influencing Human Interaction.* MI: Michigan State University.

LaBoskey, V.K. (1993) A conceptual framework for reflection in pre-service teacher education, in J. Calderhead and P. Gates (eds) *Conceptualising Reflection in Teacher Development.* London: Falmer Press.

Laycock, J. and Bunnag, C. (1991) Developing teacher self-awareness: feedback and the use of video, *ELT Journal,* 45(1): 43–53.

Lucas, P. (1991) Reflection, new practices, and the need for flexibility in supervising student teachers, *Journal of Further and Higher Education,* 15(2): 84–93.

Maehr, M. and Maehr, J. (1996) Schools aren't as good as they used to be: they never were, *Educational Researcher,* 25(8): 21–4.

McGuinness, C. (1999) *From Thinking Skills to Thinking Classrooms.* London: DfEE.

McIntyre, D. (1993) Theorising and reflection in initial teacher education, in J. Calderhead and P. Gates (eds) *Conceptualising Reflection in Teacher Development.* London: Falmer Press.

McNamara, O., Lones, L. and Van-Es, C. (2000) Evidence-based practice through practice-based evidence: the global and the local, Paper presented to the BERA Annual Conference, University of Cardiff, September.

Medwell, J., Wray, D., Poulson, L. and Fox, R. (1998) *Effective Teachers of Literacy*. Exeter: University of Exeter.

Medwell, J., Wray, D., Minns, H., Griffiths, V. and Coates, E. (2001) *Primary English: Teaching Theory and Practice*. Exeter: Learning Matters.

Merry, R. (1998) *Successful Teaching: Successful Learning*. Buckingham: Open University Press.

Moyles, J. and Suschitzky, W. with Chapman, L. (1998) *Teaching Fledglings to Fly? Mentoring in the Primary School*. Leicester/London: University of Leicester and the Association of Teachers and Lecturers.

Moyles, J. (2002) Face-to-face: Susan Greenfield, *InterPlay*, 2: 20–3, Summer.

Moyles, J. and Adams, S. (2001) *Statements of Entitlement to Play: Playful Approaches to Teaching in the Early Years*. Buckingham: Open University Press.

Moyles, J., Adams, S. and Musgrove, A. (2002) *SPEEL – Study of Pedagogical Effectiveness in Early Learning*. Research Report No. 363. London: DfES.

Mroz, M., Smith, F. and Hardman, F. (2000) The discourse of the literacy hour, *Cambridge Journal of Education*, 30(3): 379–90.

OfSTED (1997) *Literacy Matters*. London: Office for Standards in Education.

Pollard, A. (2001) Possible consequences of strong constraints on teachers and pupils: fuzzy generalisations from the PACE project, in M. Bassey, S. Hallam, A. Pollard, A. West, P. Noden and B. Stake, *Fuzzy Generalisations: Transforming Research Findings into Fuzzy Predictions which can Inform Teachers', Policy makers', and Researchers' Discourse and Action*, presented to the British Educational Research Association (BERA) Symposium at the AERA Annual meeting, Seattle, WA.

Preskill, H. (1995) The use of photography in evaluating school culture, *International Journal of Qualitative Studies in Education*, 8(2): 183–93.

Prosser, J. (1999) *Image Based Research: A Sourcebook of Qualitative Research*. London: Routledge.

Resnick, L.B. (1987) *Education and Learning to Think*. Washington, DC: National Academy Press.

Reynolds, D. (1998) Schooling for literacy: a review of research on teacher effectiveness and school effectiveness and its implications for contemporary educational policies, *Educational Review*, 50(2): 147–62.

Reynolds, D. and Farrell, S. (1996) *Worlds Apart? A Review of International Surveys of Educational Achievement Involving England*. London: HMSO.

Rosenshine, B. and Meister, C. (1994) Reciprocal teaching: a review of the research, *Review of Educational Research*, 64(4): 479–530.

Schön, D.A. (1983) *The Reflective Practitioner: How Professionals Think in Action*. New York: Basic Books.

Schön, D.A. (1987) *Educating the Reflective Practitioner*. San Francisco, CA: Jossey-Bass.

Schulz, R. (1987) *Interpreting Teacher Practice: Two Continuing Stories*. New York: College Press.

Sinclair, J. and Coulthard, R. (1975) *Towards an Analysis of Discourse*. Oxford: Oxford University Press.

Siraj-Blatchford, I. and Sylva, K. (2002) *Effective Pedagogy in the Early Years: Final Report to the DfES*. London: DfES.

Siraj-Blatchford, I., Sylva, K., Muttock, S., Gilden, R. and Bell, D. (2002) *Researching Effective Pedagogy in the Early Years*. Research Report no. 356. London: DfES.

Smith, A. (1998) *Accelerated Learning in Practice*. Stafford: Network Educational Press.

Smyth, J. (ed.) (1995) *Critical Discourses on Teacher Development*. London: Falmer.

Stenhouse, L. (1985) Action research and the teacher's responsibility for the educational process, in J. Ruddock and D. Hopkins (eds) *Research as a Basis for Teaching*. London: Heinemann.

Sternberg, R. and Spear-Swerling, L. (1996) *Teaching for Thinking*. Washington, DC: American Psychological Association.

Strauss, A.L. and Corbin, J. (1990) *Basis of Qualitative Research: Grounded Theory*. Hove: Lawrence Erlbaum.

Stubbs, M. (1976) *Language, Schools and Classrooms*. London: Methuen.

Tizard, B. and Hughes, M. (1984). *Young Children Learning*. London: Fontana.

Tizard, B., Blatchford, P., Burke, J., Farquhar, C. and Plewis, I. (1988) *Young Children at School in the Inner City*. Hove: Lawrence Erlbaum.

Tomlinson, P. (1999) Conscious reflection and implicit learning in teacher reparation. Part II: Implications for a balanced approach, *Oxford Review of Education*, 25(4): 533–44.

van Manen, M. (1995) On the epistemology of reflective practice, *Teachers and Training: Theory and Practice*, 1: 33–50.

Vygotsky, L. (1978) *Mind in Society: The Development of Higher Psychological Processes*. Cambridge, MA: Harvard University Press.

Walker, R. and Weidel, J. (1985) Using photographs in a discipline of word, in R. Burgess (ed.) *Field Methods in the Study of Education*. Lewes: Falmer Press.

Wells, G. (1993) Re-evaluating the IRF sequence: a proposal for the articulation of theories of activity and discourse for the analysis of teaching and learning in the classroom, *Linguistics in Education*, 5: 1–37.

Wilkinson, G. (1996) Enhancing micro teaching through additional feedback from pre-service administrators, *Teaching and Teacher Education*, 12(2): 211–221.

Zeichner, K. (1994) Research on teacher thinking and different views of reflective practice in teaching and teacher education, in I. Carlgren, G. Handal and S. Vaage (eds) *Teachers' Minds and Actions: Research on Teachers' Thinking and Practice*. London: Falmer Press.

Zeichner, K. and Liston, D. (1987) Teaching student teachers to reflect. *Harvard Educational Review*, 57(1): 23–48.

Appendix A
The SPRINT Scales of Concern

The SPRINT teachers' responses to the initial administration of the Concerns-Based Adoption Model Stages of Concern Questionnaire were subjected to an oblique factor analysis. A core group of five sets of items, which accounted for about 71 per cent of all the item variance, emerged. The items that made up the five factors are shown below, as well as the three unallocated items. The 'professional adoption' factor extracted 30 per cent of the variance and was the strongest. The items for the three strongest factors emerged readily from the rotated factor matrix, while separate item–whole inter-correlations were necessary to establish the weakest two. The analysis was based on the completed returns available at that time. A few late additions did not disturb the structure or have an observable effect on the means.

	Correlation with total (less item)
Professional adoption (30 per cent variance)	**N = 27**
14 I would like to discuss the possibility of using interactive teaching more effectively	0.87
15 I would like to know what resources are available to support the development of interactive teaching strategies	0.77
24 I would like my children to be excited about interactive teaching	0.83
26 I would like to know what using interactive teaching might require in the future	0.79
27 I would like to coordinate my efforts with others to maximize the effect of interactive strategies	0.80

Professional adoption (30 per cent variance)	Correlation with total (less item) $N = 27$
28 I would like to have more information about interactive teaching	0.84
29 I would like to know what other schools are doing about interactive teaching	0.82
30 At this time, I am not interested in learning more about interactive teaching (*reversed*)	0.73
32 I would like to use feedback from children to change the way I undertake interactive teaching	0.78
Overall reliability	**0.95**

Conflicting demands (10 per cent variance)	Correlation with total (less item) $N = 26$
4 I am concerned about not having enough time to organize interactive teaching each session/day	0.64
8 I am concerned about conflicts between my interests and responsibilities	0.75
9 I am concerned about revising my use of interactive teaching	0.75
16 I am concerned about whether I can manage everything that interactive teaching requires	0.69
21 I am completely occupied with other aspects of the literacy strategy	0.57
25 I am concerned about the time required to plan and monitor interactive teaching	0.66
34 Coordination of tasks, children and other people is taking too much of my time	0.65
Overall reliability	**0.88**

Cooperative development (16 per cent variance)	Correlation with total (less item) N = 27
5 I would like to help other staff in their use of interactive teaching	0.57
10 I would like to develop working relationships with other teachers and schools who are using interactive teaching methods	0.67
11 I am concerned about how interactive teaching affects the children	0.40
18 I would like to familiarize other teachers and schools with the way I am working during interactive teaching	0.68
19 I am concerned about evaluating the impact of my interactive teaching on children	0.41
Overall reliability	**0.77**

Critical concerns (7 per cent variance)	Correlation with total (less item) N = 26
1 I am concerned about the children's attitudes towards interactive teaching	0.39
2 I know of some other approaches that might work better	0.51
20 I have my own ideas about interactive teaching	0.44
22 I would like to modify our use of interactive teaching in this school based on the experience of our pupils	0.59
23 I am concerned about different kinds of teaching strategies, including interactive teaching	0.54
31 I would like to establish how to work much more interactively with children	0.39
Overall reliability	**0.73**

Lacking information (8 per cent variance)	Correlation with total (less item) $N = 26$
3 I don't even know what interactive teaching is	0.47
6 I have a very limited knowledge about interactive teaching	0.41
7 I would like to know the effect of interactive teaching on my professional status	0.61
17 I would like to know how my teaching is supposed to change	0.55
33 I would like to know how my role changes when I am using interactive teaching strategies	0.51
Overall reliability	**0.75**

Mean scores on the pre-test scales

Attitude scale	Score per item (mean ± s)	N
1 Professional adoption	5.52 ± 1.17	27
2 Conflicting demands	3.28 ± 1.54	26
3 Cooperative development	4.19 ± 1.37	27
4 Critical concerns	4.08 ± 1.14	26
5 Lacking information	3.63 ± 1.19	26

Scores on 'professional adoption' and 'cooperative delivery' correlate significantly at $r = 0.46$ ($N = 26$, $P = 0.02$). s = standard deviation.

Unallocated pre-test items: mean scores

Unallocated items	Score per item (mean ± s)	N
12 I am not concerned about using interactive teaching methods	2.81 ± 2.13	27
13 I would like to know who will make the final decision about using interactive teaching methods	3.04 ± 2.26	27
35 I would like to know how interactive teaching is better than any other kind of teaching strategy	4.96 ± 1.84	28

Appendix B

Universities of Leicester and Durham
ESRC Interactive Teaching PROJECT

SPRINT – *Initial* Interview Schedule (Tutor Copy)

It is intended that the initial interview provides data which explore teachers':

- understanding of interactive teaching;
- concerns about these strategies;
- levels of use of interactive strategies.

The interview will be taped. You will need to ensure that the teacher is happy with this and is reassured about the confidentiality of the discourse. Remember to check that the recording quality is appropriate for transcription purposes and that the cassette is labelled with the teacher's and tutor's name, the school and the date.

N.B. *If the teacher has already had the video taken and wants continually to refer to that, ask them to think beyond that particular literacy hour and at other literacy hours and other interactive teaching opportunities.*

You will need to make **brief** notes about <u>significant comments</u> or issues pertaining to each of the three key areas of interest. (Do not attempt to analyse at this stage what the teacher is saying.) At the end of the interview the tutor will need to place the teacher at one of the stages of concern and levels of use outlined by the CBAM model. Interview notes, teacher levels and the cassette will then be passed on to the Research Associate for analysis.

Introductory remarks

Thank the teacher for agreeing to be involved. Then, depending on your relationship with the teacher and their awareness, you may need to consider the following:

- Is the seating comfortable for conversation?
- Is the teacher clear about the time-scale of the interview? (1 hour and stick to it!)
- Is the teacher clear what the research is about?
- Is there anything the teacher is uncertain about?
- Is the teacher clear about the use of research outcomes? (and confidentiality issues?)
- Has the teacher completed all relevant biographical details? (elaborate where necessary)

General prompts

A number of prompts may be useful throughout the interview. The prompts are there for the TUTOR's purposes: they are intended to remind the tutor about other issues the teacher may need prompting to discuss. The tutor should think about the kind of open-ended questions they might use as part of the interview, for example:

> Can you say more about that . . .?
> What do you mean by . . .?
> What makes you say that?
> How do you know . . .?
> Is there anything further you could add . . .?

Conceptual understanding of interactive teaching

Refer to DfEE's expectations for the use of interactive teaching in the literacy and numeracy hours.

1. In your view, what is interactive teaching?
Tutor prompts:
Characteristics?
Definitions?
Wider examples of interactive teaching?

2. What do you consider to be the aims and purposes of interactive teaching?
Tutor prompts:
Own views/others?
School issues?
Policy/teaching issues?

Stages of concern

Based on the interview data, tutors need to place the teacher within one of the seven stages of concern.

3. What is your attitude to interactive teaching?
Tutor prompt:
Feelings about it?

4. Do you have concerns about using interactive strategies?
Tutor prompt:
Implications?

Levels of use

Based on the interview data, you need to place the teacher within one of the seven levels of use.

5. How knowledgeable do you feel about interactive teaching?

6. How far do you employ interactive strategies at the moment?
Tutor prompts:
Literacy hour use?
Other curriculum areas?
Future intentions?

7. What influences your use of interactive teaching?
Tutor prompts:
Resources?
Class management?
Impact on pupils?
Own knowledge/limitations?
Collaboration with others?

8. Has your use of interactive teaching changed since the literacy hour?
Tutor prompts:
In what ways?
What prompted changes?

9. In your view, what, if any, are useful alternatives to interactive teaching?

10. Do you have any other comments to make about interactive teaching?

Appendix C
Universities of Leicester and Durham
ESRC Interactive Teaching PROJECT

SPRINT – *Final* Interview Schedule (Tutor Copy)

It is intended that the initial interview provides data which explore teachers':

- understanding of interactive teaching
- concerns about these strategies
- levels of use of interactive strategies.

The interview will be taped. **Remember to check that the recording quality is appropriate for transcription purposes** and that the cassette is labelled with the teacher's and tutor's name, the school and the date. The teachers will have received a copy of the Initial Interview Summary before the final interview. They will need to consider their previous responses to answer the Final Interview questions.

General prompts

A number of prompts may be useful throughout the interview. The prompts are there for the TUTOR's purposes: they are intended to remind the tutor about other issues the teacher may need prompting to discuss. The tutor should think about the kind of open-ended questions they might use as part of the interview, for example:

> Can you say more about that . . .?
> What do you mean by . . .?
> What makes you say that?
> How do you know . . .?
> Is there anything further you could add . . .?

Conceptual understanding of interactive teaching

1. Has your understanding of interactive teaching changed since the autumn?
Tutor prompts:
Y – In what ways?
N – How might you extend your previous remarks?

2. Do the principles and purposes outlined in your Initial Interview Summary match your view of interactive teaching now?
Tutor prompts:
What's changed?
Could you extend it?
In what way?

Own view/others?
School issues?
Policy/teaching issues?

Stages of concern

Based on the interview data, tutors need to place the teacher within one of the seven stages of concern.

3. Have your attitudes to interactive teaching changed since the autumn?
Tutor prompts:
In what ways?
Feelings about it?

4. Have your concerns about/interests in interactive strategies changed since the autumn?
Tutor prompts:
Constraints?
Implications?

Levels of use

Based on the interview data, you need to place the teacher within one of the seven levels of use.

5. How knowledgeable do you currently feel about interactive teaching practices?
** *Important tutor prompts (use these!):*
What is the basis for your knowledge about interactive teaching?
Are you aware of sources of information or theory about interactive teaching?

6. How far do you employ interactive strategies now?
Tutor prompts:
In literacy/numeracy?
Other curriculum areas?
Future intentions?

7. What factors have influenced your use/non-use of interactive teaching practices?
Tutor prompts:
Resources?
Knowledge?
Class management?
Impact on pupils?
Collaboration with others?

8. Has your use of interactive teaching changed since your involvement in the SPRINT Research Project?
Tutor prompts:
In what ways?
What prompted changes?

9. FOR FOCUS TEACHERS ONLY
How do you feel about the use of video and reflective dialogues in the Project?
Tutor prompts:
What was difficult?
Was it helpful?
In what ways?

10. Are there any other comments, questions or feedback that you would like to offer us?
Tutor prompt: Are there clarifying questions, based on your reading of the teacher's Initial Interview Summary?

Appendix D
Observation variables

CONVERSATION CATEGORIES

Questions (answered by . . .)

c1 ques. recalling facts

c2 ques. offering explanations, reasons (closed)

c3 ques. offering ideas, solutions (open)

c4 ques. task supervision (what to do)

c5 ques. routine matter

Statements

c6 task state.: facts

c7 task state.: ideas, problems

c8 telling child what to do

c9 praising/evaluating work or effort

c10 informative feedback on work or effort

c11 providing information (routine)

c12 providing evaluative feedback on behaviour

c13 providing informational feedback

c14 small talk

SILENT INTERACTION

c15 Gesturing

c16 Showing

c17 Marking

c18 Waiting

c19 Story

c20 Listening to report

c21 Listening to reading

c22 Watching

NO INTERACTION

c23 Adult interaction

c24 Visiting pupil

c25 Housekeeping

c26 General monitoring

c27 Out of room

c28 Not observed

c29 Not listed

LITERACY HOUR TECHNIQUES

c31 Question: factual response
c32 Question: one answer response
c33 Question: many answer response
c34 Reading on cue
c35 Question: aural decode
c36 Choral reading

META-COGNITIVE ITEMS

c41 Learning strategy: factual response
c42 Learning strategy: closed response
c43 Learning strategy: open response
c46 Feedback on strategy: low level
c47 Feedback on strategy: high level

AUDIENCE CATEGORIES

Individual audience
Individual for class
Individual for group
Group audience (total)
Class audience (total)
Sustained interaction

Appendix E
Universities of Leicester and Durham

Teacher Copy
REFLECTIVE DIALOGUE

Using your video tape for reflective dialogue

The video tape will be used as a focus for the reflective dialogue with (tutor name)............... Before the dialogue you will need to select a 15-minute section which you think represents the most interactive teaching within the lesson.

With (tutor name)..............., you will play the section of video and stop the tape at points of significance or interest to you. You will then choose from a range of reflective questions and reflect on the clip.

We hope that your contact with the project has already indicated that we seek to value your views as a teacher and to support you. The purpose of the reflective dialogue is to explore your intentions, assumptions and experience of the lesson. It is also important that you understand that the process aims to challenge your knowledge, views and actions with the intention that you can develop your practice of 'interactive' teaching. In doing this, we hope in partnership to develop both our understandings of what it means to teach interactively.

Towards a reflective dialogue

The purposes of the dialogue are as follows:

- To surface your own personal knowledge and theories about 'inter-active' teaching.
- To highlight the assumptions you make in your thinking and teaching.
- To help you to critique your thinking and practice.

- To provide a model of reflective practice.
- To encourage you to think reflectively about interactive teaching.
- To develop your awareness of the pupils and yourself as a practitioner.

Below there is a framework for reflection that will be used in the reflective dialogue. The intention is that you will direct the focus of questioning about the lesson on video. The tutor will support you in this and draw attention to further questions or themes that may be applicable. The themes are as follows:

Intentions and purposes

The object here is to explore your intentions and goals to review what they are based on. What are your criteria for effectiveness? It is important to recognize that change is a personal process influenced by your previous experience, current school and classroom

Self-awareness

The object is to bring your attention to yourself in the moment of teaching. What do you sense about yourself – physical feelings, emotions, thinking and attitudes 'in action'?

Practical reflection

Educational ends and means are viewed in terms of the value commitments underlying them. The aim here is to explain and clarify the asssumptions and predispositions underlying teachers' practice. Practical reflection seeks out alternative assumptions, claims, perspectives and solutions and weighs competing practices

Technical reflection

Technical reflection involves identifying the educational basis for intentions and providing reasons for action. It aims to assess the effectiveness of practice used to attain defined educational goals

Perceptual awareness

The object here is to help you focus on perceptions, not your thinking. Where is the focus of your attention? What is noticed from the video that was 'unnoticed' in action? What additional foci might be developed 'live'?

Critical reflection

Both the ends and the means of teaching and its context are seen as value-governed selections from a range of possibilities. Critical reflection aims to question and critique the goals and practices of the profession; to raise awareness of the impact of unsurfaced professional aims and ideology; and take account of social, cultural and political forces in teachers' practice. Based on the desired and potential outcomes for pupils and other stakeholders, critical reflection questions the ethical and moral jujstification for educational ends and means

The reflective framework

The following framework sets out a range of possible questions which may be appropriate to specific selections from the video.

Intentions/purposes

- What were your intentions/aims/purposes in using this strategy?
- How far were you successful in this?
- How did you come to this view?
- What did you expect the pupils' response to be?
- How/why was it different?
- What does this tell you?
- On what basis were your purposes formed?
- Did the context (school policy/time of year, etc.) influence your purposes?

Self-awareness

- What were you feeling in this moment?
- What were you feeling in this moment?
- What are the roots of this feeling?
- What do you learn from viewing your self?

Practical reflection

- What assumptions are you making about teaching and learning?
- What are these assumptions based on – personal experience, teacher training, other professionals, school/professional culture, research evidence?

Technical reflection

- What were you doing/aiming for here?
- How did you decide what outcomes were appropriate?
- Why did you choose this strategy/subject matter?
- What evidence/information did you base this choice on?
- Can you break down what you were doing into different aspects/elements?
- What's significant about the different elements?
- How might different/individual children perceive/respond differently to the strategy/activities?
- How did your prior experience of the class influence your actions/thinking?
- How might your actions be improved?
- What kind of learning was promoted? How do you know that?

Perceptual awareness

- What were you aware of in the classroom at this moment?
- Where was your attention focussed?
- What do you notice now that you weren't aware of during the lesson?
- What alternative foci might there be?

Critical reflection

- What ethical/moral choices have been made here?
- What alternative moral/ethical positions are there?
- What wider historical, socio-political, cultural forces/constraints apply here – interpersonal, classroom, school?

Practical reflection (cont.)

- What alternative actions/solutions/ views might be appropriate?
- How might you decide which is appropriate to your situation?
- What source of new/alternative knowledge/information might be useful?
- What values are represented in the teaching?
- What other values might be applicable to the teaching?
- What does 'being professional' mean to you?

Critical reflection (cont.)

- How are pupils affected by your actions beyond the classroom/in subtle ways?
- What covert messages might be conveyed?
- Does the practice offer equality of opportunity? Is it just? Judged by what criteria?

Any additional questions that you found useful, or comments about the framework will be gratefully received.

Application

By the end of the session the two partners in the reflective dialogue will agree a number of action points for you to work with over the period until the next dialogue.

Name ....

As a result of the dialogue, I undertake to develop my practice of interactive teaching in the following ways.

1.

2.

3.

The date of the next dialogue is ....

Index